REDESIGNING CITIES

Principles, Practice, Implementation

Jonathan Barnett, FAICP

Foreward by Sen. Lincoln Chafee

PLANNERS PRESS
AMERICAN PLANNING ASSOCIATION
Chicago, Illinois
Washington, D.C.

Table of Contents

Foreword

In his book *Redesigning Cities*, Jonathan Barnett provides a valuable survey of the evolution of urban design standards and practices in the United States, and advocates a toolkit of new and innovative design concepts to be employed in the reclamation of our cities, the improvement of older suburbs, and the management of growth in rapidly developing areas.

This is a book that tells us clearly what the elements of smart growth policies should be, and shows how these policies have been carried out successfully in a wide range of communities all over the United States. A former director of urban design for the New York City Planning Department and a consultant to many communities, Jonathan Barnett points the way for us to make our urban areas more livable, attractive, and economically competitive. One of the most important points he makes is to demonstrate how zoning influences development and why it is so important to update zoning and development regulations in order to improve cities and suburbs.

My hometown of Warwick, Rhode Island, once was a testament to how incompatible zoning decisions create incremental and haphazard land development that was offensive to the eye and a drain on our local economy. Industrial and commercial facilities and residential homes were frequently and inappropriately sited next to each other. Arterial roads were clogged with traffic. The local newspaper described the city as a "suburban nightmare."

As mayor of the City of Warwick from 1993 to 1999, I did my best to reverse this trend. My administration fought bad zoning decisions. We updated our zoning code and development regulations. We established two new historic districts. We purchased 130 acres of open space. We created an urban forestry program. We extended sewer lines into environmentally sensitive coastal areas. We approved legislation creating a redevelopment district for a new intermodal rail/airport facility.

As Senator, I have continued to support wise growth for America. I am gratified that President George W. Bush has signed into law the Brownfields Revitalization Act. My new law encourages the redevelopment of abandoned industrial properties, especially in urban settings, into housing, offices and other uses that enhance the vitality of our cities. Of course, rehabilitation of neglected properties also brings in critical property tax revenues to financially strapped municipalities.

I also believe another legislative initiative—the Community Character Act—presents an opportunity for the federal government to play a limited but helpful role in leveraging large dividends at the state and local level. It is troubling that almost half of the 50 states have state zoning enabling laws that date back to the 1920s. My bill would provide grants to help states create or update statewide land-use planning statutes, which would allow them to take advantage of the innovative techniques described in this book.

I sincerely hope that measures such as the Brownfields Revitalization Act and the Community Character Act help empower municipal leaders throughout the country to reinvigorate our cities. I recommend they read Jonathan Barnett's book and make use of the progressive planning and urban design techniques he has assembled over a long career of public service.

Senator Lincoln Chafee
Washington, D.C.
August 2002

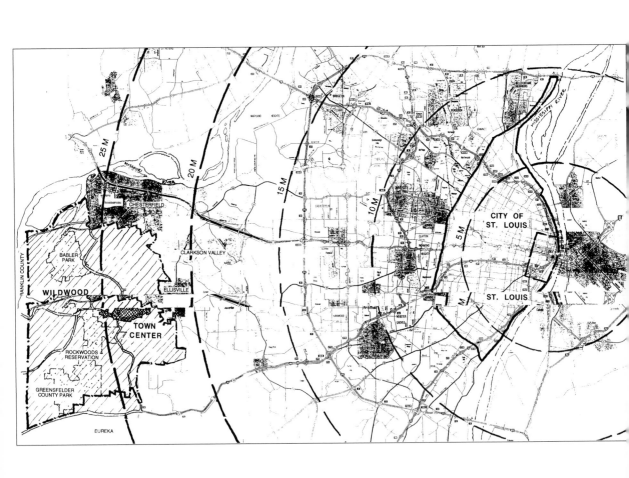

Prologue

The New Politics of City Design

In 1992, residents at the western edge of St. Louis County organized to stop the region's third ring-road from running though their neighborhoods. People were saying "Not in my back yard;" but they understood what was wrong with this highway better than the Missouri Transportation Department.

The engineers wanted a new connection so truck traffic could switch from one interstate to another, farther from St. Louis than is possible now. The residents, using common sense and their observations of what happens when other highways are built, concluded that the connecting road would inevitably become a main street for new urban development, completely changing their semi-rural residential communities.

If you evaluate an outer ring-road as a means of redesigning the St. Louis metropolitan region, rather than as a convenience for truck drivers, it is a truly bad idea.

The population of the St. Louis region grew by only four percent during the decade from 1990 to 2000, which means that from year to year the region is barely growing at all. Despite the stable population, sprawling suburban development is already moving rapidly outward, channeled along the two existing ring-roads and the main highway corridors—particularly Interstate 70, which runs past Lambert International Airport and is drawing development deep into St. Charles County, 35 or more miles northwest of downtown St. Louis. The proposed connection around the western edge of St. Louis County, 25 miles out from downtown, would pull real-estate investment from the I-70 corridor west and south into Franklin and Jefferson counties. There

1

can be big profits in turning rural land into houses, office buildings, and shopping centers; but, with so little population growth, new development on the rural fringe inevitably draws people and businesses away from built-up areas elsewhere in the St. Louis region. The city and county did not fight the proposed highway, although both are likely to lose population and tax base if it were built. Instead it was left to the local residents to stop it, at least for now.

Citizens Take Control

The same residents who had organized against the highway began to question the way St. Louis County was approving new subdivisions and stores in their area. They documented the rapidly increasing environmental damage as developers cut away the trees, removed vegetation and topsoil, and bulldozed the landscape. Creeks were running more rapidly and overflowing more frequently, undermining bridges, exposing buried sewer and electrical conduits. Citizens photographed these serious erosion problems and made presentations about them to the St. Louis County Board of Commissioners, who listened politely but continued to approve the same kinds of developments (PR 2).

The community found that they had at most one vote, the commissioner who represented their area. They took legal advice and learned that it was possible to secede from the county, create their own city government, and control land-use decisions themselves. In February 1995, after a three-year legal battle, 61 percent of area residents turned out for a referendum on incorporation and 61 percent of those voting approved it. Wildwood, Missouri's newest city, was incorporated in September 1995. Now local citizens could pass the planning laws needed to bring new development into a better relationship with the local ecology, including amendments to the subdivision ordinance that require development plans to take erosion and flooding potential into account.

Shaping the Community

I was asked to help Wildwood prepare a master plan and new development regulations right after the community was incorporated. The issues in Wildwood were not just about a new highway or about land conservation, they were about the way that people in the area wanted to live their lives. They had a mental picture of what their community should be, and they needed public policies that would help shape the community in that image. They wanted their community to be designed, and not just to be the by-product of a lot of unrelated decisions.

Wildwood's new master plan designates an area of the most buildable land as the town center (PR 3), and Wildwood has recently adopted a detailed specific plan for this center as a walkable place, with shops fronting on streets,

PR2 *The Kehrs Mill bridge in Wildwood, undermined by excessive stormwater runoff.*

PR3 *Old Manchester Road in Wildwood, saved from conventional commercial strip development, became part of the town center.*

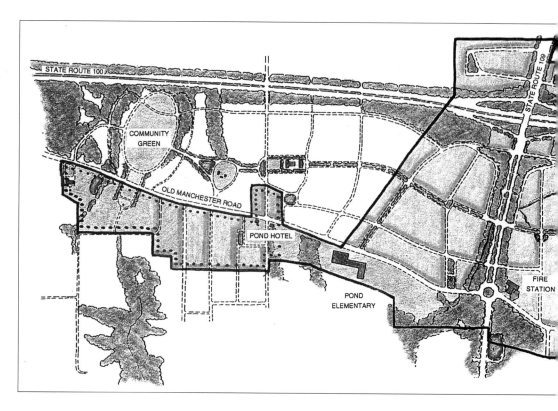

apartments and houses on small lots. It will look like an old-fashioned suburban downtown, and not the strip commercial development strung out along a highway that would have sprung up in the area under the county's zoning policies. (PR 4)

Adding yet another jurisdiction to the jumble of local governments in a metropolitan region should always be an action of last resort. But the story of Wildwood illustrates two significant trends: City design alternatives that used only to worry a few specialists are now understood as affecting everyone's daily life; and many people, dissatisfied with the way planning and city design decisions are being made, are learning to take control of events and reshape them.

Five Basic City Design Issues
The Wildwood story involves city design and planning issues that have acquired political visibility and are covered by newspapers and magazines: Community, Livability, Mobility, Equity, and Sustainability.

Organizing to fight the state highway department and county land-development policies obviously helped bring the community together, although there is always plenty to disagree about—Wildwood has had contentious races for mayor and city council. But community objectives, such as having an

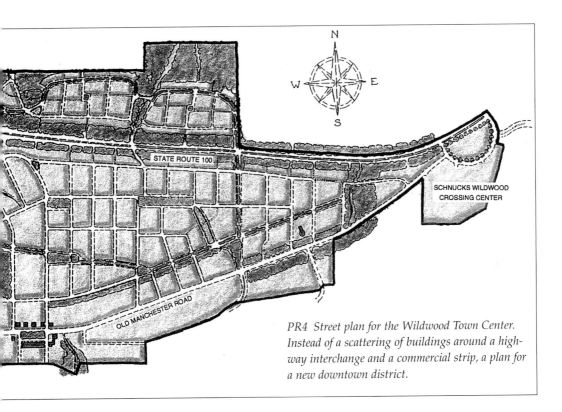

STATE ROUTE 100

SCHNUCKS WILDWOOD
CROSSING CENTER

OLD MANCHESTER ROAD

PR4 Street plan for the Wildwood Town Center. Instead of a scattering of buildings around a highway interchange and a commercial strip, a plan for a new downtown district.

identifiable downtown near where you live, used to be an automatic part of daily life. Now they have to be consciously created.

Choosing a home involves many livability decisions beyond the boundaries of house and yard: a good school system, protection from crime or fires and other disasters, a manageable journey to work, the availability of shops, the opportunity for grown children and the elderly to continue living in the community. Livability in Wildwood means meeting these needs while keeping what is there already: the natural setting, the winding country roads, the historic villages of Pond and Grover, which were its original attractions.

Letting automobiles dominate every city design decision produces a world of highways and parking lots leading to isolated offices, shopping centers, or apartment complexes—while generating more and more traffic and sacrificing livability and community. Wildwood's interest in creating a town center with residences, shops, and offices mirrors a national interest in creating 24-hour downtowns compact enough that they can be served by a bus route, if not a rail transit system, and designed so that people can walk from one place to another.

Few people in Wildwood would call themselves rich, but most are comfortably middle class. Regional equity issues, such as the concentration of poor people in the inner-city districts or in bypassed older communities, do not

affect them much in their daily lives, but they know that their community has
to be more than large, single-family houses and stores along a highway; there
needs to be a place for smaller houses and apartments.

When the proposed highway threatened to enlarge the St. Louis metropolitan area without adding to the population, it raised questions of sustainability:
Are scarce land and building resources being used in a way which safeguards
the interests of future generations? When new development created erosion
and flooding, it drew attention to the need to preserve the natural environment, a major sustainability issue. It was evident in Wildwood that typical
zoning and subdivision regulations treat land as a commodity rather than as
an ecosystem, and that this failing caused county officials to ignore the
adverse environmental effects of land-use changes. Wildwood is hardly the
only place to suffer from this blind spot in land development regulation. In
many communities, floods that were only supposed to happen once every 100,
or even 500, years have become regular occurrences.

New Constituencies for Urban and Suburban Design
Community participation in planning was once an exciting innovation. Planning had traditionally been left to experts working "outside of politics;" letting citizen representatives participate in meetings while a plan was being
drawn was a big concession. Today, no community makes major planning
decisions without public consultation, but people have often become impa-
tient with the whole process.

Zoning changes and road widenings have become hot political issues, with
protracted and contentious public hearings before local planning boards and
councils. Local government officials and members of planning and zoning
boards are frustrated also, as so often none of the alternatives before them
seems desirable.

Inner-city communities have tired of waiting for housing initiatives from
local government, or for the real-estate market to improve, and have formed
corporations to build housing themselves. Some neighborhood corporations
are moving on to economic development, utilizing the buying power present
even in low-income communities, and the advantages of a central, inner-city
location.

Merchants downtown and in neighborhood shopping streets have reacted
to poor security and infrequent trash and garbage collection by forming business improvement districts. They add a surcharge to the local property tax,
but the extra money is spent only in the district. It can pay for extra sanitation
collections, security guards to make shoppers feel safe, and extra workers to
keep the streets and sidewalks swept. The district often pays for urban design
improvements: landscaping, better lights and signs, special paving, and other

Growth Choices for the Year 2020

Consider the issues: Please indicate your preferences according to the instructions below. Do not indicate your personal preferences for the kind of future you want for yourself, but rather what you think would be best for the region as a whole.

Instructions: 1) Fill in the oval within the scenario you like best according to each topic. 2) Then rank each topic according to how important it is to you by filling in the corresponding box in the left-hand column. (1=most important, 9=least important; no two topics may receive the same ranking)

Rank	Topic	Scenario A	Scenario B	Scenario C	Scenario D
[1][2][3] [■][5][6] [7][8][9]	Example	CAT	DOG	HORSE	FISH
[1][2][3] [4][5][6] [7][8][9]	Transportation Choices				
[1][2][3] [4][5][6] [7][8][9]	Infrastructure Cost 1998-2020 (Transportation, water, sewer, utilities)	$38 billion	$30 billion	$22 billion	$23 billion
[1][2][3] [4][5][6] [7][8][9]	Air Quality (1=Best, 4=worst)	4	2	1	3
[1][2][3] [4][5][6] [7][8][9]	Total Water Demand	334 billion gallons	311 billion gallons	264 billion gallons	251 billion gallons
[1][2][3] [4][5][6] [7][8][9]	Walkable Communities (Walk to work, stores, school, transit)				
[1][2][3] [4][5][6] [7][8][9]	Average Size of Single-Family Lot	.37 acre	.35 acre	.29 acre	.27 acre
[1][2][3] [4][5][6] [7][8][9]	Single Family Homes vs. Condos, Apts. & Townhomes	SF 77% / Condos, etc. 23%	SF 75% / Condos, etc. 25%	SF 68% / Condos, etc. 32%	SF 62% / Condos, etc. 38%
[1][2][3] [4][5][6] [7][8][9]	■=Amount of New Land Consumed: 1998 - 2020	409 sq mi / 431 sq mi (Presently Used)	325 sq mi / 431 sq mi (Presently Used)	126 sq mi / 431 sq mi (Presently Used)	85 sq mi / 431 sq mi (Presently Used)
[1][2][3] [4][5][6] [7][8][9]	Agricultural Land Consumed: 1998 - 2020	174 sq mi	143 sq mi	65 sq mi	43 sq mi

Choose a Scenario: Given the priority you have assigned to these categories, decide how they should be mixed to create a desirable quality of life in 2020 and beyond. The scenario descriptions in this newspaper fold-out will tell you what mixtures are feasible in the Greater Wasatch Area. You may select one of the scenarios as described, or choose a point somewhere between the two you like best. You may also choose an option outside the range we have identified, if you feel that either Scenario A or Scenario D should be taken further in some respect.

Scenario A   Scenario B   Scenario C   Scenario D

○   ○   ○   ○   ○   ○   ○   ○   ○

PR5 Part of the ballot used by Envision Utah to help citizens participate in the planning process. The winner is Scenario C.

amenities. There are now more than 1,200 business improvement districts across the country.

People who belong to community groups have gone on from influencing their local planning and urban design agendas to the politics of regional planning, particularly the preservation of the natural landscape. There are growing numbers of ballot initiatives every election year dealing with land-use, conservation, and planning issues; many of them pass. Even the ones that are defeated generally have substantial support. This phenomenon has gained the attention of national politicians, making suburban sprawl—and the federal highway and mortgage subsidies that promote it—high-profile issues for the first time.

Whole communities and even metropolitan regions are engaging in visioning processes to decide policies out to the year 2020 and beyond, such as the *Envision Utah* process, managed on behalf of the Coalition for Utah's Future by the planning firm Fregonese, Calthorpe Associates. Four scenarios were outlined showing varying amounts of dependency on highways and varying proportions of single-family houses to apartments. Scenario C, with an emphasis on transit and walkable communities, was the alternative selected by the most people. (PR 5)

Some of these efforts suffer from a disconnect with normal decision making, and often the internal contradictions among policies are not explored sufficiently, however involving the public in long-range regional-planning issues builds a constituency for new kinds of planning and design.

Organizations That Support City Planning and Design

The National Trust for Historic Preservation is an advocacy group that began by saving buildings, moved on to include historic districts, then historic downtowns, and now finds itself engaged with regional planning and growth policy issues. It recently published a survey of other advocacy groups engaged with such issues under the title *Challenging Sprawl*. The trust counted more than 20 private national organizations dealing with some part of the growth policy agenda, including the Sierra Club, the Natural Resources Defense Council, the Congress for the New Urbanism, the American Farmland Trust, and the Surface Transportation Policy Project. The survey also described citizen advocacy efforts in 19 states, and the work of nine regional organizations, including the Greenbelt Alliance in San Francisco, the Regional Plan Association of New York and New Jersey and the Metropolitan Planning Council of Chicago. This survey did not include business organizations such as Chambers of Commerce, professional organizations, or local community organizations.

The people in these groups do not agree about everything. Only the Congress for the New Urbanism and perhaps the National Trust have a specific city design agenda. But as Dana Beach, head of the South Carolina Coastal

Conservation League, told a group of federal government officials, "The central proposition here is the need to alter the pattern and location of human settlement in America's growing cities and towns." And this is an issue that brings together, as Beach put it, "urban interests with wetland crusaders, transportation reformers with endangered species advocates, and brownfield proponents with farmland protectionists." A large, well organized segment of the public now takes a strong interest in planning and city design issues.

Metropolitics

Myron Orfield, a Minnesota state legislator and the author of the book *Metropolitics*, believes that if the residents of older central cities will work with the people who live in the first tier suburbs on issues they have in common—such as equalizing school funding and stopping the subsidies for infrastructure in outer suburbs, they can command majorities in state legislatures and even in the national House of Representatives. The Wildwood story demonstrates that such a coalition would have support in the outer suburbs as well. Almost all the issues that could unite these constituencies have to do with city design: regional transportation, distribution of a variety of housing types and jobs across the whole region, compact and livable communities, and achieving regional sustainability and protection of the natural environment by limiting exurban growth.

Can The Real-Estate Market Design Cities?

There are business and academic critics of planning and city design who say that the right way to solve all urban and suburban development problems is to allow the real-estate market to operate freely. Give everybody a choice, and let market efficiencies prevail. This may sound at first like a simple, conservative thing to do. It is really a radical, untested idea whose consequences would change the whole economy.

It is true that private investors initiate new real-estate development and decide how to re-use most older buildings. The real-estate market gives the public choices about where to live, and about the size and price of houses and apartments. The real-estate market also affects the location of work places and shopping. But what would happen if all highways were tollways? Freeways have opened up vast areas to new development; would tollways have done the same? If all public water systems were paid for by user fees, what would be the economics of developing in Phoenix or Los Angeles? What if all bridges, sewer systems, and other public works were also paid for by user fees? What would happen if all federal and state income taxes were flat percentages, and there were no deductions for depreciation, mortgage interest, local property taxes, location in an enterprise zone, and so forth? What would real-estate investment be like if there were no federal mortgage guarantees and no secondary market in mortgages organized by federal agencies, no zoning or subdivision regulations or building codes, no environmental impact assessments or growth boundaries, no pollution control laws, no laws governing the workplace?

The big decisions about cities are not made by the market. Roads, bridges, water and sewer systems, airports, schools, parking garages, convention centers and other public commitments, such as mortgage guarantees, make some investment opportunities safer and more profitable than others. The temporary abatement of property taxes, tax credits for historic preservation, or the favorable treatment of capital gains, as well as depreciation and mortgage-interest deductions, are also public investments in real estate—more subtle, and more difficult for the public to monitor, because they are indirect. Federal floodplain controls, local zoning and subdivision codes, grading and tree-preservation ordinances, and many other development regulations closely determine what a developer can build in a specific location.

How likely is it that even simple steps toward a free market, such as eliminating the mortgage interest tax-deduction or cancelling federal support for flood insurance, are going to receive political support? Most of the talk about letting the market take its course is directed at freeing a particular real-estate developer from some individual regulation.

The Public Interest in City Design

Who designed today's decentralized metropolis? No one, but paradoxically it didn't happen by accident either, as any new construction is the product of a lengthy decision-making process. Buildings must conform to development regulations and building codes. Office buildings, shopping centers, houses, and apartments must be financed by private investors. Roads, schools, and bridges must be paid for by government, with routes and sites selected after public discussion. As government is a big, if indirect, investor in all new development, satisfying the public interest in creating better communities and preserving the environment is important. The aggregate effect of all these deliberate decisions may be out of control, but, if each individual decision makes sense, there ought to be a way to impart coherence to the overall result. If people want to see the whole process managed more effectively, it is necessary to figure out how and why current decisions are being made. What are the pressure points, the decisions that are producing the unintended side effects?

The most important influences on regional development in the United States are transportation plans, and, to a lesser extent, the provision of water supplies and sewage treatment. Highway planners for years have been designing new roads to meet existing demand and assiduously not considering the potential for new highways to induce traffic by changing the land uses around the highways. The result: unplanned development and unexpected congestion on the highways. Water and sewer systems have usually been put in place to facilitate the real-estate investments made possible by new highways. Environmental protection has been a secondary issue; land is opened up for new development by transportation systems without reference to the land's carrying capacity. It is then up to advocates for the environment to fight a rear-guard action to protect what they consider to be most important.

About a quarter of the states now have some kind of growth management system based on shutting off state aid to projects outside growth boundaries or targeting state money to already developed areas. What is needed is an understanding that regional planning is a problem where design can resolve the apparently conflicting requirements of growth management. Highways and transit routes can give structure to the whole metropolitan region.

Why Better Local Decisions Are Needed

Most local land-use regulation in the United States is based on prototype enabling legislation and prototype zoning and subdivision codes prepared for the U. S. Department of Commerce in the 1920s under Secretary of Commerce Herbert Hoover. Although modern zoning codes have evolved from these early models, they do not deal effectively with the scale of today's office parks and housing tracts, or with large and complex building types like regional shopping centers that did not exist in the 1920s. While every new project must be approved under local law, these laws often produce results that neither the public nor the development industry really want. In fact, much of the recipe for urban sprawl can be found in local zoning and subdivision regulations. The endless ribbons of commercial development along highways all follow zoning; so do the big tracts of suburban houses each the same size on the same sized lots. The drastic stripping and bulldozing of the suburban landscape often results from requirements in the subdivision ordinance.

As these laws have become the literal prescription for most new development, changing them can make big changes in the design of every community. Zoning is only a mechanism, and, as the people of Wildwood have learned, it can be used to safeguard the environment, encourage neighborhoods with mixes of building types, and mandate downtowns that are compact and walkable.

The Real-Estate Industry Also Should Change

The specialization of land use required by typical suburban zoning ordinances has encouraged equivalent specialization in the development industry. Results are measured in square feet of office space or numbers of housing units, "product," rather than success in creating new downtowns or neighborhoods.

The permanent lenders have encouraged specialization by doing real-estate deals by the numbers, and not looking very hard at less tangible elements such as architectural quality and the surrounding community, despite their importance over the life of the mortgage. Securitization of real estate in investment trusts has reinforced specialization by product type. Mixed use is seen as higher risk, and more difficult to value, because development activities in categories like housing or office are measured separately and are perceived to respond to different cycles of supply and demand. The possibility that a mix of different uses can reinforce each other is understood, but the statistics to quantify such an advantage are difficult to find. Most investors evaluate the components of a mixed-use development as if each activity were in a separate location.

Some development companies are starting to emphasize community building as their product, positioning themselves as specialists in downtown mixed residential and retail, or as developers of planned towns, and a few lenders are looking at criteria for long-term value, such as giving preference to properties in locations where there is a mix of uses that create activity 24 hours a day. There are now good examples of designs that create more livable communities, and some compact, mixed-use commercial developments that are more like a downtown than an office park or a shopping center. Several of them will be discussed in succeeding chapters of this book. If these isolated examples were to become trends, they could go a long way towards making cities and towns the product of design, rather than the by product of other objectives.

What About Bypassed Older Areas?

What can city design do for distressed older suburbs, obsolete industrial districts, or half-destroyed city neighborhoods dominated by poverty and crime? Some of the clues to formulating future policies can be found in the history of downtown renewal. Since the 1960s, city centers have had to compete against the attractions of suburban shopping centers and office parks. As downtowns represent a big chunk of a city's jobs and property values, city governments have been obliged to defend them, and there are many success stories, some of which are discussed later in this book.

City officials have learned to build on what is unique about traditional urban centers by preserving historic buildings, encouraging performing arts centers for music, opera, and dance, replacing old-style shopping that has gone forever with specialty retail destinations and entertainment, building convention centers, subsidizing hotels, and supporting downtown office buildings with parking garages. Placemaking has been an important part of the repositioning of American downtowns, with emphasis on streetscape improvements, riverfront renewal, and the creation of urban plazas and squares. All these amenities bring visitors to the central city and encourage existing businesses to remain there. The public investment in these metropolitan centers has been substantial. For many years cities had access to federal grant money that was targeted to downtown revitalization, and cities also made considerable commitments of their own funds.

Building on their own unique advantages has been bringing some success in revitalizing smaller downtowns and neighborhood shopping districts and in reviving urban neighborhoods, particularly historic districts. These areas possess several inherent assets to offset the familiar list of big-city problems: an inventory of existing buildings, a complete set of utilities in place, and, usually, a central location in the metropolitan region.

There are some encouraging examples of revitalized Main Streets, reused industrial buildings, and reclaimed urban neighborhoods. What has been missing so far in the efforts to make bypassed older areas fully competitive with newer suburbs has been the kind of financial backing that was available for use in city centers during the peak years of urban renewal. The federal Hope VI program is one mechanism for turning failed housing projects into mixed-income neighborhoods. (see page 128) As major increases in value are possible for older urban areas if land can be assembled and pollution problems abated, there ought to be some financial mechanism to support redevelopment, which can be paid back from the new property values that redevelopment will create.

How This Book is Organized
This book is divided into three sections. It begins with five basic principles: Community, Livability, Mobility, Equity and Sustainability, and shows how decisions in these areas form the context for every aspect of city design. The next section describes how to create new neighborhoods, restore deteriorated old neighborhoods, and preserve and improve the residential environment in general; how to transform edge cities, commercial strips, and failed shopping centers; then describes ways to preserve and enhance older main streets and city centers. Finally, there is a section on implementation: streetscape and other aspects of public space, design guidelines that can be incorporated into development regulations, and institutions that can be created to promote urban and environmental design.

The growing political constituencies for city and regional design, signs of interest in community building in the development industry, the lengthening list of successful examples of city design at all scales and in every kind of location are all indications that a much better physical environment is possible.

Principles

1.1 *Optional and resultant activities taking place around a fountain in downtown Bethesda,
Maryland. Urban design by Streetworks.*

1.2 *(below) Jan Gehl's diagram illustrating the relationship between the quality of outdoor
spaces and the rate of occurrence of outdoor activities.*

	Quality of the physical enviroment	
	Poor	Good
Necessary activities	●	●
Optional activities	·	⬤
"Resultant" activities (Social activities)	•	●

1

Community:
Life Takes Place on Foot

"Life Takes Place on Foot," is the aphorism of Jan Gehl, a Danish architect who is an acute and sympathetic observer of the way that people interact with each other and with their surroundings. He believes that people still need the casual encounters once built into daily life, but now are made less frequent by automobiles, computers, and the Internet.

Gehl has concluded that complicated human interactions can be created by a relatively simple mechanism. People pursue necessary activities that take them through public spaces. If the spaces are a poor physical environment, everyone will get through them as quickly as possible. If the environment is attractive, people will linger and engage in what Gehl calls optional activities, like sitting down for a few minutes in a cool place in summer, or a sheltered sunny spot in winter, or just slowing down and enjoying life, stopping for a cup of coffee or tea, looking at a statue or a fountain. The more optional activities there are in a public place, the more likely that there will be what Gehl calls resultant activities, that is, sociability, people meeting accidentally, or striking up a conversation with strangers. (1.1, 1.2)

Gehl argues for the sociability created by traditional streets and squares, as opposed to the open spaces in most of Denmark's modern housing projects or the big institutional parking lots where there are trafficways but few streets next to buildings. He believes that designers can make new groups of buildings that have similar characteristics to the traditional townscapes that his research finds are still successful in fostering sociability.

Gehl's contemporary, the late William H. Whyte, studied the places where people congregate and interact in New York and other big American cities.

He also argues that design can make a big difference to behavior in public places, comparing spots that are taken over by antisocial activities with those that are safe and popular. Whyte was also an amused observer of the way people act out an image of themselves in public, and interact with the image-making of others. Whyte adds two elements to Gehl's conclusions: providing movable chairs in public places, so that people can create temporary environments for themselves, plus creating multiple activities fronting on the public space and programmed for the space. The more that is going on in and around a space, the more likely that people will be attracted, their paths will cross, and Gehl's "resultant activities" will take place.

Kevin Lynch in his *Theory of Good City Form* also looked at the components of a successful public space under headings such as the way that space is perceived through the senses, and the way that the built environment fits, or doesn't fit behavioral patterns. Lynch looks at the design of public places at a somewhat finer grain than Gehl and Whyte. He explores such questions as the functions of drama and surprise in the design of a space, and the way

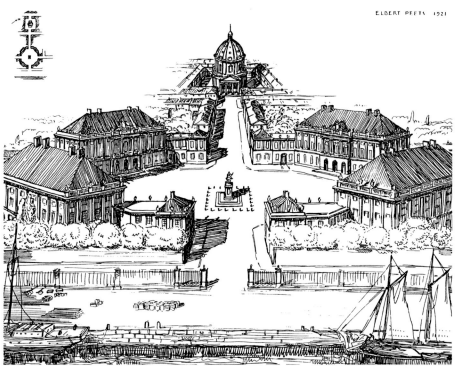

1.3 Elbert Peets' drawing of the Amalienborg Palace in Copenhagen, originally four individual houses of aristocratic families built in the late 18th century. The Marble Church in the background has its own civic square, connected by a ceremonial street to the palace. This kind of urban space is clearly a statement about power and precedence.

that people find ways to use a space not necessarily foreseen by the designer.

Richard Sennett in *The Conscience of The Eye, The Design and Social Life of Cities,* does not see the problem of community in cities as being one that can be solved through design. Instead he says that lack of community comes from a fear of exposure to strangers that is deeply ingrained in our culture. He intersperses his exploration of this issue in history and literature with accounts of his own walks through New York City. He recounts the deep, underlying cultural differences among various groups, and the ways that they manage to avoid interaction even when they occupy the same sidewalk. Sennett's descriptions make it clear how few places along these walks meet even the most elementary prescriptions of Gehl, Whyte, and Lynch. Sennett may be correct about the underlying difficulties of achieving real community in public spaces, particularly in a very large city, but there are certainly many design improvements that can make public places both more pleasant and more sociable.

The Origins of Modern Public Spaces

Traditional public spaces were not designed for leisure. Market streets and squares were crowded, functional places. Fountains were meeting places because people went there to draw water for their homes. In large parts of the world these functional public spaces continue as they always have.

The plazas in front of palaces or religious buildings were intended for ceremonies. During the Renaissance, public spaces began to be embellished to create compositions in perspective, comparable to those already seen in paintings, gardens, and stage scenery. Buildings were designed to be symmetrical around a central axis, the facades were modulated by arcades and colonnades; often the same design system was applied to all the frontages around a square. Long, straight streets were planned to terminate at the center of a public building or at a plaza with a monument. Most of these innovations were about ceremony: an enhanced street environment for the carriages of the aristocracy, a place where the arrival of important people and their entrance into a palatial building would be appropriately stately and impressive. (1.3) Richard Sennett, in *The Fall of Public Man,* explores how many of these spaces lost their meaning as much of the ritual character of urban life has faded away.

The conversion of the Palais Royal in Paris during the 1780s into what could be called a shopping and entertainment center and the opening of London's Vauxhall Gardens in 1732 were early examples of public places dedicated to leisure-time activities. Tivoli in Copenhagen is a descendant of the English pleasure garden, whose more recent evolution is the theme park.

The New England common in the seventeenth and eighteenth century was a staging area for cattle, it was overgrazed, dirty, and full of manure—not a green oasis with a white-painted pavilion in the center. The village green with a central bandstand is a nineteenth century innovation, as is a public park open to everyone, like Central Park in New York, where an artful mixture of formal and naturalistic design helped people from different social groups to share the space.

While arcades and shops along streets have long been places of commerce, the street as a place for a leisurely public promenade is also a mid-nineteenth century invention, the Parisian boulevards being the archetype. The European café with tables on the sidewalk or in the public square is a relatively recent innovation, and the pedestrian street or pedestrian district is mostly a phenomenon of the past 50 years. The Stroget in Copenhagen was one of the first shopping districts, a series of five streets closed to all but pedestrians in 1962. In Denver, Minneapolis, and a few other U.S. cities, downtown pedestrian malls remain in use, but in many other places pedestrian malls have been taken out again, as closing the streets to vehicles caused them to disappear from the mental maps of the people who once used them. In the historic centers of European cities, where public transit is much more a part of everyday life, more people live nearby, and such other options as shopping centers are still limited, the pedestrian street and plaza remain successful, particularly in countries where strolling in a public place is still a daily ritual.

Can public places in the United States attain the popularity of places in Europe that Americans go out of their way to visit when they travel?

Making Public Space Inviting

Tall buildings need space around them, and architects began designing plazas to provide an appropriate setting for towers. These plazas were not always intended to encourage people to spend time there. The idea was to create an impressive approach to the building. The owners often placed spikes on ledges so that people would not sit or lie on them, and the microclimate was frequently unfriendly, with strong down-drafts from the building when it was windy, blinding sunlight on hot days, and large unsheltered expanses in winter.

Uninviting spaces in highly accessible locations became places for "antisocial elements" to hang out, they attracted drug-dealing, they detracted from the atmosphere of corporate dignity that the owners and architects had hoped to create. In addition, some of these public spaces had been built in response to government incentives; they were supposed to be a public benefit, not a public nuisance.

Both William H. Whyte and Jan Gehl used maps to record how people use a public space. Gehl's map of an Italian square shows that people are comfortable standing in the arcade around the square, but not in the exposed open space itself. (1.4) Whyte's map of the plaza in front of the Seagram building in New York shows that people like to sit on the steps and walls along the edge, where they can watch other people walking by on the sidewalks. (1.5) From observations like these it is possible to derive some general design principles, which are discussed in more detail in Chapter 12.

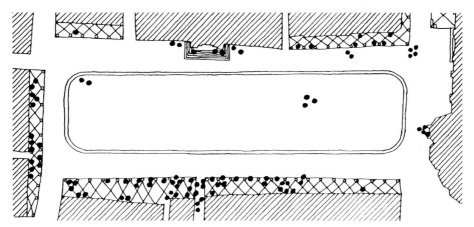

1.4 Jan Gehl's survey of where people congregate in the city square, Ascoli Piceno, Italy. Almost everyone has chosen a protected spot around the perimeter of the square.

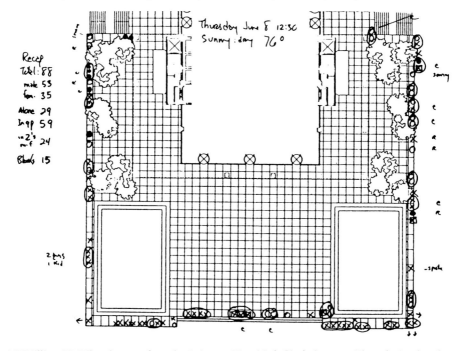

1.5 William H. Whyte's map of people sitting on New York City's Seagram Plaza during lunch hour on a mild day in June. Xs are male, Os female; a circle around Xs and Os indicates a group.

The Empty Square: Do People Still Need Public Space?
Gehl and Whyte, writing in the 1970s, discuss public spaces as questions of design, a follow-up to Jane Jacobs's famous comparison of the active social life on her street in Greenwich Village with the deserted and dangerous lawns in a public housing project.

Today, in some parts of the world, creating a sense of community has become a larger design issue than the configuration of individual streets and public spaces. An article, "The Empty Square" by Alan Ehrenhalt in a recent *Preservation* magazine asks the question: "If casual social encounters are at the heart of civic life, where did everybody go?" In most U.S. cities and towns necessary activities take place using a car, and the opportunities for any kind of casual interaction are much diminished. The commute goes from the garage at home to the garage or parking lot at work. Only the journey from the car space to the lobby takes place on foot. Shopping and errands are done by car to individual destinations. Schools, churches, country clubs, restaurants, movies—each is a separate destination reachable only by car. The Courthouse Square is empty. People drive to the health club and do their walking on a treadmill.

Architects, landscape architects, and city planners are currently debating whether it is still important to create public places that permit the personal contact found in traditional cities and towns, or whether life today requires something completely different. One side, which includes the people who call themselves New Urbanists, agrees with Gehl and Whyte that traditional streets, squares, promenades, and parks are still the essence of city design. Their opponents—among whom Dutch architect Rem Koolhaas is perhaps the most articulate—believe that the idea that cities can be designed at all is based on unexamined philosophical assumptions, and that modern transportation and communication, particularly the Internet, have made traditional urban spaces obsolete. An expert on computer technology, William J. Mitchell, has written *e-topia: "Urban Life, Jim - But Not as We Know It,"* which observes that the interactions of technology and behavior are much too complex to allow simple apocalyptic conclusions. Mitchell notes that you have to look at the totality of people's work and personal lives if you want to make good estimates about where new technology is taking us. Most of the people who have chosen to leave their offices and houses because the computer has freed them to work where they please are not living on mountaintops, but in smaller, rural communities, or in such sophisticated urban centers as Boston or San Francisco, precisely because of the face-to-face communication possible there. Many e-mail messages are about establishing meetings. The demand for hotel rooms and convention centers seems to be going up. Mitchell notes the rising interest in living in or near places that are rich in social interaction: older urban centers and suburban downtowns, older mixed-use neighborhoods and their modern imitations, as well as resorts. He concludes that the power of place will still prevail, that people will still gravitate to settings that offer particular cultural, scenic, and climatic attractions—"those unique qualities that cannot be pumped through a wire"—and will continue to care about meeting face-to-face.

Placemaking as a Larger Social Issue
William Leach, in his book *Country of Exiles: The Destruction of Place in American Life*, argues that high-speed transportation, the increasing tendencies of people to change jobs and move, the artificial environments produced by the hospitality industry, globalization policies at universities, and free trade and other international policies of government are all working to make Americans transient and rootless. These statements are an extension of the argument about the importance of public places to the larger realm of the whole environment. Rem Koolhaas in his book *S M L XL* looks at some of the same phenomenon as Leach and concludes that these trends are both exhilarating and liberating, while Leach asserts that placelessness leads to social instability, more crime, less regard for the rights of others. Tony Hiss describes in *The Experience of Place* how unsettling it is for the people he interviews to go back to places where they used to live and find the completely altered by new development, and made placeless and shapeless. Hiss notes that the future of the United States is not as open-ended as it once was. If population projections are to be believed, the built environment of the United States will approach completion within the next 50 years. While Koolhaas is right to say that places created today need not follow familiar historical patterns, the challenge to city designers is to make sure that new spaces meet people's needs as well, or better, than the places lost through growth and change.

Designing Communities as Well as Public Spaces
Excessive commuting time takes up the part of the day that could otherwise be used for more leisurely activities or spent with family at home. Attempts to solve traffic problems by building new roads are seldom successful, because the roads attract more development and induce more traffic. New patterns of working at home and commuting electronically will diminish the problem. But the real answers will come from creating places where home and work are more closely related.

The traditional main street was a place where people could meet unexpectedly walking from one destination to another. Now, designers of retail development are trying to create park-once districts, partly to foster interaction and communication, but also to create synergy among the different retail tenants. This is a trend that will make the design of public spaces more important.

Michael Porter, a professor at the Harvard Business School, elaborating on an insight first published by Jane Jacobs, postulates that the way to make a city or region more competitive is to encourage what he calls "clusters" of businesses that make related products, research laboratories that seek innovations related to these products, job-training that creates a work-force with the relevant skills, trade associations, and sales organizations that relate to these specialties and so on. This theory suggests that industrial location is as much a matter of community as a choice of residence; it is just a different kind of common interest. A successful cluster requires the interaction of a wide range of activities, and proximity is required to make these interactions effective. Business locations may be decentralized in comparison with older patterns, but scattered work places are bad for business.

The mass production of houses that began at developments like Levittown, Long Island, in the 1940s, plus the influence of local zoning ordinances that mapped large areas for the same size houses and lots (see page 101), caused homebuilders to see themselves as turning out products, rather than building communities, even when their developments were as big as a good-sized town. Today homebuilders are more aware that, whether they intend it or not, they are constructing communities, while towns and cities are deciding that zoning for neighborhoods is better than uniform tracts of a similar density and lot size.

Planning workplaces and residences so that they relate more closely to each other, designing shopping as park-once districts, creating self-reinforcing clusters of businesses and related activities, building neighborhoods of diverse housing types instead of housing tracts, and integrating school buildings back into their surrounding neighborhoods would go a long way towards making personal interactions easier and more meaningful. We will explore the ways in which a sense of community can be built into cities and towns through placemaking in the chapters on neighborhoods, commercial centers, and downtowns later in this book.

1.6 *A bench in Battery Park City can be a place for solitude in the midst of a big city, or could accommodate a family or a group. This distinctive place is created with the simplest of traditional elements, but each component has been designed with care and authority. The designers are Hanna, Olin.*

2

Livability:
Urbanism Old & New

There is talk about a crisis of livability in the United States. How can this be, when almost everyone lives at a level of comfort and safety that would have amazed people only a century ago, and still is unimaginable in many parts of the world? Most communities in the U.S. have paved streets; the water, sewer, gas, and electric utilities all work. Telephones and other communications systems are available. Police, fire departments, and emergency medical services are there when needed. There is a complete public school system. There are community parks and protections from the noise and pollution of heavy manufacturing. The housing industry builds homes with well-equipped kitchens, lavish bathrooms, and effective heating and cooling systems. Most new houses have private yards and private garage spaces. Substandard units are now less than five percent of the housing supply, and some of these are vacation houses.

At the same time, we have a breakdown of the physical environment in poor neighborhoods, inconvenient and confusingly planned suburban housing tracts, jammed local highways lined with endless strip centers and franchise stores, and the banal office parks and regional malls that have replaced traditional downtowns in many places. Within the privacy of our home and workplace we have never lived better; the problem is in the public environment, in the way our homes and lives fit together.

Livability today comes down to a discussion of city design: Not just what is being built, but also how to build it. There is also an awkward awareness that much of what has gone wrong with the design of both older cities and newer suburbs can be traced to earlier efforts at reform and improvement. To understand current prescriptions for livability, it is useful to know a little of their history, and to review the major questions where design professionals disagree.

Modernist City Design

The modern revolution in architecture and planning began early in the 20th century. The modernists knew what they were against: crowded unsanitary slums and pretentious buildings that used allusions to history to clothe contemporary structures and institutions. They wanted to open up both building and cities, getting rid of unnecessary embellishments, sweeping away old-style formal room divisions and traditional streets and squares.

In the 1920s, Le Corbusier, the French-Swiss architect, became well-known for his prophetic drawings of massive apartment and office towers composed as simple geometric masses. Vast parks and plazas separated these austere structures; high-speed highways were to be the means of organization and communication. When Le Corbusier arrived in New York by ocean liner in 1935, he was overwhelmed by his first sight of Manhattan's skyline from the harbor. Once on land, he found that the tall buildings did not live up to his anticipations. "The skyscrapers of New York are too small and there are too many of them," was his widely quoted comment. "They have destroyed the street and brought traffic to a standstill." His solution was to tear everything down, on the assumption, which he states explicitly, that the open space created will be more valuable than the accumulated property values of the buildings. His sketches (2.1) show what he proposed instead. As well as removing the buildings, most of Manhattan's streets also would be eliminated. The traffic arteries that replaced them would form cells, or superblocks. "The pedestrians will have the freedom of parks over the whole ground area and the cars will travel from skyscraper to skyscraper at a hundred miles an hour on one-way elevated roads placed wide distances apart." Le Corbusier's design ignored the subway system, which was what had actually made New York's tall buildings possible. Each tower in Le Corbusier's drawing is attached to its own parking deck. There is also nothing in these sketches that needs to be constructed in an existing city; it would be far easier to build these designs on open land.

It is remarkable how much of what has happened to modern cities all over the world is prefigured in these little sketches and terse statements. A prime modernist criterion for livability has been access to open space at ground level, plus views from the windows of tall buildings. Another criterion is fast movement for automobiles on elevated highways, with less emphasis on rapid transit. The assumption that preexisting development ought to make way for the new, and that the same kind of urbanism is appropriate in both

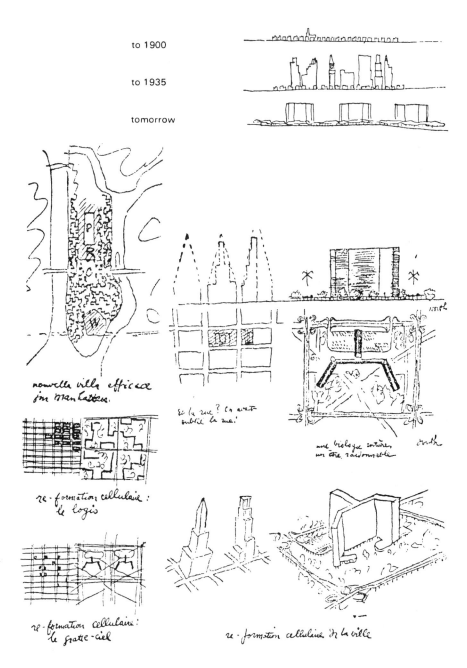

2.1 *Le Corbusier's 1935 sketches showing how to transform Manhattan into a city of highways, superblocks, and vast towers, each with its own mammoth parking deck. Only Central Park and perhaps Wall Street are left. Le Corbusier's ideas about cities have had a worldwide influence.*

city and country are ideas still powerful today. Towers and parking decks connected to highways have become ubiquitous in urban, suburban, and even rural locations.

Early Influence of Modernist City Design

Modernist images of housing surrounded by open space were especially interesting to housing reformers. Crowded, airless tenements could be replaced by bigger buildings with parks and gardens, housing the same number of people with plenty of light and air. The tenants in these new apartments would enjoy modern indoor plumbing, kitchen appliances, and central heating, which slum housing often didn't have. Modernist design ideas were rapidly assimilated into U.S. housing programs. This project at Charlestown in Boston was photographed just as construction was being completed about 1940. (2.2)

A modernist, but not Corbusian, vision of the suburbs can be seen in experimental towns like Greenbelt, Maryland, built by the U.S. government during the New Deal. (2.3) The design is influenced by modernist housing in Europe during the 1920s and 1930s, by the English garden suburbs, and by the work in the United States of Clarence Stein and his collaborators. Lewis Mumford narrates the 1939 film *The City,* which was produced by the American Institute of Planners and describes how workers could leave the ramshackle slums of a city like Pittsburgh, where water comes from a pump outside the tenement and the children play on the railway tracks, for garden apartments or small rowhouses with open interiors, plenty of windows and a plot in a communal vegetable garden in a place like Greenbelt. The children are seen walking or bicycling to school along greenways separated from traffic. Mother works in a modern kitchen, while father bicycles to a clean, modern factory, not a dilapidated, unsafe workplace, and join his friends in a healthy softball game after work.

Modernism's Implicit Social Theory

The unspoken assumption in this film, and behind the housing project and the greenbelt suburb, was that the great majority of people would always be working class; the men would labor in factories or service businesses; women would either hold low-level jobs or do housework for their families. Most people would be tenants and not homeowners; they would not own cars, and would be content with the simple pleasures to be found in the parks and green spaces near their homes. Le Corbusier apparently makes comparable assumptions, adding the possibility of individual car ownership, although his designs for automobile travel routes are highly regimented.

Authoritarian intervention also is assumed. The Charlestown project was built by the Boston Housing Authority; Greenbelt was begun by the Resettle-

2.2 Charleston housing project, Boston, Massachusetts, photographed just before it opened in 1940. A typical project for low-income families, largely separated from the surrounding neighborhood, and with buildings sited for maximum light and air according to modernist architectural theories.

2.3 The plan for Greenbelt, Maryland, by Douglas D. Ellington and R. J. Wadsworth, chief architects, Hale Walker, town planner. Greenbelt was built in the late 1930s under a New Deal program to demonstrate that garden suburbs could house low-income families relocated from urban slums.

ment Administration, established by President Franklin Delano Roosevelt by executive order as one of the emergency measures during the Great Depression of the 1930s. Le Corbusier speculated that "sooner or later" his ideas for Manhattan will be carried out by corporations, "the land-owning syndicates," or "strong, well-directed legislative measures."

The people putting together these visions were highly educated members of the upper middle class. They assumed that they themselves would continue living in large urban apartments and town houses, college towns, or country-club suburbs. They expected to be able to take their cars for a drive whenever they wished; they would travel, go out to dinner, attend elegant social events. Modernism for them was a prefabricated suburban or vacation house on their own private lot, which, thanks to the economies of new technology, could be larger and more luxurious than their current home.

The Successes and Failures of Modernist City Design
Modernist city design has been most successful in the places that best fit its underlying assumptions, the socialist democracies in the Scandinavian countries and the Netherlands, egalitarian societies with a strong commitment to collective or government ownership. The modernist design paradigm for moderate-income communities—factory towns with garden rental apartments surrounded by greenbelts—was widely used in Great Britain. A variation that included modernist apartment towers can be found all over western Europe.

The modernist vision of the future did not anticipate the wholesale opening up of the middle-class lifestyle in the United States after World War II. Mass production of automobiles put suburban living within reach of office and factory workers. Promoting home ownership over rental apartments using FHA and VHA mortgage financing overturned the assumptions of modernist design advocates and housing reformers. They had expected most suburban development to be rental communities built by the government, or by private investors like the big life-insurance companies. Mass-production techniques learned during the World War II helped the Levitt organization and other builders produce a cut-down version of middle-class garden suburbs: separate houses on separate lots. These developments lacked the design conventions that had given unity and order to older suburbs—parts of the tradition rejected by modernist planners and architects—but tract houses sold as fast as builders could finish them. There are a few post-World War II planned communities in the United States, notably Columbia, Maryland; Reston, Virginia; and Irvine, California, which can be considered descendants of pre-war experiments like Greenbelt, but most developers gave their attention to the house as the marketable product: the yard was second, the community was the result of whatever local regulations were in force in the area.

In cities, modern luxury apartment towers and tall office buildings can work well for their tenants, but the regular repeating patterns of towers and parks, so easy to draw, were almost impossible to implement in the fragmented, competitive real-estate market in the United States. Instead, towers can intrude into otherwise low-scale districts; an office building plaza will open up views of the undesigned party walls of buildings next door, and elevated expressways devastate whole neighborhoods.

The modernist supposition that large tracts of urban open space should somehow be worth more than urban buildings was given reality by government subsidies, which permitted local government to buy deteriorated pieces of the city, write down their value, and sell them for new developments. Urban renewal did permit the redesign of large tracts of urban land, but where towers are surrounded by open space, the individual buildings seldom had a coherent relation to each other. The towers could look like they would form a livable community in a presentation drawing, but there was no controlling principle. Each building was designed by a different architect, so what livability there was existed inside the buildings, not in the place.

In developing countries where modernist housing towers were imposed on people who had been living in villages or in traditional urban quarters, the result has frequently been unpleasant and uncared-for public spaces surrounded by repeating patterns of large, drab, and shabby structures—at the same time that the new housing represented big improvements in the delivery of basic services such as drinking water, sanitation, and electricity.

Well-publicized demolitions in the U.S., beginning with the dynamiting of the award-winning Pruitt-Igoe housing towers in St. Louis in 1976, have dramatized the unlivablity of modern high rises for poor tenants, often because the local housing authorities can't provide the security and maintenance needed for tall buildings.

The modernist vision of separate buildings and separate functional areas was easily attained in rapidly developing suburbs. The modernist saw nothing incongruous about tall urban buildings and massive office and shopping centers in an area that was otherwise rural, no inherent problem in exporting urbanization far into the countryside. Nature was seen as something to be subdued, paved over, rationalized.

Urban Design and Environmentalism as an Antidote to Modernism
The contemporary practice of urban design began in the 1960s as a reaction against the failures of modernism to produce a livable environment. Housing projects, where they were maintained, could produce superior individual apartments, but also unsafe open spaces that no one could use, and a danger-

ous isolation from the rest of the city. The urban plazas so important to the modernist image were also often deserted and unsafe, and broke up the continuity of retail frontages along streets. The modernist axiom that pedestrians should be separated from automobile traffic helped produce isolated shopping malls in the suburbs and, in some cities, siphoned pedestrians onto bridges and concourses, deadening buildings at street level. Elevated highways and parking decks produced other kinds of dead zones in cities, places where no one wanted to walk. The separation of cities and new suburban development into single-use "cells," as Le Corbusier had advocated, increased traffic and turned daily life into a complicated logistics problem, where trips to lunch, to school, to sports, to entertainment all had to be carefully scheduled. The isolated towers and elevated highways that were a romantic evocation of a better future in the drawings of Le Corbusier turned out to be profoundly depersonalizing, as did the modernist tendency to write off old buildings as anachronisms that ought to be scrapped to make room for architecture more suitable for today.

To make cities more livable, urban designers countered modernist ideology by protecting historic buildings, by making the street the primary element of urban open space, and by using zoning and other development regulations creatively to put new buildings into context and preserve a mix of different activities.

Neighborhood Planning Instead of Urban Renewal

The drastic slum clearance and urban renewal policies that had transformed U.S. cities after World War II were not solely the result of modernist design beliefs. Much of what was cleared was either not worth saving, or had been neglected for so long that preservation seemed unaffordable. But the idea that within the boundaries of a given district there was *nothing* worth saving, and that preserving an older building would interfere with the best new design for the area—that was modernism. With 20-20 hindsight, even the best of the total clearance urban renewal areas, like the South-West urban renewal area in Washington, D.C., suffer from a sterility that results from the removal of almost all the accretions of the past, of any trace of unpremeditated variety and incident. Something of the cold-hearted way in which the previous residents were turned out of their homes, however defective and substandard these homes may have been, was communicated by the regimented design of the new development. A truly livable community has to be created from the successive actions of the people who live there.

One of the first and most successful examples of selective urban renewal was the recreation of Society Hill in Philadelphia as an upper-income neighborhood, removing the city's wholesale market while preserving many historic houses and public buildings. Applying similar concepts to renewing neighborhoods for poor and moderate-income people without total clearance of existing buildings required complete changes in the way such projects were planned and funded. Much of the prototype work for transforming urban renewal plans into neighborhood development plans was done in New York City. Building new housing to fit into an existing neighborhood also increased community participation in planning decisions, for the obvious reason that the community would still be there when the plan was completed. Neighborhood planning caused architects to rethink housing designs. It had been the practice for housing to be sited for the best orientation of the apartments, according to modernist prescriptions, as in the Boston public housing shown on page 31, which meant that the buildings were designed on a different geometric system from the surrounding streets, leaving oddly shaped bits of open space between street and building. Instead of clearing whole districts, building "vest-pocket" housing to fit into irregular sites left when neighboring structures were preserved brought the new buildings back into a relationship with the street and preserved continuity with the surrounding neighborhood.

The Street as the Mixing Chamber

Streets occupy a big percentage of urban land. Separating pedestrians from vehicular traffic with a pedestrian bridge or underground concourse meant that the street was treated as a totally utilitarian place. Even where no separate accommodation for pedestrians was offered, modernist design meant more and wider lanes for traffic and narrower sidewalks, devoid of any amenity, for pedestrians.

Separate pedestrian concourses work well in high-density Asian cities with many competing shops. Pedestrian-only districts work in European cities where many of the people are delivered to the space by public transit or live nearby. Pedestrian bridges, underground concourses, and pedestrian malls have worked far less well in U.S. cities, resulting in deserted downtown streets in cities that had separate pedestrian concourses and even more deserted downtown streets that had been turned into pedestrian malls.

As a result, urban design practice returned to using streets as the prime means of communication in cities, adopting landscape and street-furniture designs that made it comfortable to share the space among pedestrians, transit, and individual vehicles. The design of facades and ground floors of buildings, and their relation to the street, took on renewed importance with this attention to the street as public open space.

Historic Preservation

While neighborhood planning was putting new emphasis on keeping ordinary, but perfectly sound existing buildings, sentiment also was growing to preserve noteworthy historic architecture from being torn down by the real-estate industry. The 1963 demolition of Pennsylvania Station in New York City produced the political coalition necessary to create the city's Landmark Preservation Commission. While wreckers were at work on the station, Max Abramovitz, a well-known modernist architect, told an audience at New York City's Architectural League that he could not understand why people wanted to save Pennsylvania Station. When he was a young man, he added, he would have been picketing to have it torn down. The modern movement was deeply hostile to buildings like this, where a steel structure was clad in majestic neo-Roman architecture. Historic preservationists had a reciprocal hostility to modernist architecture; all too often people preferred what was there before to the building that replaced it. The designation of historic landmarks, and, later, of historic districts, bought time for these buildings. Today, while legal safeguards are still important, the architectural merit of these older buildings is once again accepted by the leaders of the architectural profession, as well as by the real-estate market.

Restoring Continuity of Use and Structure in Cities
In the 1950s and 1960s, when cities began approving modernist urban renewal plans that promoted large open plazas, spaced housing towers far apart on open lawns, and relegated retail to separate shopping centers; they also began amending their zoning codes to bring them into conformity with their renewal plans, often giving incentives for towers and public open space.

The defects in these new codes became evident almost as soon as they were enacted, but modernist design prescriptions had now become the law. Urban designers working for cities were called upon to help modify the regulations, substituting other kinds of amenities for outdoor public spaces, requiring that buildings be built to the street line, requiring that ground floors on certain streets have shops in them, imposing height limits, or setbacks above a certain height. The principle behind all these changes were that each new building should play a part in an evolving context, not be a separate, isolated object.

New York City's special zoning districts were early instances where zoning was used to achieve urban design objectives. The Times Square special zoning district has preserved and enhanced the area's distinctive electric signs, ensuring it didn't become just another business district—an interesting inversion of the typical role of zoning in restricting private signs. (2.4) The guidelines for Battery Park City, written by Alexander Cooper and Stanton Eckstut, are a substitute for the special zoning district. These requirements are part of the purchase agreement for each property and regulate such design issues as building placement and the elements that repeat from facade to facade.

2.4 The power of zoning: Signs in Times Square, New York City, required by code to fulfill requirements of a special district. It is more usual for zoning to be used to restrict signs.

2.5 *Apartment towers along the esplanade at Battery Park City. Instead of Le Corbusier's towers in a park, towers fronting on a park—a traditional urban relationship at a new scale, controlled by carefully drawn development regulations.*

Instead of towers surrounded by parkland, Battery Park City's towers occupy traditional street-front locations along a waterfront esplanade. (2.5)

An account of some of the first applications of these four principles of urban design—neighborhood planning, historic preservation, the street as public space, and contextual zoning—can be found in my book, *Urban Design as Public Policy*, published in 1974.

The Natural Environment as the Ultimate Context for Development

While designers were learning to exert some amount of design guidance over cities, rapid urbanization was taking place in many formerly rural and suburban areas. Two important books that advocate improving the design of suburban areas are *The Last Landscape*, by William H. Whyte, originally published in 1968, and Ian McHarg's *Design With Nature*, which first appeared in 1969. Whyte advocated what he called Cluster Zoning, which is now better known by its bureaucratic name, planned unit development. By concentrating houses in relatively compact clusters, more of the natural landscape could be preserved. At much the same time Ian McHarg was developing a methodology that made it easier to select the sites that *should* be preserved. McHarg advocated mapping areas where the natural ecology and subsurface conditions were most likely to be destabilized and then building only in those areas where construction would not cause serious environmental consequences. The two concepts worked well together, producing what can be described as a fifth urban design principle: New development in greenfield areas should only take place on land where development will cause the minimum of disturbance to the natural ecology, and should be designed to be in harmony with its natural surroundings.

This principle has gained some acceptance but it does not begin to deal with all the consequences of the migration of offices and retailing to suburban and rural areas. It does, however, represent a strong contradiction to modernist assumptions that all of nature could and should be subdued by engineering.

The Congress for the New Urbanism

The Congress for the New Urbanism (C.N.U.) was founded in 1993 in emulation of the Congres Internationaux d'Architecture Moderne (C.I.A.M.) which many believe was instrumental in bringing about the triumph of modernist city planning and design. The idea was to learn from this historical example how to gain acceptance for the changes in architectural and development practice needed to produce successful urban centers and residential neighborhoods. The C.N.U. seeks to replace the modernist planning principles that continue to be used in many situations with a comprehensive way of designing cities based primarily on techniques in use before the modernist movement.

New Urbanism gives primacy to streets in planning cities. These streets should create small blocks, as in older cities and towns, not the superblocks favored by modernists; buildings should relate to the streets, not be surrounded by modernist open green spaces. Streets should be planned to create vistas, like the designs of the City Beautiful movement at the beginning of the twentieth century. Instead of the separate land-use zones favored by modernists, development should mix uses and building types, again as in older cities and towns. A new assumption is that in today's society everyone is, or aspires to be, middle class. Instead of the proletariat for whom modernist cities were intended, today's metropolitan region should accommodate everyone's aspirations.

In 1996 the C.N.U. adopted a charter, again in emulation of C.I.A.M. (2.6). Instead of creating a city from buildings, as modernism generally advocated, the New Urbanist Charter starts with the regional context, goes on to the neighborhood, district and corridor and then the block, street and building. This counter-argument is at least the outline of a design theory that gives primacy to the creation of places through shaping streets and public spaces, although there are implicit theoretical issues that are not resolved. One such issue is the importance to be given to traditional styles of architecture.

Neo-Traditionalism

At the same C.N.U. meeting that adopted the Charter there was a sharp, even angry, discussion of the usefulness of *Neo-Traditionalism,* that is designs for buildings or towns that look back to the "traditional" architectural languages of the 1920s, the design idioms that the modernists rejected. The historians Eric Hobsbawm and Terence Ranger edited a volume of essays, *The Invention of Tradition,* in which they offered evidence that most traditions, including Christmas carols, Scottish tartans, and the ceremonials of the British royal family, were invented relatively recently in response to big social changes. In architecture also the appearance of continuity with the past was counterfeited to help create stability for what were really innovations: the mansion of a newly rich entrepreneur disguised as an ancestral manor house, recent university buildings in the form of ancient colleges at Oxford and Cambridge, new suburban houses designed like a farming village.

Is it possible to revive the planning principles for civic centers, colleges, or suburban streets from the pre-modernist period without also reviving classical facades, picturesque courtyards in Tudor or Georgian styles, or Spanish and New England Colonial houses?

This is what the argument at the fourth C.N.U. Congress was about. For Seaside, the Florida resort which is generally considered a prototypical new-

CHARTER OF THE NEW URBANISM

THE CONGRESS FOR THE NEW URBANISM views disinvestment in central cities, the spread of placeless sprawl, increasing separation by race and income, environmental deterioration, loss of agricultural lands and wilderness, and the erosion of society's built heritage as one interrelated community-building challenge.

WE STAND for the restoration of existing urban centers and towns within coherent metropolitan regions, the reconfiguration of sprawling suburbs into communities of real neighborhoods and diverse districts, the conservation of natural environments, and the preservation of our built legacy.

WE RECOGNIZE that physical solutions by themselves will not solve social and economic problems, but neither can economic vitality, community stability, and environmental health be sustained without a coherent and supportive physical framework.

WE ADVOCATE the restructuring of public policy and development practices to support the following principles: neighborhoods should be diverse in use and population; communities should be designed for the pedestrian and transit as well as the car; cities and towns should be shaped by physically defined and universally accessible public spaces and community institutions; urban places should be framed by architecture and landscape design that celebrate local history, climate, ecology, and building practice.

WE REPRESENT a broad-based citizenry, composed of public and private sector leaders, community activists, and multidisciplinary professionals. We are committed to reestablishing the relationship between the art of building and the making of community, through citizen-based participatory planning and design.

WE DEDICATE ourselves to reclaiming our homes, blocks, streets, parks, neighborhoods, districts, towns, cities, regions, and environment.

2.6 Preamble to the Charter of The New Urbanism, at least an outline of an urban design theory that goes beyond buildings.

urbanist community, its designers, Andres Duany and Elizabeth Plater-Zyberk wrote a code that mandated some architectural elements, such as a uniform roof pitch for all houses, picket fences for the front yards, and front porches. However, the code was written as a series of abstract instructions. While architects at Seaside were encouraged to follow examples of traditional Florida resort cottages, the code permitted modernist buildings, and a few such designs have been constructed at Seaside, where the traditionalism is mostly in the street plan, with its emphasis on axial vistas, and in the placement of houses and fences to enclose and define streets.

Celebration, the large planned community near Orlando, Florida, developed by the Disney Corporation, is generally considered a new-urbanist design, at least in its initial stages. And at Celebration, much of the town center, following plans by Robert A.M. Stern—a leading exponent of "traditional," or even "classical" architecture—and Jaquelin Robertson, is designed in a knowing version of the kinds of vernacular buildings constructed in small towns before World War II, while the home builders are required to follow a pattern book that gives requirements for houses in such historic styles as Spanish and New England Colonial.

There is now an awkward split in the design professions between architects who consider historic revivals anathema, and urban designers who are tempted by the uniformity and coherence that historic styles can provide. It is true that there are some architects that believe that modernism was such a complete mistake that the only thing to be done is to pretend the last 100—or even 200—years never happened. This is a minority view.

Modern construction materials have changed architecture forever; it is futile to try to confine the multiplicity of modern building types to shapes that could have been built of pre-industrial materials. Most architects apply Richard Norman Shaw's late nineteenth century verdict on Gothic revival architecture to any exercise in architectural historicism: "It was like a cut flower, pretty enough to look at, but fading away before your eyes..." There are many successful modern buildings and landscape designs. It is only in city-design that modernism has been a conspicuous failure.

Historic styles are popular with home builders and the public. There used to be subdivisions of modern builder's houses, like the Eichler houses in California, or Hollin Hills, designed by Charles Goodman in Alexandria, Virginia. Very few modernist builder houses have been constructed since the late 1970s. A new speculative house has a modern plan and all the modern conveniences, but—at least in front—some kind of gesture in the direction of traditional architecture has become a customary part of individual house design.

In planned communities that are going to be constructed of builders houses there is a need to permit some kind of stylistic presentation in the design codes that control development. Few urban designers will go as far in the direction of neo-traditionalism as Celebration. At most, they will look at traditional local buildings in the part of the country where they are working, and suggest a relatively abstract code based on the most desirable features of such local architecture.

Every-Day Urbanism, Free-Market Urbanism

There are practitioners and theorists, using terms like Every-Day Urbanism, who—with a nod in the direction of French Marxist philosopher Henri Lefebvre—question the validity of the middle-class standards that underlie most planning regulations. What is wrong, they ask, with carrying on a car-repair business in your front yard or doing hairstyling in your living room? Urban designers and planners respond by saying okay: We will create a live-work zone in each community. But this kind of accommodation doesn't answer the real question, which is motivated by a more general relativism: Why should any set of top-down standards be better than decisions that people make for themselves? As cities are constantly changing and evolving, shouldn't urban designers study the process, understand what people are doing, and make any new interventions in a city derive from what is already going on? Many of the examples that illustrate books advocating this position are from neighborhoods with a concentration of recent immigrants from countries that still have strong folk traditions, which they have brought with them to decorate stores and houses. Where there is a viable folk tradition, it can be worth encouraging and preserving it. But is it possible to create the modern equivalent of folk traditions that could substitute for the regulations that seek to control the product of today's complex building and real-estate industries?

In *Learning from Las Vegas,* originally published in 1972, Robert Venturi, Denise Scott Brown, and Steven Izenour had analyzed the garish architecture and signs along the strip in Las Vegas, and concluded that they embodied a complex symbolic language that was adroitly employed to draw in the customers. They went on to apply what they had learned to the more general subject of symbolism in architecture, producing two hitherto unknown categories: the Duck and the Decorated Shed. In *God's Own Junkyard,* Peter Blake's diatribe against the ugliness of the modern world, he had shown a photograph of a building in the shape of a duck, a roadside structure where Long Island ducks were sold. A building that subordinates its design to a predetermined shape—what the modernists called "significant form"—is thus a duck. A decorated shed is a utilitarian building which has an elaborate facade. A Gothic cathedral, according to the authors of *Learning from Las Vegas,* is both a duck and a decorated shed. In their analysis, the facade of a Gothic cathedral is effectively a billboard, where elaborate iconography promotes the message offered within.

These sophisticated speculations are not the same as saying that we can learn from Las Vegas either a new architectural language or a method for how cities should be designed, although the authors do say that buildings can be "dumb" and "ordinary," that is not every building has to aspire to high style.

Rem Koolhaas and some other designers assert that cities are shaped by market forces and can't be controlled by design. They see what is happening in cities today as a great, untamed force, disregarding government decisions about highways and infrastructure, tax subsidies, the whole complex interplay between market forces and regulations.

Relativists, like the advocates for Every-Day Urbanism, and free-marketers like Koolhaas, are arguing against any kind of development regulation that relies on a pre-set pattern, in other words they are giving up the possibility of shaping the city. Understanding changing economic and social conditions is a precondition to any responsible planning, but there has actually been a consensus for most of the last century that city planning and development regulation are necessities. Modern society is so complex, and the building and development industries so specialized, that some kind of rule-making system has to be created. It is no longer possible to rely on folk traditions or community standards that may have worked in pre-industrial societies where people built their own houses and workplaces. The real-estate marketplace, far from being an uncontrollable force, is a made up of conservative institutions that look for as much certainty as possible. Developers may argue against a specific rule that applies to their individual project, but they favor a system of ground rules that apply to others. Regulations have often produced undesirable places, but this is not because they have been ineffective. They have been much too effective in imposing an outmoded design ideology.

The Consensus on Livability by Professional Urban Designers

Today designing cities is an active interdisciplinary profession made up of architects, planners, and landscape architects. I have been an urban designer since I went to work for the City of New York in the mid-1960s and have seen the profession grow from a few dozen individuals to hundreds of firms and thousands of urban designers in governmental agencies. Many professional urban designers, myself included, do not consider ourselves attached to an exclusive set of design prescriptions. Our theoretical position is well expressed in the 1977 book, *Collage City*, by Colin Rowe and Fred Koetter. Le Corbusier had drawn whole cities transformed at his direction. Rowe and Koetter remind us that cities can not be reshaped by a single designer or even a single design philosophy. Instead, designing cities is more like collage:

inventing a few things, but mostly arranging and reordering elements already at hand.

Most urban designers today share the objectives outlined in the C.N.U. charter. I myself am pleased to be a supporter of the C.N.U. as the most effective advocacy group for urban design, and I currently serve on its board. However, I understand the position of the urban designers who are reluctant to identify themselves with the Congress for the New Urbanism because of the neo-traditional architecture advocated by some of its members. For them, as for most New Urbanists, there are a series of city-design principles that have little to do with architectural style, which, if embodied in public policies, would produce more livable communities. The following is an outline of this consensus position on livability today.

1. Preserve and Restore the Natural Environment
Research shows that people have a greater sense of well-being if their lives include ready access to the natural environment. Not only should people live and work close to parks and open space, but they should not be too far from areas of natural or agricultural landscape. Ecologists have taught us that the natural environment, when it is in equilibrium, is like a design for a building in the sense that it represents the resolution and harmonization of many contradictory requirements. Once this natural design is disturbed, the environment can deteriorate rapidly. The conservative position is to avoid disturbance to the natural environment as much as possible and to restore natural systems in urbanized areas.

2. Preserve and Restore the Built Environment
A livable city needs a diversity of building types to accommodate its different activities, and a variety of incident and design which is beyond the imagination of any single designer—thus the importance of preservation and reuse not only of notable historic buildings and districts, but of ordinary serviceable buildings. Historic preservation has evolved from the concept of saving a few landmark buildings—the Mount Vernons—to a preservation ethic that suggests that any old building has value because of the energy and materials used to construct it. So, instead of the presumption that any old building may be cleared to make room for a higher and better use of the land, we now have a new presumption: Any old building should be saved, unless there are clear economic or city design reasons why it has to make way for new development.

3. Restore Existing Neighborhoods and Create New Ones
A design that encourages people to meet while they are walking through public places is a primary means of creating community, as discussed in

Chapter 1, so that the first principle of a livable community or workplace is
that it should be a walkable. From this it follows that residential districts
should be walkable neighborhoods. As mentioned above, neighborhood
planning was rediscovered in the 1960s as a way to humanize slum clearance
and urban renewal in cities. In the 1980s it was discovered again as a way to
organize master-planned new communities (see Chapters 6, 7 and 8). (2.7)

4. Make Commercial Districts Park-Once Districts

If people are going to walk between destinations in commercial districts, and
if these districts are to be served effectively by public transportation, they
have to be designed as compact, walkable places. If each separate business
has its own parking lot, and threatens to tow away the car of anyone who
dares to shop elsewhere, compact walkable business centers are impossible.
Buildings need to be grouped so that they can be accessed from sidewalks
and parking needs to be shared. Where needed, publicly financed parking
garages need to be built on suburban as well as urban sites.

5. Make Streets the Center of the Public Environment

The sidewalks along streets remain the most appropriate places for people to
walk, and the street should remain the primary means of communication in
cities and towns, the link between buildings and public spaces. Except in the
densest of urban environments, experience has shown that modernist pedestrian concourses are a mistake, because they siphon people off the streets,
leaving too few people to sustain effective retail or a safe public environment
on either the street or the concourse. The design of the street system is thus
the basis for making a community livable, and the streets should be both
pleasant for pedestrians as well as efficient for vehicles and transit.

   If the street is the basic organizing principle for the livable community, it
follows that buildings should be designed to relate to and reinforce the street.
In a residential area a street full of garage doors is not as livable a street as
one lined with porches, doors and windows. In commercial districts livability
means overcoming the fragmentation created by parking and highways to
produce the kinds of walkable places described in Chapter 1, and Chapters 9,
10 and 11.

6. Use Development Regulation as a Positive Template

Finally, the creation of a livable city requires the intervention of the public
sector as ringmaster, using the development regulations necessary in a complex society to create a context for development, so that each new project is
an addition to an evolving community, not a separate, self-contained unit. We
will return to these issues in the Implementation section of this book.

2.7 A downtown street in Orenco Station, a planned community in suburban Portland, Oregon, designed around a transit stop as a walkable neighborhood with local stores. Urban designers were Fletcher Farr Ayotte.

3

Mobility:
Parking, Transit, & Urban Form

One way to understand the difference between traditional cities and today's urbanization is to make figure-ground drawings, which show buildings as dark masses while streets and other open spaces are white space. This figure-ground drawing (3.1) of the edge city at Valley Forge/King of Prussia, Pennsylvania, is by Philadelphia architects Stephen Kieran and James Timberlake. They then superimpose their drawing over the street plan of downtown Philadelphia (3.2) to compare them. For most people interested in urban design the coherence and rationality of downtown Philadelphia is superior to

3.1 A figure-ground drawing of urban development at Valley Forge/King of Prussia, Pennsylvania, around 1990.

the diffuse and dispersed pattern in Valley Forge/King of Prussia. But Kieran and Timberlake see the potential for a new kind of development in which the landscape, by which they mean all space that is not building, takes precedence over buildings as the organizing elements of a city. Valley Forge/King of Prussia is the kind of cityscape that Rem Koolhaas refers to when he says that the modern world has swept traditional ideas of urban form away.

But does this dynamic drawing represent an equally dynamic form of urbanism? Much of what is represented as ground in this figure-ground drawing is not streets, or landscape, but highways and parking lots. The development shown in the map could be built because it was at the confluence of three major highways, and took the form it did because almost all access was by car. There was room for at-grade parking lots, and the comparatively low cost of parking gave the area a competitive edge. These commonplaces don't necessarily lead to an exciting series of urban experiences.

How Highways and Parking Lots Fragment Development

Far from being the result of the irresistible forces of modern life, the pattern of development around the typical highway interchange is the result of designing the highway as an isolated artifact, without any recognition that it will induce development. The interchange design minimizes the land needed and permits cars to maintain speed as they leave the highway. Nobody is thinking about how to fit the interchange into the buildings that will go up around it.

Highway interchanges fragment development into quadrants; the development within the quadrant is then fragmented further by at-grade parking. A parking space is generally considered to require about 350 square feet: 200

3.2 The figure ground on the opposite page superimposed over a map of downtown Philadelphia at the same scale.

square feet is for the car, the rest for aisles and other circulation. Allow 400 square feet per car if you want any reasonable amount of landscaping. The decision to provide parking in lots instead of garages is a matter of economics:

Cost of an At-Grade Parking Space: $1,000 + land (good landscaping would be extra)

Cost of a Garage Parking Space: $10,000 to $12,000 + pro rata share of land as garage is multi-story

Cost of a Sub-Grade Parking Space: $20,000 to $30,000

Providing parking is a necessity for developers. Local codes and—usually—the permanent lender require minimum numbers of parking spaces for each type of building, expressed as ratios of parking to building area. Some typical parking ratios:

Retail: 5 cars per 1,000 square feet

Office in suburb: 4 cars per 1,000 square feet

Office in city with rapid transit: 2.5 cars per 1,000 square feet

Office in a big city with a metropolitan transit system:
0 - 1.5 cars per 1,000 square feet

Hotel: 1.5 cars per room

Apartments: 1.5 to 2 cars per apartment

Industry: 1 car per employee

The figure-ground pattern at Valley-Forge/King of Prussia is a product of the interchange design and the economics of parking. The buildings, instead of shaping the space, are isolated by their parking fields.

Effect of Parking on Office Location

The economics of parking have a big influence on the dispersal of development from city centers to accessible highway locations like Tysons Corner in Virginia or Valley Forge/King of Prussia. An office building with 25,000 square feet on each floor on a suburban site needs 100 car spaces for each floor of office space. One hundred cars occupy at least 35,000 square feet. Considering only the construction costs of parking, not the full development costs, at $1,000 a car space, an at grade parking space adds $4 a square foot to the construction cost per square foot of the building. Providing garage spaces for the same building at $10,000 a space adds $40 a square foot to the construction cost. Subgrade parking would add $80 to $120 a square foot.

Land costs need to be well over $1 million an acre before land-cost, by itself, makes it advisable to build a garage instead of at-grade parking.

The moral of the story: a good way to gain a price advantage for office development is to buy cheap land with good access and get it rezoned for offices. Then the developer has enough room to build at-grade parking, which provides a big price advantage over a developer who has to build a garage. And when land at one highway location starts getting too expensive, it is time to move on to the next interchange farther out.

At-Grade Parking and Building Relationships

It is difficult to create urbanity while accommodating today's parking ratios. The continuous frontages of Parisian boulevards, which most people would agree are one of the ideal city forms, are not compatible with at-grade parking. The downtowns in most U.S. cities are pocked with parking lots.

A four-story building, with a 25,000 square feet of office space on each floor, will need a minimum four-acre site for building and at-grade parking—more with landscaping. That is at least seven times the area of the land occupied by the building itself. An eight-story building, with a 25,000-square-foot floor plate and at-grade parking will need about seven-and-a-half acres—more with landscaping. That is 13 times the area of the land occupied by the building itself.

A one million-square-foot regional mall requires 5,000 car spaces, or more than 40 acres of at-grade parking. The distance to the farthest parking space becomes so great that most malls at this scale provide part of their parking in decks.

One of the great images of modern architecture is Le Corbusier's drawing of huge, cross-shaped office towers surrounded by open space, which he showed in a number of projects, including his Voisin Plan, which erases central Paris, replacing all but a few historic monuments with towers and super-highways. This image, like his 1935 sketches for rebuilding Manhattan (page 29) helped form the modern view of the office building independent of any urban context, surrounded by parking and green space. But Le Corbusier's seductive images of such future cities are only attainable with a complete rapid transit system; if the tenants arrive by automobile, today's parking ratios produce an entirely different image. (3.3)

Drawings in Le Corbusier's book, *Urbansime*, written in the 1920s, show

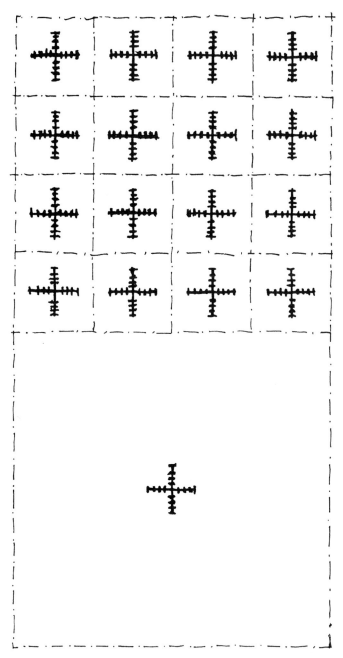

3.3 Le Corbusier's office towers for 30,000 workers grouped as proposed in his 1929 book, Urbanisme, *on the assumption that almost all of the tenants arrived by transit, contrasted with the amount of space needed for a single such tower, if most of the workers arrived by car. The original urbanity disappears.*

office towers similar to those in his Voisin Plan each accommodating 30,000 workers. The drawings also show parking for 400 cars and the spacing of the buildings is dictated by this parking estimate—or perhaps this is the number of cars that fit into his design for the spaces between buildings. When this project was designed, only the top company officials would be expected to have cars, and Le Corbusier describes most of the workers arriving by transit.

Today's suburban parking ratios effectively require one car for each building occupant, which for one of these towers would be 30,000 cars, so that Le Corbusier's building, if it were constructed in a suburban location today, would need at least 241 acres of at-grade parking. If, instead, Le Corbusier's developer decided to provide a garage, it would be a big garage. At 1,600 cars per floor, it would need to be at least 19 stories. Few garages are over seven stories, as the rule of thumb is that it takes approximately one minute per floor to enter or exit—and that is for a normal-sized garage, not one with 1,600 cars on each level. Except in New York and a few other big cities, this building would still need parking for 18,750 cars, even if there were public transit. When you look at most suburban office development you are not seeing a dynamic new design concept, you are looking at Le Corbusier's city of towers eroded by individual development decisions about parking.

Why At-Grade Parking May Be A Transitional Phase
The tide of parking spaces that has swept away traditional building relationships, might go back out again, as land values increase. At-grade parking is not an efficient use of land. Forty percent of the car spaces in shopping centers are only used on peak days, which generally occur between Thanksgiving and Christmas. (But 40 percent of sales also take place during this period.) Peak utilization of retail spaces rarely takes place during office hours; much office parking is vacant on evenings and weekends. Demand for stadium and arena parking has almost no overlap with parking used by office tenants

The Urban Land Institute has looked at the potential for shared parking among different land uses, and published modified parking ratios for such situations. For example, hotels in office centers only need half as many dedicated car spaces as hotels in isolated locations. These efficiencies depend upon effective city design. A stadium should be located near a concentration of office buildings; the right mix of retail and office also can produce parking efficiencies. Any land released from at-grade parking because of spaces shared among consolidated developments becomes available for other uses. This land is, for practical purposes, free.

The cost of "decanting" the parking from an acre of parking lot into a garage is roughly $1.25 million per acre. A garage can absorb five or six acres of parking while occupying less than an acre itself. Again, assuming the land has been paid for through the original development deal, the cost of decanting the parking becomes the cost for the land that is made available.

Townhouses and apartments could become feasible at such land prices, and could even be built over a parking deck. Another advantage of adding housing to an office district is that the peak travel requirements tend to be in opposite directions. People leaving the housing for work cross the people arriving to work in the office buildings, with the trips reversed in the evening. As the limiting factor for much edge city development is highway capacity, not zoning, adding a complementary land use is a way of increasing density and value without major road improvements. Some examples of the way garage parking can transform edge cities into something much more like real cities are shown in Chapter 10.

The increased density starts to create sites that can be served by rapid transit. If a new rapid-transit line allows a building owner with at-grade parking to reduce the parking ratio, the land made available is effectively free. Any development is made more feasible by free land.

Rapid Transit

The Washington D.C. metropolitan area transit system is the most comprehensive new rail transit system in the United States. New York, Boston, Philadelphia, and Chicago all have comprehensive rail transit systems, but they are old. The Bay Area, Atlanta, and other cities have new systems, but they don't serve the whole region the way the Washington Metro does. Washington is a good case study for what other modern metropolitan regions would be like, if well served by rail transit.

Having a good metro system has not eliminated traffic problems; Washington is often described as having the second worst highway traffic in the U.S., after Los Angeles. It has not stopped sprawl; the Washington metropolitan area is spreading fast. Planned more than a generation ago, the system is not well-designed for suburb to suburb commuting, unless your route takes you through the District of Columbia.

The Washington Metro does offer alternatives to driving for large numbers of people who can rely on the trains to take them to work in the District and to the employment centers that have grown up along Metro in Bethesda and Silver Spring, Maryland, and in Arlington County, Virginia. Metro has also had some influence in developing New Carrollton in Prince George's County, Maryland, and the nearby city of Alexandria, Virginia. Where the Metro has had the least influence has been in suburban Virginia, partly because it runs on a center island along Route 66 in Fairfax County and is insulated from development on either side, and partly because it does not reach the rapidly

3.4 *Transit-oriented design: dense development around transit stations in Arlington County. Development around the first station to open, Rosslyn, was planned according to modernist urban design ideas with raised plazas and second-level pedestrian bridges.*

3.5 *More recent development in Arlington, like this street near the Courthouse transit station, is designed to relate to traditional streets and blocks.*

developing areas of Northern Virginia out beyond Dulles Airport in Loudon County.

Metro has had a dramatic effect on the places it does influence. They have the coherence and intensity of development that some of the prophets of change, like Rem Koolhaas, have assured us would never be possible again.

Transit-Oriented Design

The presence of the federal government gives downtown Washington its basic structure, but downtown Washington, which a generation ago was as pock-marked by parking lots as most other American cities, now has the compact, intense development that can only be achieved with transit. Metro has permitted street after street to be developed with continuous urban frontages, and K Street, which was designed like a Parisian boulevard, now has a comparable grandeur—even if some of the individual buildings are not as good as they could be. Washington's height limits are also a factor in producing this distinctive form of development, see pages 252-254 in Chapter 13.

Arlington County, Virginia, has used Metro effectively to create real urban places around stations, starting in the 1960s with Rosslyn (3.4), which has the defect of using then-fashionable second-level pedestrian walkways, and later around the Courthouse and Ballston stations (3.5) The Pentagon City station, also in Arlington, is the location for a major retail center. In Montgomery County, Bethesda has grown from a being a typical suburban downtown to a significant urban center with offices, apartments, and an amazing concentration of restaurants.

The Washington Metro has some 48,000 parking spaces at stations, and in most stations the lots are filled every day. Each space intercepts a car that would otherwise have traveled farther into the area served by Metro, adding to the road congestion. Many other Metro passengers are dropped off at stations, or walk to them.

Portland Oregon's Region 2040 plan (3.6, pages 58-59) is based on the assumption that most of the projected increase in population can be contained within existing growth boundaries by intensifying development around transit stations. Peter Calthorpe was a consultant to the Portland planning process and has prepared illustrative plans showing how this can be accomplished at representative locations along projected transit lines in the Portland region. Orenco Station in the Portland suburbs (see page 47) is a partially realized example of this principle. However, while the development has a compact center within walking distance of the transit stop, the land immediately around the station has not yet been developed.

Peter Calthorpe has been able to put into practice his theory of "Pedestrian Pockets," described on page 97. Calthorpe uses rapid transit to restructure

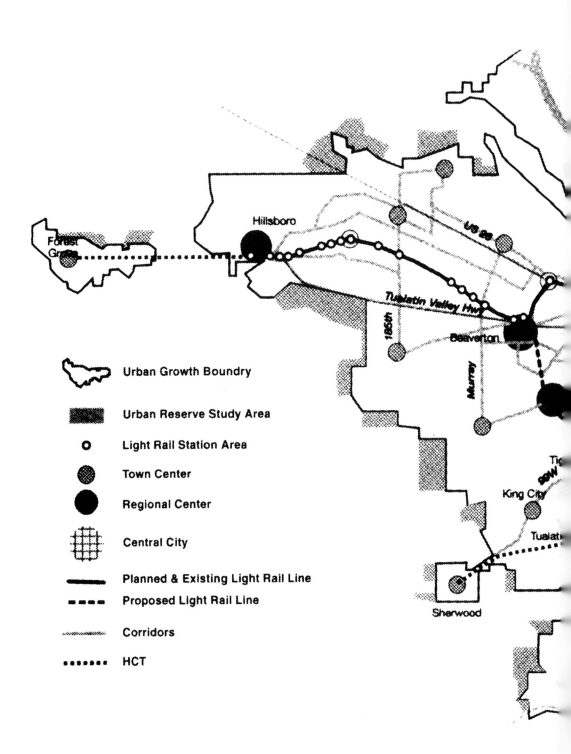

Urban Growth Boundry

Urban Reserve Study Area

O   Light Rail Station Area

Town Center

Regional Center

Central City

Planned & Existing Light Rail Line

Proposed Light Rail Line

Corridors

HCT

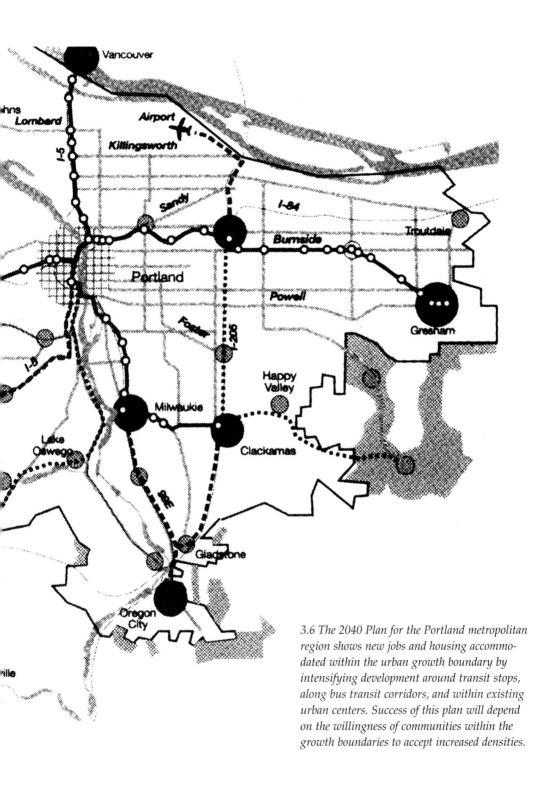

3.6 The 2040 Plan for the Portland metropolitan
region shows new jobs and housing accommodated within the urban growth boundary by
intensifying development around transit stops,
along bus transit corridors, and within existing
urban centers. Success of this plan will depend
on the willingness of communities within the
growth boundaries to accept increased densities.

3.7, 3.8 Calthorpe Associates, one of the consultants for the Portland 2040 Plan, prepared these plans for The Crossings, a redevelopment of an underused shopping mall in Mountain View, California, that takes advantage of new transit access. Calthorpe has prepared comparable plans for infill sites near transit stops to help implement the Portland plan.

suburban regions along transit lines, not to replace automobile-oriented development, but to provide an alternative. At stations along the line there are opportunities to build offices or factories, a small retail center, apartments and houses, all within walking distance of the station. A recent example from Calthorpe's practice is The Crossings, in Mountain View, California, where a dying shopping center was redeveloped as a residential neighborhood across from a new transit station. (3.7, 3.8)

High-speed Trains

The high-speed trains used in Japan and Europe to link urban centers have been much discussed in the U.S. The nearest we have so far is Amtrak's recently opened Acela service between Boston and Washington in the northeast corridor. If it makes a significant difference to intercity commuting, it is likely to help revive talk of other high-speed rail corridor proposals, such as Tampa-Miami, and Cleveland-Cincinnati. The effect of high-speed train service is to strengthen the areas near train stations in cities along the route. Many competing destinations are as close to the airport as the traditional business center, but high-speed rail can deliver passengers right downtown.

New Kinds of Mobility May Restore Old Urban Relationships

Higher densities, more traditional building relationships, intercity trains and rapid transit are not the stuff only of romanticism and nostalgia, but could make a lot of economic sense as the next generation of development takes place.

4

Equity: Deconcentrating Poverty, Affordable Housing, & Environmental Justice

In metropolitan areas across the United States twice as many poor people are white and non-Hispanic as are poor and African American, or poor and Hispanic, according to David Rusk, who is noted for using statistics to illuminate public policy issues. However, according to Rusk, poor whites rarely live in neighborhoods where poverty rates exceed 20 percent, the threshold for classifying a neighborhood as impacted by poverty. "Only one-quarter of poor whites live in such poverty-impacted neighborhoods; three-quarters live in working class or middle class neighborhoods scattered all over our metropolitan areas. By contrast, half of poor Hispanics and three quarters of poor blacks live in poor neighborhoods in inner cities and inner suburbs."

As the work of Douglas Massey and other researchers has demonstrated, the problems of being poor are magnified by having to live in a neighborhood where there is a concentration of other poor people. These are the neighborhoods where schools and social services are stressed, housing has deteriorated, and law and order are hard to maintain. If more people are to be successful in finding their way out of poverty, distressed low-income areas need to be transformed into multi-income neighborhoods, and all neighborhoods need to accept a small proportion of poor people. This is a basic equity issue.

In addition, as Rusk's statistics point out, concentrated poverty has a strong component of racial and ethnic segregation. His statistics show that it is more difficult for poor people who are African American or Spanish-speaking to find homes in mainstream neighborhoods.

Roots of Concentrated Poverty

It is easy to forget how recently ethnic segregation, and the segregation of poor people, were both official government policy.

From the beginning of federally funded public housing in the 1930s, projects were routinely segregated for people of African American descent, not just in the South but in every place where public housing was constructed. Not until Congress passed the Federal Fair Housing Act of 1968 did segregated public housing stop being acceptable public policy, and it was not until March 2000, after more than three decades of lawsuits and court decisions, that HUD Secretary Andrew Cuomo announced a policy of affirmatively ending segregation in public housing. The policy will not affect existing tenants, so its implementation will be gradual.

Public housing, whether for African Americans or for other tenants, was almost always built in low-income areas of cities because its construction was tied to the clearance of blighted areas; a finding of blight enabled governments to acquire sites by eminent domain. If a site was purchased in the real-estate market, it was also likely to be in a low-value area, as there were strict federal guidelines for the cost of land per unit. Site acquisition policies interacted with segregation policies to concentrate new housing for the poor in low-income areas. These policies were challenged in Chicago in the Gautreaux case, which led to a decision in 1969 that using public housing to reinforce segregated residential patterns in Chicago was unconstitutional. A related Supreme Court case in 1976 upheld building scattered-site housing as a remedy, but the remedy has never caught up with the original problem.

Up to the 1960s, the federal government expected public housing authorities to maintain their operations from rental income. Housing authorities accordingly restricted rentals to those families that could pay enough rent to keep up the authority's real estate. These policies were criticized as excluding the people most in need of public housing, so federal policies were changed to open up public housing to more welfare families and others in need, at the same time limiting rents to no more than 30 percent of a family's gross income. This policy change was not accompanied by enough additional federal funding to make up for the lost revenues to housing authorities. Federal policies also continued to require that public housing tenants whose income went up above the maximums permitted had to move out. The result was an increasing proportion of poorer tenants, paying lower rents, so that housing authorities fell behind in maintenance and cut back on services, including security. In many cities the most concentrated poverty can now be found in public housing projects, which have gone from being the best alternative for poor people to being the worst. Eight percent of public housing units are no longer considered habitable.

Deed Restrictions and Redlining

Deed restrictions which prevented sales of houses to buyers "not of the Aryan race"—to quote a typical provision—were declared unenforceable by the U.S. Supreme Court in 1948; but such restrictive practices continued to have tacit support by homeowners and real-estate brokers up through at least the 1970s. The Federal Fair Housing Act made segregated neighborhoods illegal after 1968; but, again the practice has a lot of momentum, and many poor neighborhoods remain effectively segregated. Some of this segregation had originally been created by government programs. Kenneth Jackson put together the story of overt federal mortgage lending discrimination in *Crabgrass Frontier: The Suburbanization of the United States*, first published in 1985. According to Jackson's research, discrimination was institutionalized in programs of the Home Owners Loan Corporation, a New Deal agency created in 1933 to refinance mortgages in danger of default or foreclosure. HOLC mortgages were long term, and uniform payments paid off the full loan, as opposed to the relatively short term, renewable mortgages that had been common up to that time. In creating national standards for mortgage lending, the HOLC systematized appraisal practice, defining four levels of neighborhood, coded green, blue, yellow, and red. Neighborhoods mapped in red were considered hazardous places to make loans. Among the factors that caused HOLC to redline a neighborhood was any evidence of African American residents. Jackson documents that neighborhoods with small lots and houses close together were generally graded yellow or red by HOLC appraisers regardless of residency and whether or not there was evidence of deterioration. Green was reserved for suburban neighborhoods with large lots, often with deed restrictions, less exclusive larger-lot areas were coded blue. The HOLC was simply codifying then-current lending practices and prejudices, but by making a code that was systematic, national, and permanent it had a pervasive influence.

Both the Federal Housing Administration, created in 1934, and the Veteran's Administration housing mortgage programs that began in 1944 used HOLC maps, or new maps following the same code system, as the basis for their lending policies. While the HOLC did make loans in areas they had coded yellow or red, Jackson's reading of FHA appraisal manuals and practices showed that the FHA and VA generally stuck to green and blue areas through the 1960s. While the FHA and the Veterans Administration had a broader range of potential lending powers than the Home Ownership Loan Corporation, which they superseded, only a small proportion of home loans went to finance renovation of existing houses, and the FHA, which has the power to finance apartments, has devoted most of its lending to individual houses.

The federal mortgage system, with its built-in bias in favor of financing new single-family houses on larger lots, interacted with the development of large tracts of single-family houses after World War II. Federal mortgage subsidies made it possible for families to buy houses in Levittown and other similar developments with a lower monthly payment than their rent for a smaller city house or apartment. The process of attracting families from cities to suburbs accelerated as the interstate highway system opened up big new areas for development after the program was passed by Congress in 1956.

While there were federal housing dollars to build public housing and middle-income apartments in cities up to the 1970s, and some federal money for code enforcement in older neighborhoods, the scale of private investment energized by FHA and VA mortgages in green and blue coded areas was far larger than the money that could be applied more directly to the yellow and red neighborhoods in the older cities. The FHA and VA began to change their lending policies in urban areas during the 1960s; although according to Jackson, "until at least 1970" the Federal Home Loan Bank Board continued to redline districts showing signs of racial change.

Private lenders generally followed the lead of federal agencies in red-lining older urban neighborhoods. In addition, the Federal National Mortgage Association (FNMA) and the Government National Mortgage Association (GNMA) made it easier for banks to put their loan funds to work anywhere in the U.S., so that even a savings bank based in an area of older neighborhoods did not have to lend there. However, the Community Reinvestment Act of 1977 now requires federally chartered banks to make some of their loans in the areas from which they draw their funds, and banks are evaluated periodically for compliance.

Federal policies carried out over 50 or 60 years helped create or reinforce today's patterns of concentrated poverty and racial segregation in distressed neighborhoods. While the federal policies no longer exist, there has been no comparable federal effort to correct the mistakes of these past programs.

U.S. Housing Policies Did Enlarge and Improve the Housing Supply

Among the benefits of federal housing policies was a big increase in home ownership, mostly in new suburban areas, and a substantial increase in the overall housing supply. As recently as the 1960s, there was still a severe housing shortage in older cities. The bias in favor of suburbs and the national increase in the total number of houses and apartments translates into lower population in most urban areas. As a result, the most deteriorated—or hardest to maintain—urban housing "took itself off the market." This phrase, which sounds relatively benign when spoken by experts at conferences, describes a horrifying reality of burnt-out, abandoned buildings, the vanished life savings of small investors, and distressed older neighborhoods where the people with little choice about where they can live are increasingly concentrated.

Statistically, the U.S. is winning the war against housing shortages and substandard buildings. Nationally, the census found only 1.1 percent of homes lacked complete plumbing facilities; less than .6 percent lacked some kind of heating system (and these statistics include Hawaii, where more than half the housing units have no heating); less than 5 percent of housing units were considered crowded, and severe crowding—defined as more than 1.5 persons per room, was found in only 2.1 percent of housing units. As there are around 110 million U.S. housing units (not including vacation housing), substandard conditions still affect a lot of housing. The worst is increasingly concentrated in a relatively few urban neighborhoods and a few severely impacted rural areas.

Affordable Housing

Unfortunately, while as a nation we have greatly reduced housing shortages and raised the overall standards, The Center for Housing Policy still estimates that one out of every seven American families has a critical housing need, some 13.7 million families. This crisis is primarily about affordability. Affordable housing is generally defined as costing less than 30 percent of gross family income. Information from the U.S. Housing Survey indicates that people in the bottom 20 percent of income in the U.S. spend, on average, 58 percent of their income on housing. The Center for Housing Policy estimates that three million moderate or even middle-income families are forced to pay more than half of their income for housing.

No one has exact figures, but something like another 600,000 people are homeless. While many homeless people have mental health or substance abuse problems, there are also people who have full-time jobs who are unable to afford housing.

There is agreement that the affordability problem is getting worse. Rents are rising at twice the rate of general inflation. For every 100 households seeking affordable housing, only about a third as many affordable units are available. Of course, housing costs vary in different parts of the country, and some places are a great deal more affordable than others. Many people believe that the private market can't solve the affordability problem on its own, and that the federal government is needed to help resolve the situation. There are many different federal programs that can help alleviate housing affordability problems, tax subsidies for building affordable housing, direct rental supplements, and various "bootstrap" programs to help families invest in their own homes, particularly older structures or new houses built by not-for-profit organizations. These existing programs could solve the problem, if sufficient funds were allocated to them. The National Low Income Housing Coalition estimates that the federal government allocates $40 billion a year to a combination of direct payments and tax subsidies for low-income housing. They then estimate that around $82 billion a year goes to subsidize home-owners through the mortgage-interest tax deduction, with many of these homeowners in the top 20 percent of all U.S. incomes. The implication is that the argument is not about the principle of subsidy, but over the politics of who gets the subsidy.

The Montgomery County Moderately Priced Housing Program

Is there an alternative to federal subsidies? David Rusk in his book *Inside Game/Outside Game* calls attention to the Montgomery County, Maryland, Moderate Priced Dwelling Unit Program. In an ordinance passed in the mid-1970s, Montgomery County required that 15 percent of all housing in any development of more that 50 units must be affordable for the lowest one-third of the county's households. One-third of these affordable units, or 5 percent of the total, are available for purchase by the county's housing authority. To prevent this requirement being considered a taking by the courts, the same ordinance permits a density bonus of up to 22 percent. (4.1, 4.2)

Rusk recounts that almost 11,000 such units have been produced, two-thirds purchased by teachers, police officers, retail, or service workers who could not otherwise afford to live near their jobs in this affluent suburban county on the fashionable side of Washington, D.C. More than 1,500 units were purchased by the housing authority. Scattered among some 200 subdivisions, the public housing is constructed in buildings that look as similar to their market-rate neighbors as possible, so that the presence of the public housing tenants is almost invisible.

Rusk estimates that similar policies pursued throughout the Philadelphia metropolitan area during the same period that the Montgomery County, Maryland, ordinance has been in force could have produced enough afford-able housing and public housing units to bring poverty rates below 30 per-cent in all of the high-poverty census tracts in Philadelphia, Camden, Chester, and other places of high poverty concentration throughout the Philadelphia metropolitan region. Rusk has done similar calculations for the Chicago met-

4.1, 4.2 Montgomery County's moderately priced dwelling unit program requires affordable housing as part of any development of more than 50 units—but also gives a density bonus. The two dwelling units at left, above, sell for about $88,000, the townhouses at right from $250,000 to $300,000. Single-family houses in the same development sell for $450,000 to $500,000. Below, the affordable units on the right side of the picture are stacked, with one-bedrooms at ground level, and two-bedroom apartments above.

ropolitan region and other areas. His conclusion: If, and it is a very big if, housing policies similar to those of Montgomery County had been pursued in all the metropolitan regions of the United States during the past generation, concentrated poverty could have been virtually eliminated in the United States and public housing projects could have been replaced by mixed-income communities.

The Hope VI Program

In 1993 new federal legislation authorized what the Department of Housing and Urban Development calls the Hope VI Program. Under Hope VI, the 100,000 most deteriorated public housing units in the U.S. are being demolished and replaced by mixed-income communities, which include public housing tenants but also residents who are paying closer to a market rent. The buildings and site plans are designed to create a sense of permanent community, whereas conventional public housing projects all too often conveyed a sense of being a temporary holding area. The program has produced some excellent early results, some of which are illustrated in Chapter 7. However, the creation of mixed-income communities on public-housing sites, although it is the right social policy, reduces the number of available public housing units. Many of the projects in the Hope VI program were so badly deteriorated that they were no longer inhabited and relatively few families have had to be relocated. In theory, families not returning to the new Hope VI project will be placed in conventional housing through a voucher program that subsidizes rents. This way, not only are mixed-income communities created in formerly segregated areas, but also former public housing tenants will be dispersed throughout the larger community. The theory is excellent, but it is not yet clear that the performance will live up to the theory. There is also a question whether some or all of the low-income apartments in Hope VI projects will eventually be converted to market-rate housing, further reducing the supply of housing affordable by the very lowest income groups. In addition, many of the other public housing units are being renovated through conventional rehabilitation programs, some of which look like the Hope VI projects in design, but leave the same concentration of poor people in place. So far, Hope VI is only a promising prototype, not a corrective, to the ways in which public housing contributes to concentrating poverty.

Environmental Justice

President Bill Clinton issued an executive order in February 1994 directing federal agencies to consider adverse impacts on low-income and minority communities in making decisions about Federal programs. This order recognizes that people in such communities have often been subject to the more environmental pollution than people living in affluent areas. Pollution problems are closely related to long-established land-use patterns. In every community, rich people choose to live in the most pleasant areas: on higher land where the microclimate is better, upwind of local industry, and in places which command the best views. This pattern is recognized in expressions like "the wrong side of the tracks," the name for the district where people who have choices do not live. These "wrong" areas of cities and towns have always been the location for factories, refineries, and other activities that cause the most environmental pollution. When zoning codes were enacted, they ratified existing land-use patterns and made them compulsory; activities that cause pollution can only take place where they are zoned, generally the places where they have always been.

The concept of environmental justice directs attention to these issues, working against the unthinking acceptance of long-established real estate and zoning patterns. However, making significant changes is hard to do. The acronym NIMBY (not in my backyard) is often used to describe the politics of this issue. Saying that one neighborhood already has more than its fair share of undesirable industrial installations, and it is time to locate them somewhere else, is a reasonable political statement but where should they go? For example, every region needs mixing plants for concrete, where cement and aggregates are stored, mixed, and loaded into heavy trucks for delivery to building sites. Such a use does not raise the obvious pollution problems of a trash incinerator or a sewage treatment plant, but no neighborhood wants the storage yards and truck traffic associated with concrete plants. Where should they be located? Solving this problem without offending any substantial interest group is possible, but only in the context of effective regional planning. Industrial districts in older cities and towns are usually close to residential neighborhoods that date from days when workers lived within walking distance of the factory. Either the remaining industrial uses in these areas should be discontinued, or the older residential areas should be relocated. Easy to say, as a theoretical proposition, but almost impossible politically except in a long-range context. Industrial districts in the suburbs are usually more separated from residences, but are not necessarily planned for minimum impact on surrounding areas. Regional plans should consider industrial location in the context of wind direction, soil suitability, and water runoff issues, as well as transportation access.

Environmental Reparations

Many old industrial districts are barely used today; pollution, or suspected pollution, causes them to be labeled "brownfields," as opposed to the green fields where developers prefer to build. Nearby older neighborhoods are probably still suffering from the blighting effects of years of industry, plus the environmental impacts from highway viaducts, railway lines, electrical sub-stations and other installations likely to be found in or near industrial districts.

These two drawings from the Regional Plan Association of New York and New Jersey's Third Regional Plan illustrate what could be done with a relatively modest infusion of capital into an old inner-city neighborhood. The scene is the Passaic River in Newark, New Jersey, with the Manhattan skyline in the background. The first view (4.3) shows conditions today: Old industrial areas, now hardly used, polluted land, the river banks artificially constrained and hardly supporting any kind of natural life. The second view (4.4, see page 74) shows the river edges restored to a natural wetlands environment that helps to clean the river; the park-like river edges have in turn made the land adjacent to them into a valuable location, perhaps as desirable as a greenfield site on the fringe of the metropolitan area and certainly much better located. The drawing shows new non-polluting industrial uses and residences. This scene, although it is fiction, is a plausible depiction of what could happen, but the initial funding almost certainly has to come from outside the private real-estate market. Such improvements could be paid for by the increased real-estate values that would be created once the area had become an attractive location for private investment. In fact, federal government bond programs have been proposed that would finance park development in brownfield locations. The bonds could be paid back from increased property values. The investments required are not that large: a comparable riverfront restoration near Boston was done in the early 1990s for $62,500 an acre (see page 87).

The restoration of neglected urban areas that have been bypassed by real-estate investors also will require infrastructure investments in repairing old bridges, as shown in the drawing, providing soundwalls to protect residential areas from noise pollution by highways and railroads, enclosing power substations to the standard provided in affluent suburban areas and so on. Such investments ought to generate increased property values, not to mention relieving development pressures at the edge of the metropolitan region. A major reason why public investments are needed is the systematic official neglect of these areas in the past, often accompanied by overt discrimination. In the circumstances, reparations is not too strong a word to describe such an investment program.

The Equity Agenda
Equity in city planning and urban design means recognizing that a history of official discrimination and injustice has helped create the distressed, deterio-

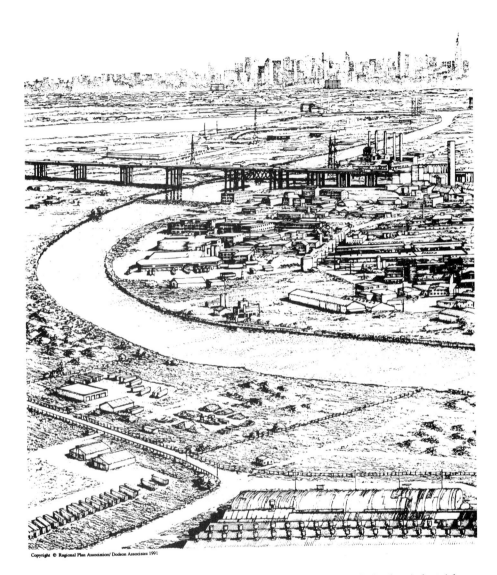

4.3 This drawing made for the Regional Plan Association shows a typical urban industrial area, where most of the jobs are gone and only marginal businesses are left.

4.4 This second Regional Plan Association drawing shows the areas in the previous view entirely rebuilt because the river and its surrounding environment have been reclaimed. A real-life example of such a riverfront restoration can be seen in the illustrations on page 87.

rating areas of cities and towns. The public has an obligation to compensate for this history with new investments to make these areas competitive. It means the conversion of all public housing projects into mixed-income neighborhoods, and the integration of poor people into mainstream neighborhoods. It means meeting the crises of affordability and homelessness.

Highways, railway lines, and electrical substations in low-income neighborhoods and towns should be given the same kinds of landscaping, sound barriers, and enclosures that they get in high-income areas. Disused industrial land and land that has been scarred by extractive industries should be reclaimed and environmental problems corrected.

The long-term locations for heavy industry, power plants, incinerators, and other elements that no one wants in their back yards should be determined for whole regions, as part of regional and statewide planning processes.

Public policies have created many of the inequities that underlie the design of cities and regions; public policies are required to correct them.

5

Sustainability:
Smart Growth versus Sprawl

The population of the world has now surpassed six billion people. While the Reverend Thomas Malthus may have been too pessimistic in his *Essay on the Principle of Population*, his name is identified with a fundamental problem: Population increases at an exponential rate, while the amount of habitable land is fixed. Population has been found to stabilize in mature societies, however, and improved agriculture has produced food at a level of productivity unknown in 1798, when Malthus's essay was first published. Currently, experts believe that the world population will stop growing at around 10 billion and that there will be sufficient food to sustain population at this level without the Malthus correctives: war, famine, and disease.

What kind of lives will these 10 billion people lead if the world is indeed successful in reaching population stability without nuclear war, worldwide plagues, catastrophic droughts, or other causes of famine? If China, with almost 1.3 billion people becomes a developed country with 60 percent of its population in urban areas, up from 35 percent now, it will need to house 300 million new urban residents, the equivalent of 20 New York metropolitan regions or 10 Tokyos. Comparable changes could happen in India and parts of Africa. Will everyone want the automobiles and labor-saving appliances they can see on television or in movies? What happens when the ratio of car ownership for families in China and India reaches levels similar to those in the U.S.? What kind of strain will they put on the world's resources, and will the consumption of these resources overwhelm the earth's ability to process pollution?

Malthusian predictions that the world is running out of resources have proved untrue up to now. So far, new sources of petroleum and other natural resources have always been found, or new technology has made older forms of dependency obsolete. So far, combustion products and other pollutants have not destabilized the ecosystem, although holes in the ozone layer and rising global temperatures are serious warnings. Perhaps the answers to pollution problems could come from new inventions that suppress pollution in automobiles or provide electricity from photovoltaic sources, rather than from enforcing difficult choices about consumption.

These questions are the context for the issues discussed in this book; they are a reminder of how important sustainability is, and how necessary that the United States and other developed countries help create a sustainable future.

Sprawl and Sustainability

Current metropolitan growth and development patterns are our biggest single sustainability issue. The U.S. needs to solve these problems not just for itself, but as a model for rapidly developing countries elsewhere. While the 2000 census of 281 million is higher than predicted, the U.S. population is not increasing at a rate that would explain current metropolitan development. Forests and farms are being converted to built-up areas at the edges of metropolitan regions at a rate 4 to 15 times the local population growth. In some places, such as metropolitan Cleveland, rural land is being converted when the regional population is actually shrinking. Much of what is called growth is actually moving people from one part of the country to another, or from older cities and suburbs, as in St. Louis City and County, to new locations on the metropolitan fringe. Old urban neighborhoods with existing streets, utilities, schools, churches, and other institutions have been emptying out. Philadelphia, for example, has 15,000 vacant residential buildings and 30,000 vacant lots. Development at the urban fringe requires new roads and utilities, new schools, churches and other institutions. In this context, a conventional house built as infill on an existing city street is a far bigger contribution to a sustainable future than a solar house built on a rural site.

In terms of resources expended in structural steel, copper pipes, wood paneling and so on, renovating an existing downtown office building is superior as sustainability to building a new "green" office building in a suburban office park.

Dispersed development patterns mean more traffic. Total vehicle miles traveled in the U.S. have increased four times as much as would be explained by the number of new drivers. In 1970, individual drivers averaged 4,485 automobile miles, 6,330 miles per person in 1990. During the same period the average length of an automobile trip went from 8.68 to 9.45 miles. Americans have been estimated to lose more than 1.6 million hours a day stuck in traffic. Despite reductions in pollutants from individual automobile exhausts, nitrogen oxide emissions from vehicles are already higher than they were when pollution control devices were introduced. The EPA predicts that ozone and particulate matter pollution will begin to rise above previous highs after 2005, demonstrating that technical fixes alone have not so far solved vehicular pollution problems.

Dispersed development is destroying prime farmland, which is often located close to cities which began as centers of an agricultural region. Dispersed development means more runoff from lawns and parking lots, which means more erosion and water pollution. It diverts resources and development away from existing cities and suburbs and makes it harder for people in such areas who need jobs to get to those jobs. To the extent that older cities and suburbs are part of the same sewer and water districts as newer areas, people in the older areas are paying part of their rates to subsidize the cost of extending these services outward.

Smart Growth and Portland, Oregon

Advocates of better metropolitan development policies have come up with a clever brand name: Smart Growth. There are three essential elements of smart growth. First, policies to discourage the continued conversion of rural land at the edges of metropolitan regions. Second, finding ways to make infill development and the restoration of older areas more attractive to investors and consumers. Third, knitting the metropolitan region together with transportation systems that reduce dependency on automobile trips.

The Portland, Oregon, metropolitan area is a place that has carried out a program of limiting growth at the metropolitan fringe. It is sufficiently successful, and sufficiently unusual, that it is cited as an example over and over again, to the point where many knowledgeable people are getting sick of hearing about it. They point out that Portland is not the typical American city, and the Portland experience won't necessarily be repeated elsewhere. Meanwhile Portland residents are quick to explain that things are far from perfect; they have not gotten where they are without a lot of controversy, and what progress they have made could still be reversed.

Oregon has had a comprehensive land-planning act since 1973. The original purpose was partly to save valuable orchard and farmland that was being overrun by hit or miss development. It also was clearly a forward-looking move by the then governor, Tom McCall, and a coalition of advocates for good planning. There have been attempts to repeal this law in every legislative session since. The act requires each city in Oregon to draw a growth boundary line, beyond this line the infrastructure to support urban growth would not be funded. The boundaries were set loosely enough that they could contain a long period of expansion, and within the boundary there was nothing to change conventional development patterns. There were also provisions in the law that permitted the boundaries to be redrawn once growth limits had been reached.

Nevertheless, this law has given Portland a metropolitan character that is different from most other U.S. cities. There are places in the region with dense suburban development on one side of the road, and nothing but farms on the other side. It is like being on the edge of a European city, where similar boundaries are often enforced. Within the growth limits, while much recent development is like suburban sprawl elsewhere, several older Portland neighborhoods are seeing reinvestment not found in comparable places in most other cities. Downtown Portland is also stronger and more dominant in the region than would be likely without the act.

Portland's light-rail transit system is another element that has helped pull the region together. The Metropolitan Service District was established in 1979 to harmonize the region's growth plans and design its transportation systems. In 1992, Metro was transformed into an elected regional government. One of its major achievements has been the adoption in December 1994 of the Region 2040 Growth Concept (see map pages 58-59), which demonstrates that new construction can be kept almost entirely within current growth limits by completing a comprehensive rapid-transit system and focusing intense residential and commercial building around the stations. The public has recently backed this plan by adopting bond issues to construct the next increment of the light-rail system and to fund open-space acquisition and park improvements.

Other State Growth Management Programs
The power to regulate land use and development belongs to the states, but the states have traditionally delegated this authority to local governments. Keeping control over the future of their community continues to be an important local issue, but metropolitan regions can contain dozens, sometimes more than a hundred different local governments. What is especially interesting about the Portland model is that the growth boundary, a relatively simple state planning requirement, set in motion a process of regional growth management carried out by cities.

At present about a quarter of the states require local governments to participate in some kind of regional growth management. Tennessee has recently enacted growth boundary legislation. Florida law seeks comparable results through the principle of concurrency, that is development may not be approved in areas that do not have the necessary transportation and utility infrastructure. City and county plans for future growth are reviewed by regional planning councils coordinated by a state agency. Washington State's growth management law uses both concurrency and growth boundaries.

Some states take stronger measures. Hawaii has a statewide plan and has retained the authority to give out permits for development. Vermont has taken back the authority to grant permits for projects with regional impacts.

At the other polarity are state planning procedures that are essentially advisory. Georgia law sets requirements for local planning, backed by state funding policies: Localities that comply are supposed to get more funds. New Jersey's state plan is a policy document directed at preserving existing open space and farmland and giving priority for state funds to existing urbanized areas. The plan was approved through a "cross-acceptance" process involving the state planning commission, county planning commissions, and local governments. As the maps in the plan are only advisory, it is not yet clear whether it can accomplish its objectives. Utah has recently established a Quality Growth Commission, whose role is to advise the state legislature and to provide technical assistance to local government. This commission was considered a big step, brought about in part by a public participation in Envision Utah, which sponsored a series of workshops whose participants were asked to decide where future growth should go (thereby teaching themselves that it is impossible to avoid higher densities if the state grows as predicted), followed by a ballot asking the public to choose among four growth scenarios. The ballot is shown on page 7. The winner, scenario C, is based on channeling new growth into walkable communities, estimated to have the least expensive infrastructure cost and best air quality of all the alternatives, plus big savings in land requirements and water use compared to Scenario A, the standard sprawl model.

The Maryland Planning Act of 1992 sets standards for local comprehensive plans. It was followed by Smart Growth legislation of 1997, which is a package of different complementary measures designed to restrict growth at the metropolitan fringe and redirect it towards existing communities. The words "growth boundary" are never mentioned, but state support for infrastructure improvements is to go only to areas that are already at least partly developed. There is money to acquire and preserve critical pieces of rural land. There are also incentives for development in enterprise zones in older areas, and measures that make it easier to clean up brownfield sites.

Additional states have planning legislation, environmental impact review laws, or other types of growth management, but there is still a long way to go before all the states have addressed these issues and there is anything like a system of growth management that covers the whole country.

Because the idea of limiting growth is still widely considered to be un-American, it may be that the most effective way to achieve smart growth would be to deal with underlying causes of sprawl. Developers converting rural land would have to pay the full price for all the necessary new infrastructure, for example, as is required in the Canadian province of Ontario. Another interesting approach would be to relate smart growth to education spending.

Fiscal Inequity as a Cause of Sprawl

Current development patterns pull tax values out of older communities, particularly first-ring suburbs on the unfashionable side of big cities. At the same time, new communities on the rapidly developing fringe of metropolitan areas face big costs to create a complete new infrastructure of schools and utilities. Fiscal needs set up a ruinous competition among communities in the same metropolitan area as each offers incentives to shopping malls, car dealerships, office parks, and other non-residential land uses that produce tax revenue without adding children to the school system. New malls and office parks attracted to edges of a metropolitan area pull values from older malls, commercial strips and office buildings closer in. At the same time, they create new development pressures on rural communities farther out.

In the few places where there is a system of regional sales-tax revenue sharing, individual communities are under less pressure to make development decisions based on tax considerations. Many states have an equalization formula to help reduce disparities of revenue among school districts. In exceptional metropolitan areas, notably the Twin Cities, there is some form of property-tax revenue sharing. However, the Minneapolis-St. Paul region has now sprawled out beyond the area where revenue is shared.

Ultimately, tax base sharing is a way of creating a sustainable metropolitan region. With equalized educational funding, older communities would be free of the concern that declining property values can set off a downward revenue spiral and the collapse of their schools. An improved urban school system would remove one of the big obstacles to infill residential development on vacant land in older neighborhoods or former industrial sites. Families would have more options to stay in the city or even move back to a convenient close-in neighborhood.

Thinking of a metropolitan area as a single fiscal entity would improve the chances of creating fast, reliable transit systems, which in turn could help create more walkable neighborhoods and compact business centers as destinations, and would reduce people's dependence on automobiles. In addition to decreasing air pollution, less automobile travel could have a useful effect on the family budget. It is estimated that every car costs 5,000 (usually after-tax) dollars to operate each year. People who live and work within walking distance of a good transit system, like the Washington, D.C., Metro, do use it.

Why All Communities Should Adopt Environmental Regulations

In his book, *Design With Nature*, Ian McHarg assesses how various types of natural landscapes sustain development, and describes ways of choosing the most suitable sites for roads and buildings through a system of maps that exclude inappropriate areas. McHarg's mapping concepts lend themselves to translation into zoning requirements, and the connection has been made by Lane Kendig and others. Most zoning codes base the amount of development permitted on the area of the lot. Kendig suggests a simple amendment to local zoning that discounts the lot's area according to the land's sensitivity to environmental damage. Land that is most suitable is counted fully. Land that is most unsuitable, like land under water or wetlands, would be fully discounted. Land that is somewhere in between these two polarities is assigned a percentage discount, based on sensitivity to damage. This system is simple and objective, and can be added to any ordinance without changing its other provisions. It can apply uniformly to every property, which means that it meets an important constitutional test.

The subdivision ordinance, which regulates the division of tracts of land into building lots, can also be a means of bringing environmental considerations into land-use policy. It can specify that there should be no changes to natural drainageways and steep hillsides, and it can require the developer to show how buildings will be kept away from sinkholes, easily eroded soils, and landforms or any floodplains and wetlands. In addition, there can be retention requirements that water should leave the property no faster after development than it did before.

Communities that wish to add environmental regulations to their zoning and subdivision codes also will need to enact grading and tree-protection ordinances. Bulldozing the land into new shapes and chopping down big stands of mature trees should not take place without a permit, and the permit should be conditioned on an approved development plan. Agricultural activities and minor domestic changes in landscaping can be exempted in a well-drafted ordinance. Without such protection a developer can simply strip and regrade the property before applying for approvals.

Environmental zoning, plus the planned unit development options found in most local codes, combined with environmental safeguards in the subdivision ordinance, can preserve natural drainage and ecological systems, which then form a frame of open space around the areas more suitable for development. (5.1, see page 84)

Although environmental impact laws require the assessment of significant impacts, both favorable and unfavorable, a development that follows environmental zoning should have fewer unfavorable impacts on the natural environment. Environmental zoning should also lessen conflicts between what is permissible under local land-use law and what is permitted under Coastal Zone Management and other forms of environmental review. However, while environmental zoning and subdivision laws, plus grading and tree-protection ordinances, can protect a community against some of the damaging effects of sprawl, they can make other aspects of sprawl worse by thinning development and spreading it out over more of the natural landscape. Other regulations, that encourage the creation of compact walkable communities also are needed; we will come back to this issue in the chapters on Neighborhoods and Development Regulations.

Direct Methods of Preserving Open Space

A developed area with its most sensitive natural systems preserved is still a developed area. In many places it is desirable to keep the natural landscape intact. The simplest way to preserve a natural landscape is to buy it for a

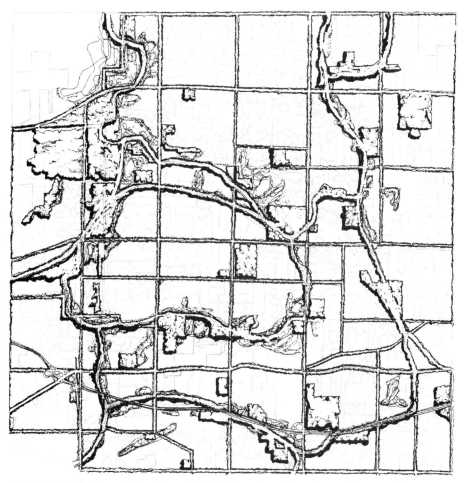

5.1 A plan by the Cunningham Group highlighting the parks and natural systems that run through the city of Brookfield, Wisconsin. It is possible to create a park and open space system that will not only frame the city's neighborhoods, but can retain and manage stormwater to prevent flooding.

park system or a landscape trust, or for a park or landscape trust to accept land as a gift.

If the land is a farm or working waterfront it is possible to buy—or be given—the development rights in the form of scenic easement, or some other form of easement, so that the property can never be used in a more intensive way. Purchasing land or development rights is expensive, and the funds available for it are always limited. But referenda for funds to secure open space often pass. There is clearly public support for preserving the natural landscape.

If state and local governments used more forethought, they could save much of the money they spend on landscape preservation. Natural areas come under development pressure when they are made more accessible by a new highway. State departments of transportation have a lot of control over where new highways go and in what order they are built. One of the criteria for highway route design ought to be not opening up sensitive scenic areas to potential development. It is unlikely that this issue has been considered explicitly in most highway decision making.

Public acquisition of open space becomes necessary, and also is made expensive, because agricultural and forest lands have already been zoned for development, usually in large-lot residential districts. Why? Agriculture and forestry are both land uses, and zones permitting only such uses are accepted as legal in many states, and could be everywhere if a state legislature so decided. Zoning farmland as a residential district invites local governments to tax it that way, and encourages banks to lend the farmer money secured by potential real-estate values, a combination which makes future development almost inevitable.

Some communities have dealt with overzoned agricultural land through the transfer of development rights. Farmers can sell their zoning rights to developers who would be able to build denser developments in some more appropriate location. In theory this idea ought to work; in practice, most local governments have gotten into the habit of giving developers higher densities in the form of zoning changes. Why should a developer buy rights that the local planning board is prepared to give away? For an air-rights regime to succeed, local governments have to take a pledge: No more approvals for higher densities unless the developer buys the rights. There are other complications. Development rights that someone may buy in the future are not worth as much as the right to develop now. The ability to transfer development rights into another zone also calls into question the validity of the original zoning. If you can double the number of houses on your property by purchasing air rights, what is wrong with someone building at the same density next door without purchasing the rights? If it is legitimate zoning for one owner, why not for the others? Development-rights transfer sounds like an easy answer, but it isn't.

Regional Planning as a Design Problem

Ideally, no rural land would be converted to urban uses except as part of a regional natural resource plan. Local governments would work from maps of local natural systems that would show the drainage patterns, the areas of steep slopes, of mature woodlands, of soils sensitive to erosion. Mapping techniques such as those advocated by Ian McHarg and Philip Lewis would highlight the areas most suitable for development.

Highways and other transportation would be planned to connect only those parts of the natural landscape capable of development without serious environmental damage. Parts of the countryside that should not be developed would be zoned as agriculture or forest land. Other infrastructure, such as water and sewer systems, would also only be planned for areas that were environmentally suitable for development.

This type of regional planning would not show whether areas that could be developed, should be; nor would it determine what type of development should take place. But it would make the stability of the natural environment a public policy issue and not a by-product of other considerations. It would give an additional objective basis to decisions about growth boundaries and concurrency.

Reclaiming Natural Landscapes in Urban Areas

It is easy to forget that even heavily urbanized areas are also still subject to natural forces. Anne Whiston Spirn has documented the connection between deteriorated housing in poor urban neighborhoods and bad subsurface conditions, which should have precluded building there. She traces newspaper accounts of subsiding and collapsing houses in West Philadelphia and shows, by comparing street plans with earlier topographic maps, that all these houses were built over a stream that had been put in a culvert.

It has always been an axiom of urban life that the rich people lived on the hill and the poor people down in the hollow. Now that urban populations are so much less dense than they used to be, low-lying, flood-prone areas, as they become vacant, are probably best put into parkland, as a new generation of buildings is likely to have problems also.

Vacant industrial land along the Mystic River in Boston has become an inspiring example of an urban park created from a derelict area, where much of the soil was toxic to plants. The ground was made into a growing medium by blending layers of clay, silt, sand, and peat, without importing topsoil stripped from other locations. In the first stage, 80 acres were redeveloped at a cost of $5 million (5.2, 5.3, 5.4)

5.2 *Derelict urban land along the Mystic River in Boston before restoration as parkland following a plan by Carol Johnson Associates.*

5.3 *Land restoration in process. Much of the existing soil was toxic to plants. The ground was made into a growing medium by blending layers of clay, silt, sand, and peat. No topsoil was stripped from other locations and imported.*

5.4 *The completed park, a neighborhood and regional amenity.*

The Second Nature Experiment

What about urbanized areas that are always going to remain developed? More than 60 percent of the land surface in the city of Los Angeles is covered with buildings or pavement. The water needed to sustain Los Angeles is imported by aqueducts over long distances. Most of the 15 inches of rainfall every year, which could supply as much as half of the city's water needs, is channeled into wastewater systems rather than replenishing the groundwater or irrigating lawns and trees. Leaves, twigs, branches, and lawn trimmings make up 30 percent of the city's overloaded landfill sites, instead of being returned to the soil as mulch.

An organization in Los Angeles, TreePeople, which originated as group to promote planting trees, has created the T.R.E.E.S. project, advocating natural systems to help manage the whole urban infrastructure. Individual houses and buildings can have cisterns to catch and store rainwater from the roof, as is customary in Bermuda and other places where water has always been scarce. Water from the roof can be filtered and treated for household use or can water lawns and plants. Stormwater on driveways and parking lots can be directed into storage and filter systems to replenish groundwater, and reduce or eliminate flooding. Trees and drought resistant plants can improve local micro-climates, and reduce air pollution. A coalition of federal and local agencies sponsored a design charrette in Los Angeles to apply ideas like

Issue	Amount Changed	Value / year	Value / 30 years
Irrigation water use	100% reduction (from 108 acre-feet/year to 0)	$353,300	$10,600,000
Domestic water use	40% reduction (from 54 acre-feet/year to 32 acre-feet/year)	$70,000	$2,100,000
Flood management	100% reduction (from 21 acre-feet to 0 during a 133-year flood emergency)[28]	$88,250	$2,647,500
Water pollution	200% reduction (All average annual rainfall is treated on-site)[29]	$26,600	$798,000
Air pollution	300 shade trees and vines on trellises	$1,058	$468,000
Green waste	100% reduction	$7,000	$210,000
Total value of all remediation measures over a thirty-year period =			$16,823,500

5.5 A presentation of the dollar value of environmental interventions studied in a workshop in Los Angeles. This is a way of getting the attention of business executives and public officials.

these to five specific sites: an individual house, an apartment complex, a high school, a strip commercial development, and an industrial site. While the costs of adding such features to individual houses would probably have to be supported by government grants—at least in low and moderate income neighborhoods, money for improvements at the Los Angeles high school could be found in a current renovation program, and the cost for retrofitting the other sites could be incorporated in future renovations or reconstructions. The benefits in reduced pollution, flooding, and improved water supply could be immense. (5.5) If these concepts were applied consistently to all houses, government buildings, and commercial properties, they could transform an entire region in a generation (5.6, 5.7, 5.8, see page 90).

Brownfield Redevelopment

A brownfield originally meant an urban site that was contaminated by industrial pollution; but the term is now used more loosely to mean all vacant urban land, as opposed to rural greenfields. Unfortunately this terminology leaves the impression that all urban land has contamination problems, whereas serious contamination is actually unusual, and is almost always confined to former factory and storage sites.

Congress and state legislatures have passed strict laws to protect the public from environmental contamination. The problem is that anyone who acquires a contaminated site and wishes to put it to use becomes responsible for cleaning it up. As it is difficult to know the extent of the contamination without instituting the clean-up, the amount that it will cost is hard to estimate. The new owner also acquires the liability for damage that the contamination might have caused in the past, to groundwater, for example, although the new owner had nothing to do with creating the problem. The laws also have required a site to be completely cleaned up, regardless of what use is planned. It is common sense that paving a piece of land and using it for parking should require a lower standard of clean-up than building housing, where not only will people be living on the site, but they might plant a vegetable garden and children might be playing in the yard.

A great many old industrial sites have been vacant for years, not because there is no potential new use, but because open-ended liabilities and high costs of clean-up have scared off prospective developers.

Now states are helping developers who want to acquire potentially contaminated sites by creating funding sources for clean-up programs, assuming off-site liabilities, and relating clean-up standards to proposed future uses. These measures in turn are starting to unlock investor interest in vacant inner-city properties.

5.6 *Landscaped islands between rows of cars in a parking lot include a bio-filtration system, drought-tolerant plants, and shade trees. The parking lot is sloped to detain and filter stormwater during a flood.*

5.7 *Planters along the wall of a school cover cisterns that store stormwater from the roof, which can be used to irrigate the adjoining athletic fields*

5.8 *Section shows a porous parking lot with drainage swayles that support shade trees. Under the parking aisle is a crushed stone bed to store runoff water.*

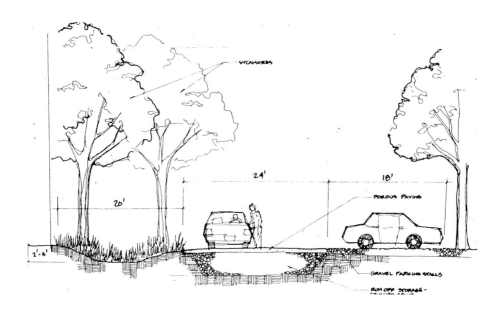

Macro-environmental issues

Federal air and water quality legislation have set standards that have not yet been attained. The worst sources of industrial pollution have been identified and are in the process of being cleaned up, sewage treatment plants have been built; what remains are the sources that are part of every-day life, air pollution from vehicle exhaust and water contamination running off the land and into streams and the watertable.

For a long time it was assumed that cleaner cars would solve the problems of the metropolitan areas whose air quality did not meet federal standards. But the increase in the number of automobile trips, and the lower pollution standards for truck-based sport-utility vehicles, are cancelling the benefits of technology.

If the only way to meet federal air-pollution standards is by reducing the number of automobile trips, reducing air pollution becomes an urban design problem.

Similarly, the EPA has only recently begun enforcing the legal standards for waterways. Meeting these requirements also will involve urban design and planning issues. Some of the contamination consists of animal waste and fertilizers from farms, but suburban yards and golf courses also produce these contaminants, and runoff from parking lots puts petroleum products into streams and groundwater. In urban areas stormwater often flows into a piped drainage system, which creates conventional water pollution treatment concerns. Where there is no piped system, water needs to be retained and filtered, and these systems have to be designed into individual developments.

What Are the Chances for Sustainability?

How likely is any smart growth scenario? To answer this question we have to ask another: What is the alternative?

A continuation of current de facto growth policies means a process in which older urban neighborhoods and aging suburbs are in effect written off, to be replaced with new communities on the urban fringe. Schools in old neighborhoods and older suburbs close, as new ones are constructed at the edge of the metropolis. Older urban neighborhoods with existing water, sewer, electric, and other utilities sit half empty, while new infrastructure is constructed for newly urbanized land. Because the new development is so spread out, and because it is so far from older, established centers, providing services is very expensive. Writing off old areas and replacing with new development is ultimately unaffordable. Governor Parris Glendenning of Maryland, who has led his state to enact strong smart-growth measures, say that Maryland would otherwise "go bankrupt building the roads, schools, and other facilities needed to accommodate the kind of sprawling suburban growth patterns that have characterized development in the last few decades."

It is the cost to the taxpayers of current policies that will force regional revenue sharing and smart growth. Instead of moving development outward into greenfields, the green can be brought into existing urbanized areas as demonstrated in Boston and Los Angeles. As mentioned in the prologue to this book, the political coalition for regional policies has been identified by Myron Orfield as voters in the old central cities and the older, less-fashionable suburbs. Adding in people who have become disenchanted with the way suburban growth is happening, as in Wildwood, and together they constitute a majority of voters in a metropolitan region.

Practice

6

Designing New Neighborhoods

Neighborhoods are not created by planners or builders, but by networks of people who know each other, share some of their social life, help each other out in emergencies, and get together to manage community projects. Many neighborhood links are created by children and children's after-school activities. People can make a neighborhood out of different kinds of places, but the design and physical condition of the community have a big effect on whether people create neighborhoods or not.

The *Washington Post* runs a feature every week, "Where We Live," profiling neighborhoods in its metropolitan area. Some are traditional streets and blocks within the city, others are suburban subdivisions built-out a generation ago, some are in planned communities. Each one has its own character, and the residents interviewed by the newspaper all cherish their neighborhood and feel it is an important part of their lives.

What you don't see in the *Post* are profiles of the big suburban housing tracts, or of places where all the houses are on large lots. There are no profiles of suburban garden apartments corridors, or of high-crime inner-city districts and housing projects. Mass-produced housing tracts full of same-sized houses and lots, too-wide streets lined with garage doors, and no local parks or landmarks are hostile to neighborhood formation. If your neighbor's house is a five-minute walk, as happens when lots are two acres or more, there is not much casual daily contact. Suburban apartment clusters, relegated by zoning to otherwise unwanted sites adjoining commercial corridors, make their residents feel like transients. Highly stressed inner-city districts where law and order are not maintained, and people stay behind locked doors, are obviously not friendly to the kinds of neighborhood activities chronicled in "Where We Live."

"Neighborhood" can also be a way to categorize the social and economic

6.1 Seaside, Florida, a resort designed as a traditional neighborhood.

character of parts of a city, and the term can have connotations of discrimination and segregation.

The Neighborhood as a Design Concept

We are in the midst of an impressive revival of community designs that are friendly to neighborhood formation. It happened first in the inner cities, where old-style urban renewal was replaced by community-based neighborhood planning, as described in Chapter 3.

The unlikely source of the neighborhood revival in the suburbs is Seaside, Florida, designed in 1980 by Andres Duany and Elizabeth Plater-Zyberk to duplicate the atmosphere of early twentieth century summer resorts. Seaside's architectural code encourages front porches, picket fences, and pitched roofs. There is no parking at the beach, and only a small number of beachfront lots. Residents leave their cars at home and stroll the artfully designed narrow streets to access pavilions that guide them on boardwalks and stairs over the dunes to the water. On the shore road that runs parallel to the beach is a center with a village green, the post office, and shops. (6.1)

Masterfully publicized by its developer Robert Davis, Seaside attracted national, even worldwide attention. Its sense of community and place, however artificially produced, was clearly missing from most new suburban areas. Developers began calling Duany/Plater-Zyberk, asking them to design something similar to Seaside, not as a resort but for the suburban tracts they planned to build.

Peter Calthorpe and Douglas Kelbaugh were promoting a planning concept that they called Pedestrian Pockets at much the same time as Andres Duany and Elizabeth Plater-Zyberk were applying lessons learned at Seaside to the design of new residential neighborhoods. Kelbaugh, then a professor of architecture at the University of Washington, organized a workshop in 1988 to demonstrate different designs for walkable neighborhoods related to transit stops. These designs were later published as *The Pedestrian Pocket Book.* The "pocket" nomenclature comes from Peter Calthorpe's regional planning studies. He advocates giving structure to sprawling, automobile-based suburban development by building rapid transit lines—where possible along disused existing rail corridors. Higher intensity development, consisting of employment, stores, and apartments can take place within walking distance of the transit stops, with less dense, but still transit-oriented, residential development just beyond. As noted earlier, Calthorpe was a consultant in the development of the 2040 Plan for Portland, which demonstrates how most of the projected population growth in the Portland metropolitan area can be accommodated within existing growth boundaries by building transit lines and encouraging higher-density neighborhoods around station stops.

More recently, neighborhood design has come back to the inner cities through the Department of Housing and Urban Development's Hope VI Project and other sources. These inner-city neighborhoods are discussed in Chapter 7.

There are currently 305 new developments designed to create and foster neighborhoods in various stages of completion in 32 states and the District of Columbia, according to a list kept by *New Urban News.* These communities, designed by Duany/Plater-Zyberk, Calthorpe, and many other firms, are often referred to as Traditional Neighborhood Developments (TNDs), because they attempt to reproduce the virtues of traditional, pre-automobile cities and suburbs.

The Theory of Neighborhood Design

Much of the theory of neighborhood design refers back to an essay written by Clarence Perry for *Neighborhood and Community Planning,* volume 7 of the *Regional Plan and Survey* published by the Regional Plan Association of New York in 1929. Clarence Perry was the executive director of the Russell Sage Foundation; the foundation was the developer of Forest Hills Gardens, a pioneering garden suburb in New York City's borough of Queens, where Perry was living while writing his definition of neighborhoods. (6.2) His innovation

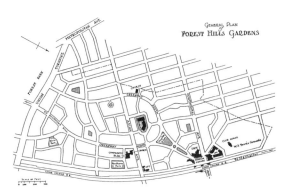

6.2 *The plan of Forest Hills Gardens, a planned community designed by Grosvenor Atterbury and Frederick L. Olmsted, Jr., begun in 1912.*

6.3 *Clarence Perry's diagram of a suburban neighborhood unit. He also drew an industrial neighborhood and a high-density neighborhood that was almost all apartment houses.*

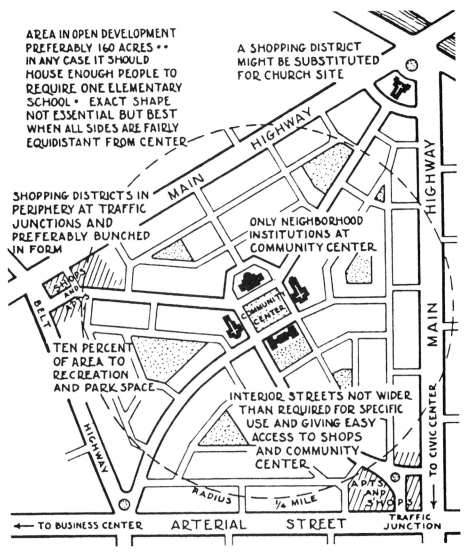

was to derive from Forest Hills Gardens, and various other examples that he admired, such as Hampstead Garden Suburb in London and Kohler, a company town in Wisconsin, a series of principles that would produce what he called the Neighborhood Unit, 160 acres where residents could reach schools, playgrounds, and local stores without crossing a main highway, and where about 10 percent of the land would be set aside as park space.

Perry wrote of the *Neighborhood Unit* at a time when old certainties about city design were beginning to erode and automobiles were helping to produce new suburban developments that Perry criticized:

> "If there is a school, it is too far away, or it can be reached
> only by crossing a dangerous thoroughfare. Playgrounds are
> too small, or absent altogether. The grocery is in one direc-
> tion and the drug store in another..."

Perry was emphatic that walking distances were still the right measure of the constituent parts of a city or suburb. The 160-acre size came from a judgment by Perry that the distance across a neighborhood should be no more than a 10-minute walk. At an average walking speed of three miles an hour, a person who walks for 10 minutes will cover about half a mile. A square one-half mile on each side is 160 acres. Perry's graphic explanation of the same idea was to draw a circle with a half-mile diameter over the map of an ideal neighborhood. (6.3)

Perry also defined the neighborhood as housing the number of families that would support a public elementary school, his diagram left sites for religious buildings and other neighborhood institutions at the center, and showed apartments and shops at the corner where four such neighborhoods could be expected to meet.

Early Influence of the Neighborhood Concept

The neighborhood unit was a basic element of the famous plan for Radburn by Perry's friends, Clarence Stein and Henry Wright. (6.4, see page 100) Note, however, that the circles drawn on the Radburn plan have a half-mile *radius*, so that each circle encompasses four neighborhoods, as defined by Perry. The walkable neighborhood-elementary school relationship was adopted in the 1930s by the Congres Internationaux d'Architecture Moderne (C.I.A.M.) as a basic design principle which has been built into housing projects all over the world. (6.5, see page 100) The concept of neighborhood influenced each of the three Greenbelt towns built by the federal government before World War II, and a few post World-War II planned communities, such as Columbia, Maryland, and Reston, Virginia.

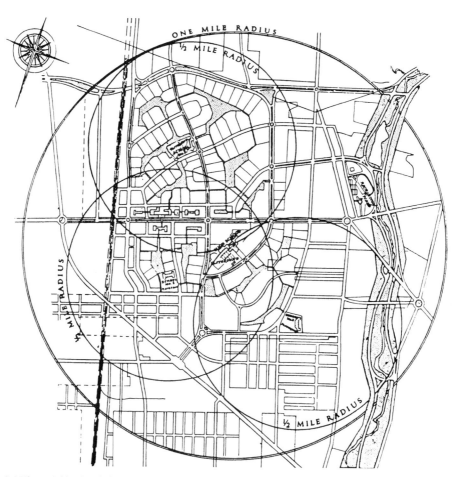

6.4 *The neighborhood theory applied to the plan of Radburn, New Jersey, by Henry Wright and Clarence Stein. Note that the radius of the circles is twice that used by Perry.*

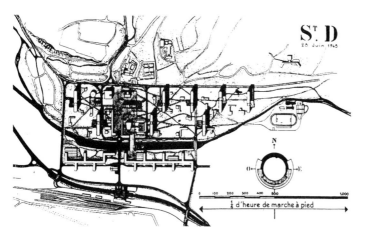

6.5 *Le Corbusier's plan for a walkable residential area, the proposed reconstruction of Saint-Die in France, 1945. Modernist architects adopted Perry's neighborhood theory but reinterpreted it.*

In the late 1930s, when something like a third of all U.S. housing was substandard, the American Public Health Association published a handbook, *Planning the Neighborhood*, which firmly associated neighborhood planning with housing reform. The concept of neighborhoods also was promoted in publications by the Urban Land Institute, the American Institute of Architects, and other professional organizations.

Nevertheless, the neighborhood unit rapidly eroded into the subdivision after World War II. Levittown, Long Island, begun in 1947, was a prototype of the large-scale housing tract with mass-produced houses. It originally was laid out as several neighborhoods, with an elementary school in each and even local convenience stores. However, houses were designed on the same sized lots, at about four houses to the acre, and the primary means of transportation was intended to be by car. By the 1980s, thousands of master-planned communities were being built around the United States where automobile access was essential, houses were separate from all other activities, and walking was solely for recreation, serving no functional purpose.

Zoning Versus Neighborhoods

The designs of Forest Hills Gardens and Radburn both included apartment houses and different house and lot sizes. The typical house at Radburn was actually part of pair, and there are also attached rowhouses. At the time Perry was writing, urban and suburban neighborhoods had this kind of variation, and Perry must have thought it was axiomatic. Unfortunately, zoning codes, another planning concept just coming into general use at the time, typically assign a different classification to every residential lot size, and segregate two-family houses and apartments. The proliferation of different residential zones was an attempt to avoid nonconforming lots when older neighborhoods were first given zoning classifications, There is no planning theory that says that single-family houses on 40-foot lots should be in a different zone from houses on 50-foot lots, or 100-foot lots, and that individual houses and small apartment buildings can't be compatible. However, once different zoning designations were on the books, communities had to choose one when they mapped a new residential district.

If there is a master plan for a new area, it can show a mosaic of different zones that fit the plan. But zoning first, planning later is the usual order—despite the statements in planning textbooks that zoning is the means of implementing master plans. In most communities the zoning code is the real master plan. A large area all in a single zone, and following recognizable geographic or geometric boundaries, looks like uniform administration and is probably legal. A mix of small, different-sized zoning districts mapped over open land looks like discrimination among various property owners and can

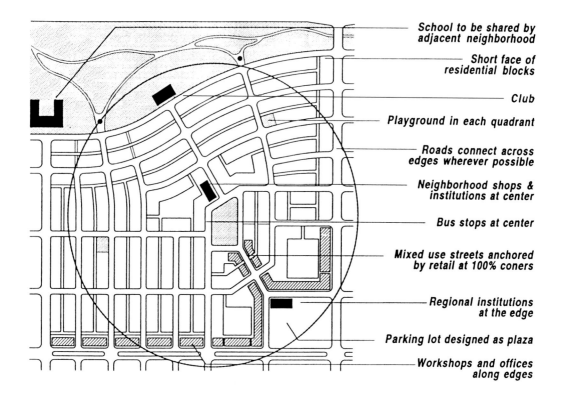

6.6 The neighborhood unit as rethought by Andres Duany and Elizabeth Plater-Zyberk.

be challenged in court. So mapping big, separate residential zones based on lot-size became the norm, and no one stood up to say that this practice made little or no sense as a plan for new development.

As each zone has a minimum lot size, all the houses in the zone are usually built on the same-sized lot. It is largely because of modern zoning codes that builders' houses at different price-points are found in separate subdivisions. It is not good planning, and it is not even good merchandising, because house buyers need different sized houses at different stages in their lives, and shouldn't be forced to move away from familiar surroundings to modify their lifestyle.

While most people would say that they live in a neighborhood, if it was constructed since World War II, zoning laws make it unlikely it resembles Perry's neighborhood unit. Some rowhouses and apartments are needed to achieve the densities necessary to support neighborhood schools and services, while still preserving open space and creating a desirable diversity of places to live.

Neighborhoods Lose Favor With Planners
Starting in the late 1960s, the idea of building new neighborhoods began to lose favor with planners and reformers. Richard Llewelyn-Davies, whose firm prepared the 1967 master plan for the English new town, Milton-Keynes, saw neighborhoods as a limiting concept, observing that social relationships in the modern world are networks. He rejected neighborhoods in favor of a one-kilometer street-grid system for maximum flexibility. Milton-Keynes was seen as the prototype of a new kind of planned community not based on sentimental, village-like images from the past. Certainly a well-traveled, highly educated person like Lord Llewelyn-Davies did not choose his friends from people who happened to live close by, and he didn't see why anyone else should either.

Other planners came to a similar rejection of neighborhoods for the opposite reason; they saw them as exclusionary: safeguarding the rich and ghettoizing the poor. In *Beyond the Neighborhood Unit*, published in 1984 and one of the few scholarly studies of the subject, Tridib Banerjee and William Baer interviewed subjects in nine Los Angeles neighborhoods and concluded that, in practice, neighborhoods were a way of separating people by social class, race, or ethnicity. They also concluded that the prime neighborhood relationships took place in an area much smaller than 160 acres. In looking beyond the neighborhood unit, they suggested a grid of streets on half-mile centers (Llewelyn-Davies's grid of streets at one-kilometer intervals is only a little bigger) with two or three dwelling clusters of people at similar income levels occurring within each half-mile square. The grid helps permits equal access to schools, parks, and shopping, while the clusters accept the inevitability of some form of segregation, whether by income or by elective affinity.

Walking Distances as the Measure of the Plan
Duany and Plater-Zyberk make explicit their debt to Clarence Perry by redrawing his 1929 diagram with its circle denoting easy walking distances. (6.6) Perry's hypothesis about the appropriate size of a neighborhood relates closely to the principle expressed by Jan Gehl as "Life takes place on foot," as discussed in Chapter 1. If relationships among families living in the same general area are important, and if people relate to each other meeting in an unplanned casual way as they go about their lives, it is logical to base neighborhood size on the distances that people can comfortably walk.

Perry's formulation about neighborhood size conformed to characteristics he could observe in New York City at that time. The 10-minute walking distance across a neighborhood, with five minutes from any point to a center, corresponds to the five-minute walking distance demonstrated to define the primary influence of transit stops, and also considered a practical maximum for the length of a shopping mall. A 10-minute walking distance is usually considered the limit of influence of a transit stop. The maximum distance that people will walk from a parking space to the farthest destination in a mall is also about 10 minutes.

Mixed Housing Types as a Key to Neighborhood Design

Bannerjee and Baer assumed that it is not possible to eliminate segregation by income, and probably for other reasons as well, and concentrate on eliminating disparities of access to schools and other facilities. But the neighborhood unit was meant to be an egalitarian concept, and an egalitarian neighborhood is necessary to implement the concepts of deconcentration of poverty and environmental justice discussed in Chapter 4. An egalitarian neighborhood requires a full range of housing types within the walkable area, but not necessarily all on the same street. The Kentlands, and its sister community Lakelands, in Gaithersburg, Maryland, were both designed by Duany/Plater-Zyberk on neighborhood principles. They have four-story apartment houses, rowhouses, detached single-family houses on small lots, as well as a district of big houses on relatively large lots. Some of the moderate-sized detached houses also have an additional rental apartment over the garage. Some other jurisdictions that permit garage apartments specify that the house must be owner-occupied if the garage unit is rented. Should the apartment tenant give loud parties, the landlord gets to hear them too. (6.7, 6.8, 6.9, 6.10)

While a few jurisdictions, like Miami-Dade County and Orlando, have adopted special Traditional Neighborhood Development zoning, Seaside, the Kentlands and most other new "traditional" neighborhoods are made possible by planned unit development procedures available in most zoning codes. As the name suggests, the development is planned as a unit, and the plan becomes the zoning. Lot sizes and building types can be mixed, but the overall density should remain the same as the original zoning. More important, all the land in the development has to be under one ownership, and approval of such a plan is almost always a special alternative, which a local community may or may not permit; sometimes they do not. How such neighborhoods can be a rule and not an exception is discussed in Chapter 13.

Neighborhood Schools

During the school-busing era, the idea of being able to walk or ride a bicycle to school fell into abeyance, but today many people have come back to neighborhood elementary schools as an important aspect of a livable community, having concluded that busing for small children is not a substitute for achieving integrated neighborhoods.

Clarence Perry's prescription for an elementary school in every neighbor-

6.7 A mid-block walkway in the Kentlands, designed by Duany/Plater-Zyberk

6.8 A street scene in the Lakelands, also designed by Duany/Plater Zyberk. The Lakelands has more rowhouses than the Kentlands, a street of live-work units can be seen in the distance.

6.9 Single-family houses in the Lakelands face an open-space preserve. The typical suburban apartment houses in the background improve the mix of housing available, but are out of scale with the rest of the development.

6.10 An alley in the Kentlands, with additional apartments over some of the garages.

hood is repeated in planning textbooks without anyone answering the follow-up question: How many children in the elementary school? Clearly the size of the school has to relate to the population density of the district. Perry suggests a population of 5,000 for the neighborhood illustrated in the diagram, which is mostly single-family houses with some apartments at one corner, and goes up to 10,000 residents for a neighborhood that is all apartments. For the apartment house district he projects an elementary school population of 1,600; which suggests a school with 800 students for the primarily single-family neighborhood.

These are big primary schools, concentrating more young children in one place than most people would consider appropriate; but Perry's densities are also high: 30 to 60 people per acre. Today neighborhood plans face the opposite problem. At what is considered a moderately high density in neighborhoods today, 12 people per acre, there would not be enough children to justify an elementary school just for the 160-acre neighborhood.

Assuming that a neighborhood is zoned for four families to the acre, or about 640 families in a Clarence Perry neighborhood-unit of 160 acres, an elementary school serving only the one neighborhood would have about 200 pupils. Schools of around this size were often built in suburban and low-density city neighborhoods in the 1920s and 1930s. Because of their small size, the auditorium, gymnasium and cafeteria would generally be the same multipurpose room, and the building didn't have the learning centers and other amenities expected in a school today. Most experts would say that a 200-seat elementary school is no longer an economic size, although, in retrospect, these small schools had a big advantage. They were small enough that the principal could know all the students and most of their families. To have a true neighborhood school at today's school sizes would mean doubling the density of the neighborhood to an average of eight families per acre.

One alternative is to place the school where it can serve more than a single neighborhood, although the arithmetic doesn't change, and at lower densities some of the children in each neighborhood will be outside of easy walking or bicycle distance. The 400- or 600-seat elementary schools being built in some jurisdictions are far too large to ever be a neighborhood school at today's typical residential densities. Many people would say that they are far too large for such small children in any case. In communities where the average size of house lots is a half-acre or more, the densities are just too low to support a neighborhood elementary school today. And, as noted above, when average lot sizes get larger, the possibilities for residents forming any kind of neighborhood get lower and lower.

School Funding and Suburban Planning

Today many school districts include more than one city or town. Even elementary schools are planned to serve a large geographic area and are located on big sites often selected because the land was available and affordable, assuming that just about all the children will arrive by bus or car.

If a community is going to go back to neighborhood schools, big changes will have to take place in the way school boards make their decisions, and the school boards will have to coordinate their plans with the land-use decisions made by the local governments in the district. If neighborhood elementary schools are to be smaller than usual, it may well be necessary to combine the school with other uses, such as a community center or recreation center, in order to share the cost of meeting rooms and playing fields.

Nobody really likes to talk about it, but in most rapidly growing areas today, a house with an assessment of less than $250,000 is probably not paying fully for its costs to the school system, which can make a community wary of a approving a mixed-income neighborhood with apartments and small houses as well as large ones. If residential property taxes are not enough to support the schools and other services, the community has to find the money some other way. Office parks tend to pay more property tax than they require in services, so do shopping centers. If the community receives a percentage of sales-tax revenue, a car-dealership is a nice asset: lots of sales-tax, not much in the way of demand for services. Michigan has managed to decouple school funding from the property tax and other states have equalization formulas that help overcome deficits and disparities in school funding. But until there is true equalization of school funding for a whole state, local communities have to worry about what their land-use decisions are doing to their school budget.

Neighborhood Streets: Connectivity Versus Traffic Safety

Designing and placing streets is one of the oldest and most established powers that local government has, but it has become the custom to have the streets in new areas constructed by the developers; the local government then accepts the streets and maintains them if they meet their standards. The standards for street design are usually found in the subdivision ordinance, although the actual construction specifications are probably administrative.

 A study of streets in San Francisco neighborhoods by Donald Appleyard demonstrated that the more traffic ran down the street the fewer contacts residents had with the families on the opposite side. Busy streets tend to be neighborhood boundaries. Keeping through traffic off local streets within neighborhoods is a big issue in local politics.

There is currently a debate going on between advocates of neighborhoods designed as a continuous grid of streets, and advocates of dead-end streets, often called cul-de-sacs. Raymond Unwin and Barry Parker needed an act of Parliament to use dead-end streets in their 1910 plan for Hampstead Garden Suburb, because such streets had been outlawed after landlords used them to create airless interior buildings in the slum blocks of nineteenth-century English cities. The 1929 plan for Radburn, New Jersey, by Clarence Stein and Henry Wright took Unwin and Parker's garden suburb to the next logical step by alternating dead-end streets with greenways that connected all the houses to a central open space. One side of each house faced the street, the other faced a greenway. The Radburn plan has been widely admired, particularly as an alternative to the mechanical layouts of streets and blocks that typified other new development at the time. The prestige of the Radburn plan helped make cul-de-sacs synonymous with good suburban planning in the years after World War II.

Pedestrians living on a street that connects only at one end have to walk from their cul-de-sac to a more important "collector" street and follow it to another cul-de-sac which leads to their destination—seldom the shortest distance between two points. At Radburn this problem was solved by the greenway system, which let people walk across the central open-space to go from one cul-de-sac to another. The influence of the Radburn plan at first caused developers to adopt both cul-de-sacs and greenways, not just cul-de-sacs. Greenways were important features of some of the most famous post World War II planned communities, including Columbia and Reston in Maryland, and Irvine, California. They were also sometimes used in smaller planned communities.

However, these greenways were all planned before widespread use of portable radios, and at a time when street crime was relatively low. In the 1970s, communities with greenways discovered that they had become hangout places for teenagers playing loud music, and then, later, that greenways were hard to police. People became afraid to let their children use greenways on their own. So builders went on planning subdivisions with cul-de-sacs, and left out the greenways.

A cul-de-sac saves the builder money, providing the largest number of house lots for the least amount of street. It is often popular with the residents on the street, as there is no through traffic and exclusiveness helps create a social unit. Children can improvise greenways by cutting through contiguous back yards; but big tracts laid out using only cul-de-sacs are seldom successful neighborhoods.

After Seaside, city designers began rediscovering the advantages of using grid plans where all the streets connect, without going back to the surveyor's street and block plan of most older U.S. cities and towns. Designers began looking at more artful street systems, such as John Nolen's plans for Mariemont, Ohio or Venice, Florida, or the layouts of pre-World War II country club suburbs. Streets in these plans do not need to be dead straight, and they are designed with a consciousness of the vistas people experience while walking or driving through them. At the end of each street there is a park, or a scenic easement, or an important building, so that pedestrians always have a destination in view. Placement of houses is important at T intersections, so that the vista doesn't end in one half of a driveway or garage door.

Controlling Driving Speed in Neighborhoods

Suburban subdivision ordinances routinely require street rights-of-way of 50 or even 60 feet, the width of a typical right-of-way for a crosstown street in Manhattan. It is understood that such wide streets are not necessary in low-density residential neighborhoods, but it used to be considered good practice to require wide streets in case a neighborhood was redeveloped at a higher density later. Paradoxically, such radical change was only likely in the days before zoning and subdivision ordinances. Today, in most places, it is just not going to happen.

In any discussion of street widths, it is important to distinguish between the *right-of-way*, which is the total width of the street controlled by the local government, and the *cartway*, which is the paved area of the street itself. Where there is a 60-foot right of way, it is easy for the local engineering establishment to require a wide cartway. A typical disposition might be the following: an inadequate four feet on each side of the street for sidewalks, and six feet on each side for a planted verge of grass and street trees. That leaves 40 feet for the cartway, divided as follows: two parking lanes of eight feet each, and two traffic lanes each 12 feet wide.

A 12-foot traffic lane is a width you would provide on a high-speed arterial highway. On a local street, at low speed, 10 feet or even nine feet for a traffic lane ought to be adequate. And is it necessary to have two full lanes of parking on a street where the homeowners all park their cars in driveways or garages? If two parking lanes are required, there can be one traffic lane of 14 feet, enough for two cars to squeeze by each other if they are careful. (6.11)

Within a residential neighborhood planned with a connecting grid plan, the streets should be designed to limit speed, so that through-traffic does not take shortcuts through the neighborhood. Sometimes called *traffic calming*, such designs limit lane widths, and reduce the radius of curvature at corners to 15 or 20 feet from 25 or 30, to slow down cars making turns. Such plans also create deflections around parks and traffic circles to prevent drivers from

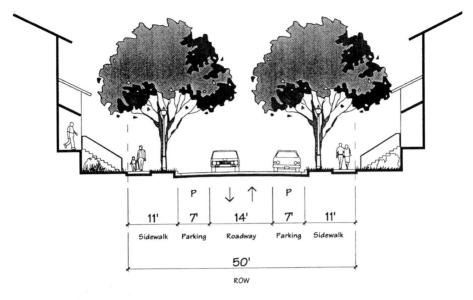

Neighborhood Streets

6.11 An appropriate section for a neighborhood street, by the ROMA Design Group.

6.12 An appropriate section for a service lane, or alley, also by the ROMA Design Group. The 5-foot setback and 2.5-foot verge are enough to allow cars to go in and out of garages safely.

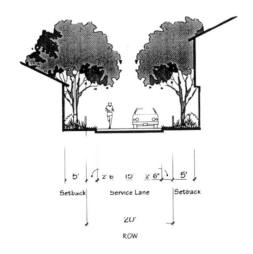

Service Lanes

speeding up on straight stretches.

A comfortable six-foot sidewalk on each side of the street, plus one lane of parking and two 10-foot traffic lanes adds up to a width of 40 feet. If the ordinance asks for a 50-foot right of way the other 10 feet should be divided into verges between the sidewalk and the street. Sixty feet should ordinarily be reserved for unusually important streets. A cartway in a one-way alley shouldn't need to be wider than 16 feet, and could be less. (6.12) The cost difference between the 40 feet of cartway in some suburban streets and the 28 feet of cartway in a better-designed street is almost enough to pay for an alley. Of course, if a boulevard with a landscaped center island is designed for a neighborhood, then the right of way will be wider.

Making a Neighborhood Friendly to Pedestrians

People will walk for five or 10 minutes, but, as William H. Whyte observed, you have to keep them interested if you want them to walk at all. So making a residential district small enough to be walkable is not sufficient by itself; the design has to encourage people to walk. Some ways to do this:

1. Keep the Garage Doors off the Street Front

When houses had stables, it went without saying that they belonged away from the house and at the back of the lot. When the horseless carriage arrived, it remained the custom for garages to be set back from the street. Well-designed early suburbs, like Forest Hills Gardens, enforced garage set-backs through community regulations. Garages in city neighborhoods often faced the alleys, still a good arrangement. Small houses had one-car garages, and, if they were on narrow lots, often shared driveways with the house next-door. Gradually, as the two-car garage became more usual and houses became less pretentious, the garage worked its way to the front.

Walking by a garage door is not as interesting as walking by the windows and doors of a house, and, when a small house has a two-car garage facing front, half of the street facade of the house is going to be garage door. On a street with small lots, even more of what a pedestrian sees will be garage doors. If the builder is trying to save money on paving driveways, the garages may be pulled out to within 20 feet of the sidewalk, and the house tucked in behind. The street frontage can then become almost all garage door.

This is why city designers often promote regulations that garage doors should be set back from the street or, even better, face away from the street. This does not normally mean going back to the pre-World-War II practice of building garages as separate structures at the back of the lot. People have become accustomed to the convenience of using their garage door opener to drive straight in and then enter the house directly from the garage.

2. Use Alleys or Lanes

On narrow lots there is no substitute for entering the garage from an alley or lane, if the front of the garage is to be kept away from the street. Builders object to alleys because they are paying to build a second street. On the other hand, they should be able to save money on paving driveways—as the alley is essentially a collective driveway—and also save money on paving streets if they follow sensible cartway dimensions. To make the alley cost-effective, it is probably necessary to let home builders provide only a five-foot apron between the garage and the paved surface of the alley. Requiring a 20-foot setback of garage doors from the alley eliminates some of its cost competitiveness. Alleys can be made one-way and provided with speed bumps to ensure the safety of cars entering and exiting garages close to the alley. Alleys are also a good place for trash collection and for locating utility wires. Above-ground utility wires may be acceptable in an alley location where they would not be on the street front.

Shared driveways have become less satisfactory now that most people own more than one car. It is too easy to leave one car in the driveway and go out in the other one, leaving the neighbor blocked and frustrated. So house lots without alleys have to be big enough to allow for a full driveway to bypass the house. On these larger lots, driveways can bypass the house and swing around to garages entered from the side or rear, or there can be a turnaround and the garage can be built into the house but entered from the side. Front-facing garages can also be acceptable on a larger lot, if they are at the side of the house and set back a reasonable distance like 25 feet from the front of the house.

3. Keep the Houses Close to the Street

A wide expanse of perfectly manicured front lawn is certainly impressive, but it is a lot of work to keep up and not much use to anyone. Most people want a large lot so they can have a big back yard. Big front and side yards are a setting for the house but generally are not worth having unless the whole lot is so big that the back yard is as large as it needs to be anyway. So, as house lots get smaller, it makes sense to pull the house toward the street. Houses that are within hailing distance of the street help keep a neighborhood friendly and interesting to walk through.

Front porches and picket fences have become in some people's minds the hallmark of good neighborhood planning. Seaside, its design based on streets in Key West, encouraged front porches on all the houses as well as white picket fences around the yards. People out for a walk after dinner can say hello to people sitting out on their front porches, so that a walk becomes a social occasion.

Seaside is a resort designed to recreate the summer places that people remember from their childhood, or, more likely, wish they remembered from their childhood. Sitting on the front porch is part of the deal, so people conscientiously do it. While traditional resort houses had wrap-around verandahs, this architectural feature vanished from most other houses before World War I. Narrow city rowhouses often continued to have front porches, and, before air conditioning, people would sit outside on the porch in the evenings because it was far more comfortable than sitting in the house. In more affluent neighborhoods, the front porch had long been replaced by the screened side or back porch, an outdoor room with cushioned furniture. From the street the side porch was revealed by the glow of parchment-shaded bridge lamps filtering through the cedars and azaleas.

But porch life everywhere has been strongly affected by air-conditioning and television on the one hand, which tend to keep people inside the house, and more active outdoor lifestyles, with people cooking at the barbecue or sitting by the backyard pool, rather than on a porch.

Does it make sense to build front porches to restore a tradition that vanished a long time ago, and for many people never existed at all? Maybe. Sometimes people with front-facing garages turn them into porches by leaving the door open and sitting there in lawn chairs, a sad commentary on the inadequacies of typical suburban design. Most houses have some kind of shelter over the front door, and extending that shelter to be big enough to hold a few chairs is not a big incremental cost. The symbolism of the front porch is desirable, a way of inviting people into the zone of the house, without having to worry if the house itself is presentable. But the front porch is not a necessity in creating a livable neighborhood. It is more important to keep the front door relatively close to the street.

Although they look charming in Key West and Seaside, frontyard picket fences are a maintenance nightmare, unless you have Tom Sawyer to organize their upkeep for you. And, so far, vinyl fences are not convincing in real life although they may look appropriate in photographs. Enclosing front lawns with fences, walls, or hedges is the usual practice in England. The American tradition is to leave the front yard unfenced, so that the front lawns and planting merge into a continuous garden landscape. And if there are going to be front fences, it is important that everyone do it, as a street where some yards are fenced and others are not seldom looks right. Fencing back yards for privacy makes perfect sense, but fences are likely to be taller and less transparent than pickets.

4. Provide a Network of Open Spaces
Clarence Perry suggested that 10 percent of the land area in a neighborhood

be set aside for parks and open space. Some of that land goes to the school and parks that are focal points for different places within the neighborhood, other land may be steep slopes and parts of the local drainage network.

5. Find a Way to Have a Neighborhood Store

Walking to a neighborhood store is one of the conveniences of urban neighborhoods, but unless there are more than 35 housing units per acre throughout the neighborhood, it is difficult to provide the customer base even for a convenience store. Clarence Perry recognized in his neighborhood diagram that shops had to be located on the perimeter arterial streets at the interface of two or more neighborhoods, meaning that some customers arrive by car. Seaside has some retailers in its town center, but they are exclusive specialty shops that serve a larger area. At Seaside you can walk from your cottage to the town center for for morning coffee and a muffin, but the 27 different brands of olive oil on the shelves indicate you are not in an ordinary corner store. Developers of some planned communities have decided that a convenience store is an amenity, like a park, and has to be provided even if the operators can't pay an economic rent. Through a process of trial and error, as different tenants try to survive in these neighborhood store spaces, a bakery restaurant is emerging as a business likely to survive and prosper in such a setting. People come for breakfast, lunch, or a light dinner, and can pick up some household necessities and luxuries at the same time.

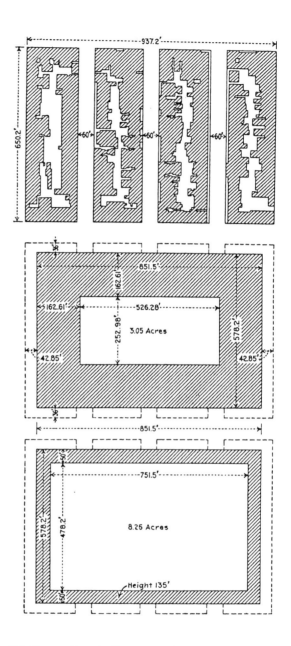

7.1 Clarence Perry's diagrams explaining how conventional New York City slum blocks in the early twentieth century can be combined into superblocks, replacing streets and back yards with significant open space.

7

Reinventing Inner-City Neighborhoods

In the days before building codes, housing for low-income people seldom offered more than minimal shelter. When a few requirements were enacted, like having a window in every room, they didn't make low-income housing much better. Middle-class buildings that lost their original social standing, and were divided up into small apartments, deteriorated quickly under such conditions. People lived in these places because they could not afford anything else that was close enough to their jobs. In the 1930s, a third of the U.S. housing supply did not meet minimum standards, such as having indoor plumbing and central heat. While some of the worst housing was rural, much of it was concentrated in crowded city neighborhoods.

The Superblock: Slum Clearance and Public Housing in the 1930s

The superblock was meant to improve housing for the poorest city-dwellers just as the neighborhood-unit was meant to improve living conditions for the middle class. In the same volume of the 1929 *Regional Plan and Survey for New York* in which he discusses the neighborhood unit, Clarence Perry illustrates the basic theory of the superblock. He shows four typical inner-city blocks, and then illustrates how eliminating intermediate streets produces a three-acre open space while providing room for the same amount of building. (7.1)

When slum clearance programs began in the 1930s, deteriorated housing was regarded as a form of cancer. If these bad areas could be excised, the city would stay healthy. Public housing was built on cleared urban sites consolidated into superblocks, a strategy that both provided more open space and separated the new buildings from the surrounding cancerous slums. Buildings, almost always two- and three-story walk-ups, also were given the best orientation for sunlight, which meant pulling them back at an angle from the remaining streets, reinforcing separation.

For most families, selected from long waiting lists to live in these buildings, it would the first time they had a toilet and bathtub within their own apartment, and a kitchen with a modern stove and refrigerator. There was central heating. The buildings were fire resistant, and the windows looked out on lawns and trees and not on air shafts or back yards filled with rubbish. Early reports on public housing are full of accounts of how well these new buildings functioned as communities; tenants formed clubs and mutual-assistance committees, planted and maintained flower gardens, formed softball teams and bowling leagues. These illustrations of flower gardens planted by tenants at Old Harbor Village were published by the Boston Housing Authority in a 1940 report. (7.2)

As discussed in Chapter 4, the signs of future trouble were there, but hard for people to read at the time. All public housing segregated people of African American descent; this was government policy and nobody questioned it. Most public housing was built on cleared land in low-income areas, reinforcing income segregation. Families whose incomes exceeded the limits had to move out immediately. This regulation seemed only fair, given the long waiting lists, but it meant that the housing was officially a temporary expedient, not a permanent home. The design and administration of the housing also made it clear that people were living in an institution. It feels better to live at 11 Lily Pond Lane than in Unit 132B in Building 14. Public housing projects, while separated from their surroundings, were also not complete communities; they still depended on whatever shops and other services the neighborhood offered.

Slum Clearance and Public Housing after World War II

After World War II, housing projects got bigger and also taller. Where land prices were high, local housing authorities began building elevator apartment towers, first at six and eight stories and then as high as 22 stories, in order to meet federal limits on land price per housing unit.

Decisions to put public housing tenants in elevator buildings appear to have been made primarily for economic reasons, perhaps also influenced by images of the modernist city as drawn by Le Corbusier and other visionary architects. The middle class had been living in apartment towers for generations, but a typical middle-class building would have doormen or security guards at the entrance, and a full-time maintenance staff to keep everything in repair, clean public areas, and make sure garbage and rubbish were taken away. Housing authorities could not provide enough of this kind of support.

EXAMPLES OF TENANT MAINTENANCE WHICH HAVE THE FULL APPROVAL AND ENCOURAGE-MENT OF THE HOUSING AUTHORITY

7.2 Housing authority tenants before World War II were pleased to move into clean new apartments with kitchen appliances and indoor plumbing, and spent time improving their new surroundings.

Oscar Newman's book, *Defensible Space*, published in 1973, documented how vandalism and crime could overwhelm high-rise buildings that did not have secured entrances. Newman found that high-rise buildings for subsidized middle-income housing, where the finances did not permit guards at doors, had the same kinds of problems.

Another typical public housing type was a long, low row of attached duplex apartments. The apartments were like small, separate houses, potentially much more manageable than a tower; but the design of the buildings as utilitarian barracks laid out in rows did not create a controllable environment. At the time these projects were built, public housing tenants were not allowed to own cars, so there are few internal streets in these projects and wide open spaces between the buildings which became uncared for and unsafe. (7.3, 7.4)

As construction of public housing continued it became a larger percentage of a city's housing supply. As most of it was built in low-income areas, the projects began to link up with each other, creating belts of public housing that replaced whole neighborhoods. Government officials became aware that slum clearance was a self-defeating strategy, as the people displaced from

7.3 Public housing in the West End of Louisville, Kentucky, a modernist version of the row-house type; the public environment is very institutional.

one area were overcrowding others. They also became aware that the physical condition of buildings was not the only index of a community's health. People read Herbert Gans's 1962 book, *The Urban Villagers,* and became convinced that the City of Boston had made a mistake, tearing down a viable neighborhood out of arrogance and ignorance. In a few more years, the misgivings of public officials, fair housing laws, plus growing community opposition, had brought about an end to slum clearance policies in most cities.

The Deterioration of Older Neighborhoods

Rapid new development in the suburbs opened up good urban apartments and houses to people who had been living in the worst housing. As demand went down for slum buildings, their landlords often sold out to more cynical operators, who created dummy ownership corporations, stopped paying for maintenance and taxes, and collected rent as almost pure profit. When tax foreclosure threatened or the tenants stopped paying rent, the owners walked away from their buildings, and cities were unable to hold them accountable. Cities, the reluctant new owners through foreclosure, were left to rehabilitate the buildings themselves or to demolish them.

7.4 Another rowhouse public housing project in Louisville's West End. Here the public environment has deteriorated. Both of these projects have been cleared for the Park DuValle mixed-income development shown on page 129.

It was an ugly process, producing results as if whole neighborhoods had been heavily bombed. It created great misery for the tenants caught in the middle; it was a waste of resources. However, some of the reasons why these neighborhoods deteriorated were actually by-products of favorable developments. The overall supply of housing in cities and suburbs was growing. More families were making enough money to have some choices about where they lived. Anti-discrimination laws were working.

Unscrupulous real-estate operators engaged in what was called block-busting in some of the neighborhoods where former slum dwellers were moving, scaring building owners into selling out to them at distress prices because the neighborhood was changing, and then overcharging the newcomers. Sometimes, when homeowners sold out to homebuyers, the neighborhood stabilized with a new population. Sometimes when the newcomers were mostly tenants and the owners let the buildings run down, the cycle of destruction extended to neighborhoods that had not previously been slums.

Even in deteriorated neighborhoods, as the worst housing is taken off the market, a higher percentage of houses and apartments now meet minimum standards. They have workable bathrooms and kitchens, they have heat. The buildings meet the fire code. Dwellings may be isolated, surrounded by vacant lots, but housing conditions have improved even where neighborhood services and institutions have deteriorated.

In many cities public housing has become the last resort; instead of waiting lists, there are vacant apartments. Embarrassingly for local governments, some of the worst housing conditions are in public housing projects.

The current situation is both a tragedy and an opportunity. The tragedy is that the people with the least resources have been concentrated into badly deteriorated neighborhoods and public housing projects. The large amount of vacant land and buildings, much of it in public ownership, is the opportunity. These sites are in good central locations and comes equipped with all the necessary utilities, unlike raw land at the edge of the metropolitan area. It should be possible to rebuild these significant areas of older cities without perpetuating racial and economic segregation. (7.5, 7.6)

Turning Public Housing into Neighborhoods
There has long been federal money for rehabilitating housing projects, but the funds were restricted to repairs and reconstruction, which made it hard to correct original errors of planning and design.

Typical public housing, barracks-like two-story rows of duplex apartments, can be made into a community if the environment around these buildings is improved. One useful concept, which followed from Oscar Newman's research into what he called defensible spaces at Clason Point Gardens in the

7.5, 7.6 Derelict land near downtown Detroit, a tragedy but also an opportunity, as utilities and some community institutions are still there. The downtown skyline can be seen in background of the photo at top.

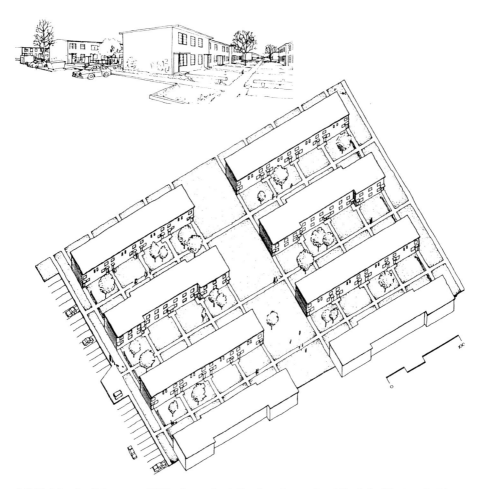

7.7 Sketches by Peterson and Littenberg of existing housing units at the Lake West project in Dallas.

Bronx during the early 1970s, was to enclose the open areas adjacent to the duplex rowhouses into fenced front and rear yards—the front yards with low fences that delineate a private area and the rear yards with six-foot high metal railings. At Clason Point Gardens, 80 percent of the public areas could thus be controlled and maintained by the tenants.

Lake West, 3,500 units of barracks-like duplex housing covering much of a square mile in Dallas, was a badly deteriorated, high-crime area. Architects Steven Peterson and Barbara Littenberg suggested enclosing the front and rear yards, as at Clason Point, but they also revised the site plan to add more streets and make them connect to the surrounding neighborhoods, which had been deliberately avoided in the original design. The buildings originally had

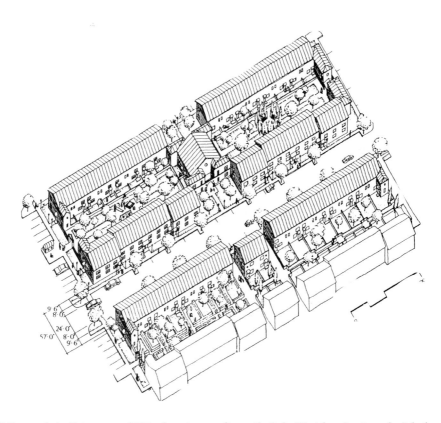

7.8 Proposals by Peterson and Littenberg to reconfigure the Lake West housing to make it look like middle-income garden apartments and add streets to make a real neighborhood instead of a project. This 1981 design anticipates much of current practice in renovating and replacing public housing

presented blank end walls to streets; Peterson and Littenberg proposed opening them up with doors and windows. In addition they proposed altering the architectural character of the buildings, raising the roof pitches, adding front porches and some simplified Colonial Revival detailing to doors and windows. The effect was to change the symbolic character of these buildings from looking like the cheapest and barest housing possible—a place where no one would expect to live a moment longer than necessary—to something resembling middle-class garden apartments. The plan also proposed adding more shops and other kinds of housing on vacant land within the project. In 1981, these proposals were ahead of their time, and only the renovation of a small part of this project has been carried out while much of the rest has been demolished. (7.7, 7.8)

The Norfolk Redevelopment and Housing Authority has recently implemented a similar approach at the much smaller Diggstown Project in Norfolk. The site plan was revised by UDA Architects to create a normal pattern of streets and blocks, so people can park their car in front of their house. Front yards were enclosed with picket fences and rear yards with strong metal railings. The typically barracks-like buildings were rebuilt, with doors and windows on formerly blank end walls and with Colonial Revival doors and windows and elaborately detailed front porches, which convey the symbolic message that the authority thinks the people who live at Diggstown are just as good as the people who live in Colonial Revival suburban houses. There has been a big improvement in safety and morale in the project, and the tenants have taken over the maintenance and improvement of their newly private yards, gardens and porches. The result is strikingly like the 1940 photographs of Old Harbor Village on page 119. Diggstown is still a low-income housing project, and, a legacy of earlier segregation policies, its tenancy is all African American. However, it is now more connected to its surrounding neighborhood.

Renovating Public Housing Towers

The fashionable thing to do with high-rise public housing at present is to write it off as a failure and demolish it. Blowing up a housing tower is a crowd-pleaser; it acknowledges past mistakes; it looks like action. There may well be situations where the tower has been allowed to deteriorate to the point where it is more expensive to save it than to replace it with some other form of housing. It may also be true that families with young children should not live on the upper floors of such towers because it is too hard for parents to supervise them.

However, high-rise public housing is managed successfully in some places, notably New York City. With a different mix of tenants and more management staff, some of these towers could be rehabilitated. A few towers were saved and rehabilitated at Boston's badly deteriorated Columbia Point where a largely vacant project that was all towers has been turned into a mixed-income community of different housing types. The possibility of saving some public housing towers and integrating them into a community of townhouses and other low-rise buildings needs to be explored further. It is most likely to be possible as part of a Hope VI Project.

7.9 A derelict housing project on the edge of Washington's Capitol Hill neighborhood ....

7.10 ...became the Town Homes at Capitol Hill, a mixed low-income and market-rate neighborhood designed by Weinstein Associates. One of the earliest Hope VI projects, this development was being planned years before the Hope VI initiative began, and is in some ways its prototype.

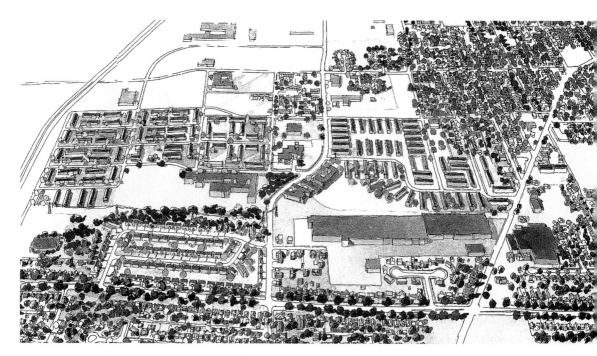

7.11, 7.12 These drawings by UDA Architects show the public housing projects in Louisville's West End and the Park DuValle Hope VI development that is replacing them.

The Hope VI Program

The U.S. Department of Housing and Urban Development's Hope VI program has a name emblematic of the cycles of high expectations followed by disillusionment that have been the history of U.S. housing programs. Nevertheless, early results look promising. The program addresses two big issues, the deterioration of public housing projects and the policies that had segregated poor people in high concentrations. It gives grants to local housing authorities to help them replace their most deteriorated projects with mixed-income communities. The program was originally intended for the 100,000 most deteriorated public housing units in the U.S., about 8 percent of the total amount of public housing. The original target of the program was to replace the deteriorated units with 40,000 subsidized and market-rate houses. Public housing tenants not accommodated in the new development are given Section 8 certificates which allow them to find housing outside the confines of the original project. Many of the public housing projects in the worst 8 percent were so badly deteriorated that they had been abandoned, or relatively few people still lived in them. This helped make lower densities and much lower numbers of public housing tenants feasible.

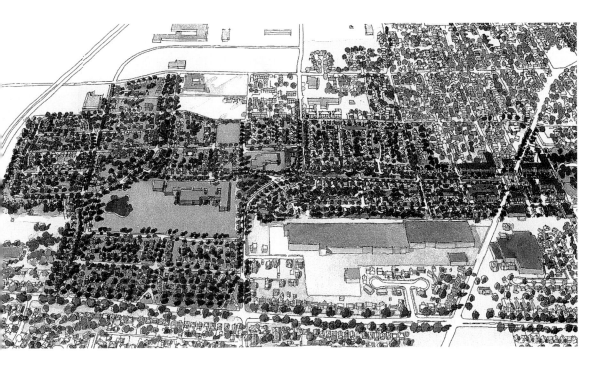

One of the earliest Hope VI grants funded Ellen Wilson Houses, a replacement for an abandoned housing project in Washington, D.C., that had already been under study before Hope VI became available. The design by Weinstein Associates opened up new streets through the project area and lined them with buildings that resembled the houses in the adjacent Capitol Hill neighborhood. (7.9, 7.10) It attracted the middle-income buyers needed to create a mix of subsidized and market-rate residents.

Realizing that many public authorities had little experience in creating housing that would appeal to middle-income tenants, the Department of Housing and Urban Development enlisted the help of the Congress for the New Urbanism, many of whose members had been instrumental in the neighborhood design revival described in the previous chapter. The C.N.U. worked with HUD to provide training sessions for housing officials, and create handbooks and other instructional materials on neighborhood planning and design. Sometimes C.N.U members were retained to plan Hope VI projects. The best projects reverse the previous superblock policy and reintroduce normal streets and block sizes. This strategy helps create places that are desirable neighborhoods in themselves and reconnect what had been isolated

7.13 One of the streets of houses in Park DuValle.

projects into the surrounding community, as in the redevelopment of the Park DuValle project in Louisville to a plan by UDA Architects, with houses designed by Stull and Lee and William Rawn. (7.11, 7.12, 7.13)

Two strategies have emerged for introducing parking into these inner-city neighborhoods when garages are too expensive and parking lots are hard to police. One is to use on-street spaces in front of each unit, as in this design by Goody, Clancy Associates for the renovation of Longwood, a privately owned rental property in Cleveland. (7.14) The other is to provide parking in the courtyards, as in Flag House Courts, designed by Torti Gallas and Partners, a Hope VI funded renovation of a public housing project in downtown Baltimore. (7.15)

The early success of the Hope VI program has encouraged replacing public housing projects that are not so badly deteriorated. Should all housing projects be replaced by with mixed-income neighborhoods? In principle this would be the right policy; in practice the latest generation of Hope VI applications reveals some serious problems that will have to be overcome to make such a policy workable.

The rule of thumb for a Hope VI community has been two-thirds market-

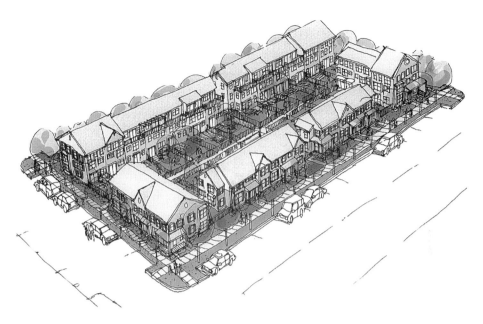

7.14 *This sketch by Goody, Clancy Associates of the housing planned for the redevelopment of the Longwood apartments in Cleveland shows that, with the right block size, on-street parking can provide a ratio of better than one car-space per unit, while letting residents park within sight of their townhouses.*

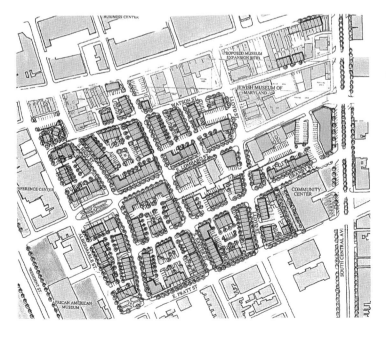

7.15 *Torti Gallas and Partners plan for Flag House Courts Hope VI project in Baltimore puts the parking behind the houses, inside the block.*

rate housing, one-third public housing. Most Hope VI projects have been built at the equivalent of high suburban densities, 10 to 15 families per acre, using single-family houses on small lots and attached houses. What happens when applications come in for rebuilding urban public housing projects that are still fully occupied and where the densities, even in low-rise buildings, may be twice as high as most Hope VI projects so far? If the city promises housing tenants they can come back to the rebuilt neighborhood, and most of the tenants elect this option, population densities could go to 60 or more families per acre, to allow the ratio of two market-rate units for every subsidized unit.

One way to hold densities down is to expand the project area, condemning the additional land if necessary. The problems with this policy became familiar in the days when cities made heavy use of urban renewal. It can take a long time to assemble contiguous properties, and may require relocating existing tenants and businesses.

A second alternative is to accept higher densities. In some places this will mean elevator buildings—which are what created the problems in many of the housing projects in the first place. Columbia Point in Boston illustrates that it is possible to have elevator buildings in mixed-income communities, but design and management have to be done right for such a neighborhood to succeed.

The third alternative, is to keep densities the same, and send a high proportion of the public housing tenants out into the real-estate market with Section 8 certificates. In the Section 8 program, government subsidies make up the difference between what the tenant can afford to pay and the actual rent. The availability of these certificates is limited, and there would have to be enough to meet the relocation needs of the Hope VI project. Not every landlord will accept a Section 8 certificate, and rents for available apartments or houses often don't meet the guidelines of the program.

In theory, dispersing public housing tenants throughout the region meets many of the equity issues raised in Chapter 4. In practice, it is a daunting task for people who may well have been born in a housing project, whose whole social network is there, and who may not own a car. They have to go out into communities they don't know in search of an apartment eligible for Section 8. These tenants will need help in making such a major change, and housing bureaucracies are not good at this kind of individual assistance.

If the Hope VI program expands into conversion of relatively sound housing projects in good real-estate locations, some people can have their lives drastically altered in the process.

Scattered-Site Public Housing

Mayor Joseph Riley of Charleston, South Carolina, came to the conclusion in

7.16, 7.17 Infill public housing in Charleston, South Carolina. The building on the left, above, is public housing, as are the units below.

the early 1980s that public housing projects were a bad way to house people. He decided to put as much public money as possible into repairing individual houses in Charleston neighborhoods and into building houses, or clusters of houses, on vacant lots. Public housing tenants would then move into these individual properties. Riley had observed that one deteriorated house on a block, particularly a corner house, could set off disinvestment and decay all the way down the street. Using public housing money to mend the rips and tears in Charleston's close-in, older neighborhoods not only helped integrate public housing tenants into the larger community but encouraged private repair and infill investments. Riley persuaded the city council to expand Charleston's Old and Historic District, which originally included the business center and the homes of wealthy people south of downtown, to include old and deteriorated, but historic, neighborhoods north of the center. The infill public housing has met the standards of the historic district. (7.16) Charleston has been able to vacate some deteriorated barracks-style housing projects, while creating 113 units in individual homes or small apartment buildings, in 14 locations with real street addresses, just like everybody else. So far this program accounts for a little more than 7 percent of Charleston's public housing units. (7.17)

Charleston is unusual in having so much historic architecture, and it helps a scattered-site public housing policy that the city is not too big. Philadelphia's scattered site public housing has created administrative problems that the city has found hard to solve. Charleston's public housing has still attracted a lot of attention as a prototype.

Eventually most public-housing should be replaced with mixed-income neighborhoods and lower-income people will disperse into homes which are not easily distinguished from the rest of the population. But it is going to be a long, difficult process.

Rebuilding the Vanished Neighborhood

There are places in some cities where decades of disinvestment, fires, and demolition have removed almost all the buildings, leaving the streets and sidewalks, some valuable utilities, some trees, and virtually nothing else. These vacant areas, often in excellent central locations, ought to be opportunities for new real-estate investment, but there are problems. First of all, just because the land is vacant doesn't mean it is easy to buy. Titles are often clouded and the ownership of each lot is different, and requires a separate transaction. Turning the land into building sites also can be a problem. Demolished houses were often simply bulldozed into the basement, so site preparation work is complicated and filled with the potential for unpleasant surprises like fuel oil tanks. The utilities in the area may have deteriorated

7.18 *New housing gradually replacing cleared land in the Central neighborhood in Cleveland. Downtown is in the background.*

from lack of maintenance. Few private companies have the finances and administrative staff to take these complex problems on; the local government is needed as an intermediary to condemn the land and clear the titles, do some of the clean-up and put the properties together into parcels that will be large enough to appeal to developers. Cleveland has been inducing some new development this way in the inner-city Central and Hough districts, including some big, single-family houses. (7.18) Detroit is also beginning to capitalize on its vast resources of vacant property. It will take time for a city to get its money back, but these neighborhood can become valuable real-estate. Thirty or 40 years ago, such large tracts of vacant land would have been pulled together into superblocks, but cities have learned from the neighborhood revival to leave the streets and blocks in place, or, if missing, to put them back.

CHAPTER

8

Restoring and Enhancing Neighborhoods

This is a short chapter about two big topics:

1. What is the best way to maintain the many aging and distressed neighborhoods in cities and older suburbs?

2. Is it possible to extend the benefits of neighborhood design to housing subdivisions and apartment complexes that were developed after World War II and are unfriendly to neighborhood formation?

Much energy is going into designing new neighborhoods and in reinventing neighborhoods and housing projects that have deteriorated beyond repair. As we will see in Chapter 11, downtowns are turning into new kinds of neighborhoods. Except in historic districts, much less attention has been given to the vast amount of residential real estate that is not downtown, is not historic, and is not really new either. So far, there are not a lot of good examples of what should be done for these places.

The Decline of the Neighborhood Concept
Before World War II most Americans thought of themselves as living in a neighborhood, although by 1929 Clarence Perry was already writing about an absence of good neighborhood qualities in suburban development. People can make a neighborhood out of many different configurations of streets, houses, and apartments, but neighborhood identity was almost inevitable in older cities and towns where houses were close together; shops, schools, and religious buildings were within walking distance or a short ride on public transportation. Small businesses were individually owned, so that people got to know the shopkeepers, who also knew a lot about them. Compared to today, people were much less mobile; only a small percentage owned cars,

and most car-owning families owned only one. People were less mobile in another sense, being more likely to live for a longer time in one place. Neighborhood associations were proportionally more important.

By the 1960s when Jane Jacobs wrote about street life in Greenwich Village and Herbert Gans described urban villagers in Boston, such close-knit neighborhoods had become unusual. In *Middletown*, the sociological study of Muncie, Indiana, done in the mid-1920s and published in 1929, Robert and Helen Lynd document that neighborhood traditions had eroded, particularly among the wealthier residents that the Lynds called the "business class." One woman of this class is quoted as saying, "My friends and I don't go back and forth to each other's houses much except for definite social engagements." Another says, "I like this new way of living in a neighborhood where you can be friendly with people but not intimate and dependent." As their title suggests, Muncie, which the Lynds did not name in their study, could be considered a representative U.S. city. The Lynds used newspaper reports from the 1890s as a comparison for their survey, and cited a number of statements that people were less prone to drop in on neighbors unannounced because of the telephone. Clubs, associations, and church groups were also a more important part of social life in the 1920s than they had been in the 1890s. In a follow-up study, *Middletown in Transition*, published in 1937, the Lynds found more separation of social classes than they had seen a decade before, because the city was larger and because of an exclusive real-estate development by the city's most influential family. This new country club district was drawing the business class out of their elegant but stuffy old houses near downtown into a more spacious, suburban way of life.

Thus, even before World War II, a transition away from traditional neighborhoods had begun; and it accelerated rapidly with post-war construction: FHA and VHA mortgages, the interstate system, the whole process of rapid suburbanization. New development consisted mostly of subdivisions of singe-family houses on large lots priced to attract people living in cramped, dark urban apartments, or small, equally dark, urban houses. The big advantages for individual family living took precedence; people were willing to ignore such inconveniences as having to drive to shops and drive children to school. The social fragmentation caused by tract developments, with hundreds of houses and lots, all the same size and not an apartment in sight, did not become an evident problem until later.

Meanwhile, back in the older city, neighborhoods that were losing their inhabitants to the suburbs were being taken over by people moving up from less desirable areas. City officials were enthusiastically knocking down the worst neighborhoods: helping them to empty out through relocation programs, clearing out the old houses, and reorganizing the street system into superblocks for housing projects. In some cities whole areas became derelict as the urban population grew smaller, and people with any kind of choice moved away. Of course, many other well-established city and suburban neighborhoods continue much as they always have been, but, instead of being the only way of living, they became one alternative.

Families in large-lot subdivisions know people in nearby houses, but much of their day involves closely timed engagements that require travel by car. Many people like this way of life, but others miss the kind of neighborhood they remember from childhood, or from visits to their grandparents.

The Historic District Revival

In once exclusive neighborhoods of old cities, Victorian and Edwardian houses became relatively inexpensive. Some of the old houses were broken up into apartments or offices, others were torn down for parking, or replaced with new offices and apartments. And some of these houses attracted the attention of young, well-educated people who could see the original elegance under layers of badly applied paint, sagging roofs, and a thicket of improvised partitions. These buyers found suburban life boring. They liked the idea of a neighborhood. Air-conditioning tamed the heat that had driven the original inhabitants to their country houses during the summer. The semi-derelict old houses promised an elegant lifestyle in return for a few years of really hard work.

As more of these houses were purchased and restored, the new owners became concerned with what was happening in the rest of the neighborhood. They wanted the remaining houses to be lived in and fixed up by buyers like themselves, not left to deteriorate or be torn down to make way for apartments or medical office buildings. The mechanism that came to hand is the historic district. More information about historic district legislation is given in Chapter 13. In essence, enacting such a district makes it difficult to tear down existing buildings. It sets standards for renovation which discourage cheap, expedient repairs in favor of restoration to something as close to the original appearance as possible. It can require that new, infill buildings be in keeping with the historic character of the district.

Attracted originally by individual houses, these owners found that they needed to engage in political action with their neighbors to create and maintain an appropriate setting. Historic preservation became more than a concern of a few historians and a small group of enthusiasts; it turned into a powerful political movement. It also helped create other neighborhood activities, and the concentration of relatively affluent families in historic neighborhoods attracted restaurants and other amenities.

The achievements in neighborhood restoration have been remarkable.

8.1 The historic Garden District in New Orleans.

Almost every community now has at least one well-maintained historic district lived in by people who are enthusiasts for the architecture and vigilant about what is happening to their neighborhood. (8.1)

The Gentrification Issue

The restoration of a historic district is a boost for local tax revenues, and good news for most property owners. But what about the tenants in the houses which have been broken up into apartments, and what about people who own houses in the neighborhood and can't afford to do the kind of restoration district rules require? The British coined a wry description of this problem: gentrification, a term now widely used. Although the income tax credits for restoring owner-occupied houses are no longer available, real-estate tax abatement programs for historic districts can help owners struggling to keep up with restoration requirements. The root of the problem for tenants is the shortage of affordable housing; if there were plenty of acceptable alternatives for displaced families, moving would seldom be an issue. Sometimes not-for-profit groups are able to organize affordable housing within the same neighborhood, including several examples in the Mission district in San Francisco, a traditionally Latino neighborhood that has recently attracted many information technology professionals with a lot of disposable income.

Neighborhood Self-Help

Many inner-city neighborhoods are scarred by failed or incomplete government intervention that leaves vacant lots, or a single isolated tower of apartments for the elderly. The private market has given up on the area, stores are closed and buildings show the deterioration that comes from years of little or no maintenance. The owners can not afford to repair their properties, or are disinclined to do so. While deteriorated buildings are usually in violation of the building code, code enforcement efforts by a local government are double edged. They can cause the owner to abandon the building, leaving the government with the obligations of ownership. If the building still has tenants, the local government becomes responsible for repairing the furnace when it breaks down on a weekend night in the middle of winter.

Not-for-profit corporations have stepped in where city officials and the real-estate market have been afraid to go. Sometimes these nonprofits are created by tenants banding togther to save the building where they live. Often they are operated by faith-based charities or are created by a consortium of business leaders. Habitat For Humanity has been an especially effective means of intervening in neighborhoods, using volunteers and donations to make the housing affordable, and involving the future residents in constructing their homes—a great psychological mechanism for encouraging commitment to house and neighborhood.

Often local religious organizations are the most stable and best-financed institutions in the neighborhood and are able to create a series of co-ordinated programs that go beyond housing to education, job-training, and even economic development. Bringing back a grocery store to one of these neighborhoods can be a major step toward returning the area to stability.

These neighborhoods usually deteriorated because of a blighting influence: railway and highway viaducts, derelict factories, areas that flood or have unstable subsoils. What local government can and should do is obtain money to repair these problems, using money from federal programs as well as local funds to install sound barriers and landscaping for viaducts, clean up brownfields, and restore parks and landscapes. These efforts can provide a supportive context for the work of local self-help organizations.

Local governments can also provide a plan that coordinates individual

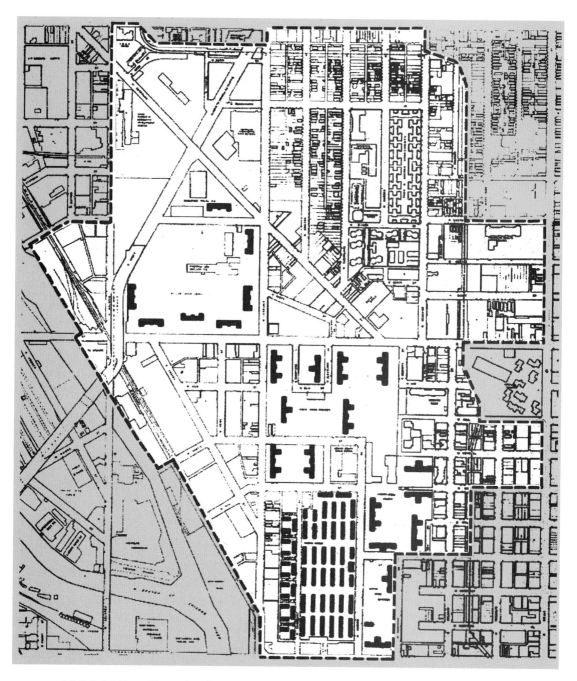

8.2 Cabrini Green Houses in Chicago and their surrounding neighborhood.

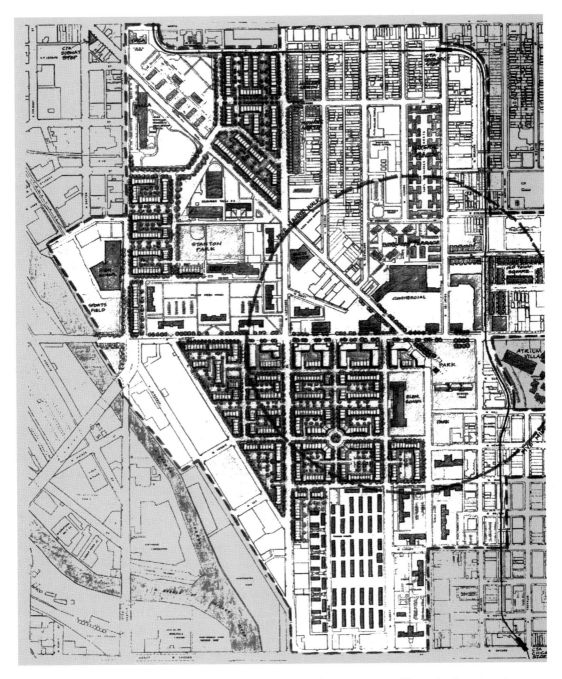

8.3 Plan by Goody, Clancy and Associates to replace housing towers with a mix of apartments and town houses, plus infill townhouses in the surrounding neighborhood.

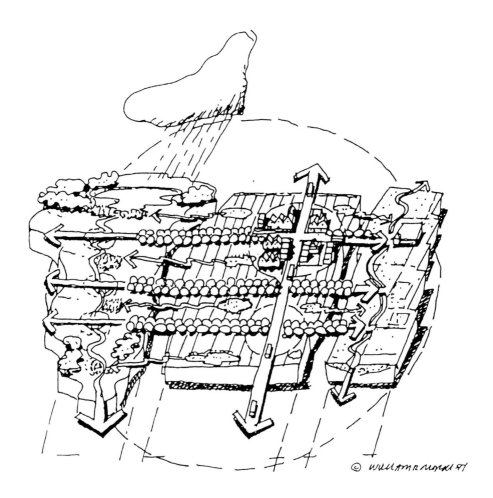

8.4 Diagram by William Morrish illustrating that reclaiming natural systems can provide inner-ring suburbs with an improved setting, comparable to greenfield development on the metropolitan fringe.

projects. This neighborhood plan by Goody, Clancy Associates was developed for the city of Chicago to pull together several different proposed developments including the Hope VI project that replaces the notoriously deteriorated and crime-ridden Cabrini-Green housing. (8.2, 8.3)

Problems for Neighborhoods in First-Ring Suburbs

Most houses built during the first wave of suburban expansion after World War II are smaller and much less luxurious than then houses the market builds today. These post-war houses are often built directly on a concrete slab, without basements; they have a carport or garage for one car; the front

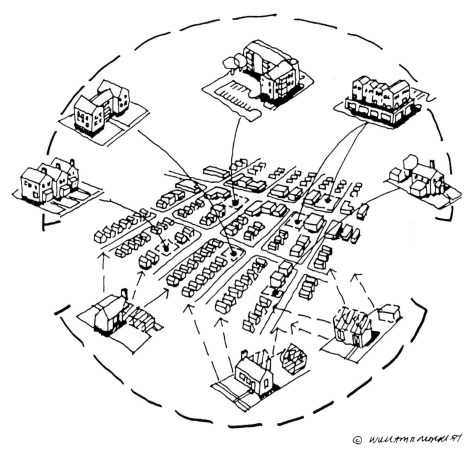

© WILLIAM R MORRISH 91

8.5 Diagram by William Morrish suggesting that vacant sites found in older suburbs can be redeveloped to increase the variety of housing available.

door opens directly into the living room; the dining room is an alcove, the kitchen is small; there are two or three small bedrooms and maybe only one bathroom. They are a big step up from a four or five room urban apartment, or from a four or five room rowhouse, but they are half the size of today's average builder's house.

In some neighborhoods the original house became a canvas for each owner's creativity. Roofs were raised to add bedrooms, garages were enclosed to make a family room, wings were added on. In preferred real-estate locations an original post-war house is a candidate for a teardown; in effect the lot is worth more than the house. But in some modest post-war suburbs street after street of houses remain much as they were when they were first built, except that the appliances are worn out and the houses need

8.6 Aerial photo of Suisun City, northeast of San Francisco, with a deteriorating waterfront where industry was no longer viable.

8.7 Aerial perspective of the plan by the ROMA Design Group for Suisun City giving it a central park, a new retail district, and a neighborhood of houses along the water.

8.8 Suisun's new central park.

8.9 A new residential street in Suisun City.

8.10, 8.11 Drawings by Duany/Plater-Zyberk for a planning study of northern Hillsborough County, Florida, showing how to add a neighborhood center to the edge of areas developed as conventional subdivisions.

a lot of repairs. These house are still move-up housing for people coming from smaller urban apartments and houses, but these suburban neighborhoods are now at risk of the kind of deterioration that has afflicted older inner-city neighborhoods.

The diagrams on pages 144 and 145 by William Morrish describe some of the policies that can be used to transform first-ring suburbs, including using infill projects to enlarge the variety of housing types and enhancing natural systems to provide a more attractive living environment. (8.4, 8.5)

Suisun City an old industrial town in Solano County, northeast of San Francisco, shows what can happen when the natural environment is reclaimed. The industry along the riverfront was almost derelict. Rebuilding the waterfront as a central park with new residential and commercial districts, according to a plan by the ROMA Design Group, has completely transformed the community. (8.6, 8.7, 8.8, 8.9)

Turning Housing Tracts into Neighborhoods
Are there ways to make large-lot subdivisions more like traditional neighborhoods? At present, this is not an urgent question. Many people who live in these places are perfectly satisfied with them just the way they are. However, there are opportunities to make such places more walkable when it is time to repave the streets. One step would be to put in sidewalks, which are often

missing from these subdivisions. Room for the sidewalks could be found by reducing the often excessive widths of the paved portions of the street. At the same time the radius of curves at street corners could be reduced to fit with the now narrower streets, and make it easier for pedestrians to cross at corners. Driveways could be reduced to one lane where they cross the sidewalk. Perhaps a site could be found for a convenience store, possibly combined with a service station at the edge of the neighborhood, as shown in these drawings made for a planning study in Hillsborough County, Florida, by Duany/Plater-Zyberk. (8.10, 8.11) As neighborhood elementary schools start being built again, one might be built at the edge of the neighborhood. It would be controversial, but perhaps the zoning could be changed to permit accessory apartments over garages. This change would permit young people who can't yet afford a house to rent in the community where they grew up. It could also provide a way for local school teachers or other government employees to live in the area.

Preserving Successful Neighborhoods

Mayor John Norquist of Milwaukee would come back to his office from meetings of the Congress of the New Urbanism complaining that the city's zoning code did not permit him to implement the innovative policies he was hearing about at the congress. Many of Milwaukee's residential neighborhoods had been established before zoning, and contained precisely the mix of lot sizes and building types that are now considered an asset. The problem was that Milwaukee's zoning laws no longer permitted the corner stores, and the mix of houses, even in established neighborhoods. So the old store buildings were empty and new houses being built in the neighborhoods did not fit in. The mayor had the zoning changed.

Once considered outmoded, the traditional neighborhood is back in favor. We may not live in it the way people did generations ago, but it provides an antidote to the rootlessness and constant mobility of modern life.

9

Redesigning Commercial Corridors

The local highway lined on both sides with franchise restaurants, strip shopping centers, car dealerships, and all sorts of other commercial development can be found so often in the United States that most people assume it has been created by market forces. But the commercial strip is actually a zoning concept, derived from an outmoded model adopted long ago by most local governments.

In small towns shopping had always been organized along a main street, and up through the 1920s—when zoning districts first began to be mapped—streetcars helped create continuous commercial frontages along important traffic arteries in big cities. After World War II, when cities and suburbs began expanding, the kinds of zoning districts originally devised for main streets and streetcar streets were mapped along suburban and rural highways. At first, this pattern had advantages, creating sites with plenty of parking for businesses that had been constricted by downtown locations. Strip zoning helped empty out traditional downtowns, especially in small communities, where much commercial activity migrated out to the "bypass."

Today, in most places, the only available retail locations, and most office and hotel sites, are along commercial strips or in traditional downtowns. The market has had little choice.

Why Commercial Strip Zoning Is Dysfunctional

Today real-estate investors and planners, especially transportation planners, are coming to believe that the strip-zoning pattern has been a mistake, because it creates two incompatible functions. The highway's original purpose is to connect one place with another; in many suburban areas, such connections are scarce and badly needed. At the same time, the highway is being used for access to individual stores and other businesses. The more people make left turns into businesses along the strip, the more congested the traffic becomes. At the same time, even short trips between different destinations along the strip usually have to take place on the highway. Eventually the highway ceases to function well as a traffic route while access to each business becomes more and more difficult. Much of the worst suburban gridlock takes place along commercially zoned arterials.

Highway departments are under pressure to do something about traffic congestion. The option most easily available is to widen a highway, but widening can deprive highway-oriented businesses of the synergy that comes from participating in the same commercial location. This problem is generally thought to begin when there are more than three lanes in each direction. Highway improvements also can create other problems for local businesses. Transportation engineers want medians that restrict left turns, and recommend that right turns between intersections be as few as possible. Such changes can reduce access to an individual property to only half the passing traffic, or less, if the only access is from a service road.

Meanwhile the retail market suddenly has all kinds of new options. Catalog and Internet shopping have become significant alternatives to traditional trips to retail stores, and no one is sure how far these trends are going. Established retailers, in addition to starting their own Internet sites, are starting to pay much more attention to making shopping a pleasant and interesting experience for people who actually go out to a store. There has been a revival of traditional streetfront retail in downtowns, where it is possible to walk along a sidewalk from store to store, and where offices, apartments and other destinations make for a more lively environment. There has also been a trend towards creating a downtown experience in "park-once" shopping developments, which are laid out along internal streets. Such settings can provide the optional activities referred to by Jan Gehl in the discussion of community in Chapter 1. The use of the term "Town Center" for a shopping development, whether it resembles a town center or not, is an indicator of this new direction in the retail market. Another evident trend is towards bigger and bigger retail malls, which include entertainment and restaurants, and can create an experience comparable to going to a downtown.

Much of the existing development along commercial strips can't compete with the new malls, "town centers," and revived downtown retail districts. Strip commercial zoning districts are narrow, sometimes as shallow as 100 feet back from the highway, seldom more than a few hundred feet deep. Most communities have ample amounts of commercial land zoned in strips along highways, which has encouraged development to spread out into many small, inefficient buildings. But there is seldom much commercially zoned land at any one place. What there is has been divided among multiple owners. There is little opportunity to create the kinds of street-front retail and mixed-use centers that the market now seems to prefer. Instead, many strip-commercial highways are showing signs of the deterioration that long-ago happened in older downtowns: empty stores, sometimes whole empty malls, marginal tenants. At the same time, a few, old-style commercial strips are redeveloping into almost urban commercial corridors, with multi-story office buildings, malls, hotels, and entertainment retail destinations. Here the problems are those of too much success: heavy traffic congestion, not enough parking, difficulties with access and with getting from one destination to another.

OK, What Do We Do Now?

It was an easy political decision to map commercial frontages along busy streets and highways. It seemed to be a standard zoning practice. It meant a potential increase in property values for owners. Commercial zoning for miles of frontages meant no landowner was left out. It took a generation or more for the full effect of these decisions to become visible, so there was little opposition at the time, except in higher-income residential districts where property owners, not interested in selling-out and moving, objected to traffic generation and the intrusion of outsiders. Where local highways do not have commercial frontages, it is often because they run through a high-income neighborhood.

The commercial strip has been created by land-use regulation, and new types of regulation will be needed to correct it. But this time around the decisions may well generate controversy and will be more difficult to make. Property owners with commercial zoning continue to expect future profits, even if these expectations are not realistic. Reducing zoning potential can be a political problem, and may, perhaps, be a legal problem as well. So, if commercial-strip zoning was a mistake, what can local communities do about it?

Three Important Questions

Commercial-strip zoning can cover many different situations. In considering remedial action, there are three important questions to ask: What is the market potential for the commercial strip in the future, what are the traffic demands in the highway corridor, and what stage of development has been reached along the strip?

1. Relating Zoning to Market Potential
What is a reasonable estimate of commercial development along a highway

corridor in the next 10 to 25 years and how does that estimate compare with the amount of land already zoned, or potentially zoned for commercial uses? The trading area helps describe the market; usually highways in affluent areas will have more potential for higher intensity development than strips in poorer neighborhoods. The community should use professional real-estate market studies to help it predict the likely amount of development in the next generation and relate it to the development potential of land already zoned. Many communities are grossly overzoned for commercial uses along highways. Overzoning not only creates scattered low-density development, but also causes owners to let existing land and buildings run down, waiting for a real-estate payoff that may well never happen. Other uses, such as multifamily housing, may be more valuable to property owners than some kinds of commercial uses, particularly where future commercial development potential is low, with the apartments oriented to adjacent neighborhoods rather than to the highway.

2. Relating Zoning to Traffic Patterns and Highway Design

Zoning provides a mechanism for sorting out commercial uses based on traffic generation. Shops, restaurants, and professional offices—the uses that generate the most traffic—can be grouped in one commercial designation, and less intensive service commercial uses in another. Development that generates the most traffic can then be zoned only in the locations most suitable for it.

Traffic has to stop at important cross streets anyway, and they are also where significant amounts of traffic enter and leave the highway corridor, so the most intensive commercial development should usually occur near an important cross street. In many parts of the U.S., major cross streets are spaced a mile apart because of the original surveyor's grid when the area was first settled.

In between the commercial districts located at the cross streets, access along the highway can be much more severely limited, in accordance with requirements for maintaining traffic speeds. These areas can still be zoned for businesses that can operate from a service road and don't need immediate highway access.

The design of the highway itself should vary with the zoning. In high intensity commercial areas mapped near major intersections, the highway can become more like a street in a town, with buildings close to the street, turn lanes, sidewalks, curbs, and artificial drainage. In between, the highway can be in a landscaped corridor using natural drainage swayles, with center medians to reduce or eliminate left turns and with right turns limited to entrances for service roads, as the uses zoned for this part of the corridor should not need direct visibility and immediate access from the highway.

3. *Relating Zoning and Street Designs to Development Intensity*

Finally what stage has development reached along the strip: a few commercial properties here and there, fully developed at low density, developed at low density and deteriorating, or redeveloping at almost urban densities? The general land-use strategy should remain the same in each case: concentrate commercial development that generates a lot of traffic at important cross streets, promote lower density development and other land uses in between—but each set of circumstances requires different means of implementation to correct past mistakes in regulating commercial corridors. It may be that more commercially zoned land should be mapped at highly accessible locations near important intersections. High intensity commercial corridors have the potential to be supported by mass transit: first by buses, and later, if usage warrants, by light rail or even heavy rail—if the development is concentrated in places along the corridor at densities that support rapid transit.

One Strategy, Many Variables

Considering the relationships among the real-estate market, highway and transit planning, and development regulation leads to the strategy of concentrating the commercial development that generates the most traffic at important intersections along a highway corridor, with the amount of land set aside for these uses based on a realistic estimate of market forces. In between areas of commercial concentration, the highway function of the corridor should dominate over access to fronting land uses. Service roads or parallel roads should be used for access in these areas; and the zoning should call for land uses that do not require immediate access from a highway. Applying this strategy requires different actions in different sets of circumstances.

1. *Expectations for commercial development, but not supported by zoning or official plans*

Most properties fronting along Highway 111 in Indian Wells, California, had remained undeveloped in expectation of commercial projects in the future, but Interstate 10 had taken much of the traffic off the highway, and the market for such development did not appear to be present. In the mid-1980s Indian Wells adopted a specific plan by Johnson, Fain and Partners that zoned these frontages for resort or multifamily, with a substantial required landscaped setback. Commercial frontages were confined to either end of the corridor, next to commercial development in neighboring communities. The city has successfully defended 11 separate lawsuits and the plan is now substantially implemented. (9.1)

9.1 Highway 111 in Indian Wells, California, runs along a landscaped corridor, created by deep setbacks for the fronting properties.

9.2 This diagram by Landers, Atkins indicates that development should take place at major intersections where there will be a grid of local streets, with landscaped service roads in between.

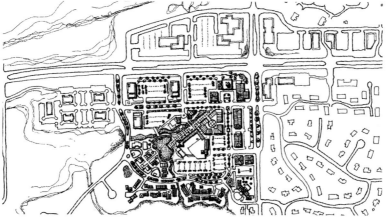

9.3 Where possible, most of the development should take place in one quadrant of an intersection, as shown in this plan by the Cunningham Group for Capitol Drive in Brookfield, Wisconsin.

2. Commercial corridor policy in place, but only a few developments

Metropolitan regions are expanding so rapidly that there are still highway corridors in outlying areas where commercial development is officially expected, but has not yet taken place. There may be strips along the corridor that are already zoned commercial, and a policy map may exist that shows strip commercial development in areas not yet zoned for it.

In this situation, where most of the development is potential, local government has the most flexibility to locate zones of intense commercial development, the size and number to be determined based as much as possible on real-estate market studies, and the locations on points of greatest access

Other locations along the corridor can continue to have commercial zoning or light-industrial zoning, but in districts that do not contain uses that are high traffic generators. Multifamily housing may be an appropriate alternative to the commercial zoning. This plan for the Pine Island corridor in Cape Coral, Florida, by Landers, Atkins is a proposal for organizing development in such a situation. (9.2)

In Brookfield, Wisconsin, a suburb of Milwaukee, the city has anticipated commercial development along Capitol Drive, and has adopted a policy of placing development only at major intersections. The design illustrated by the Cunningham Group shows development at one such intersection, concentrated primarily in one quadrant. (9.3)

Wildwood, the community in St. Louis County described in the prologue to this book, is clearly in the path of commercial corridor development. Old Manchester Road running west from St. Louis through next-door Ellisville is already a complete commercial strip. Wildwood, instead of enacting strip-commercial zoning, has adopted a master plan that makes an area along the Old Manchester Road in the center of the community a mixed-use Town Center for stores, offices and a higher density of residential development than is permitted elsewhere in the community. The street plan is laid out to create a park-once district that will also ultimately be dense enough to support rapid transit (see pages 4-5). Again the development is concentrated in one area, not grouped equally around the four sides of an intersection.

3. Zoned, partially developed

Many arterial streets are zoned for commercial development, but development has only taken place at some locations, while others are still in rural or residential uses. Again, an evaluation should be made of the market potential for the whole corridor. The best outcome would be like those discussed above, where development is concentrated in the most accessible locations, and the areas in between have lower intensity commercial development, or are zoned for another use like multifamily housing. The difficulty is changing

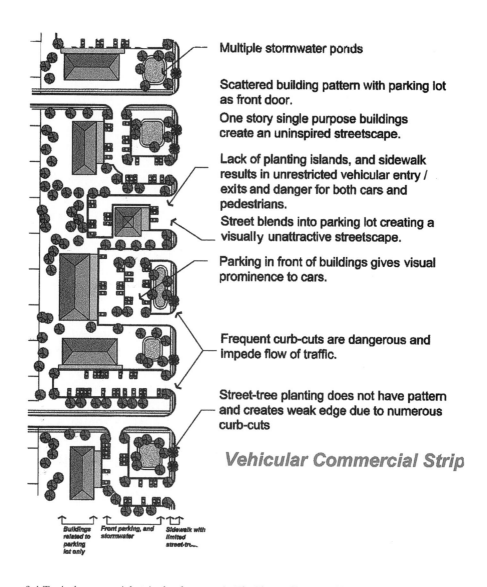

Multiple stormwater ponds

Scattered building pattern with parking lot as front door.

One story single purpose buildings create an uninspired streetscape.

Lack of planting islands, and sidewalk results in unrestricted vehicular entry / exits and danger for both cars and pedestrians.

Street blends into parking lot creating a visually unattractive streetscape.

Parking in front of buildings gives visual prominence to cars.

Frequent curb-cuts are dangerous and impede flow of traffic.

Street-tree planting does not have pattern and creates weak edge due to numerous curb-cuts

Vehicular Commercial Strip

Buildings related to parking lot only

Front parking, and stormwater

Sidewalk with limited street-tre...

9.4 *Typical commercial strip development in Florida, as diagramed by Landers, Atkins.*

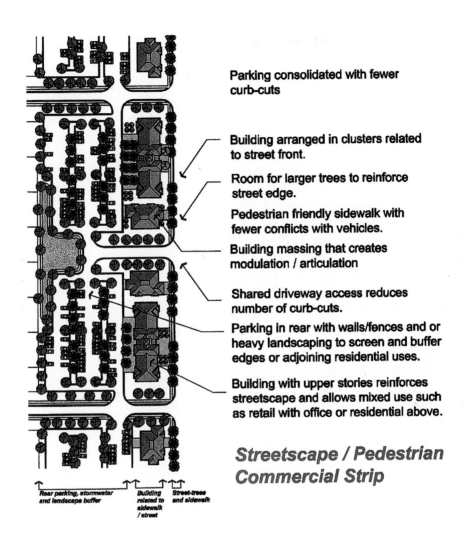

Parking consolidated with fewer curb-cuts

Building arranged in clusters related to street front.

Room for larger trees to reinforce street edge.

Pedestrian friendly sidewalk with fewer conflicts with vehicles.

Building massing that creates modulation / articulation

Shared driveway access reduces number of curb-cuts.

Parking in rear with walls/fences and or heavy landscaping to screen and buffer edges or adjoining residential uses.

Building with upper stories reinforces streetscape and allows mixed use such as retail with office or residential above.

Streetscape / Pedestrian Commercial Strip

Rear parking, stormwater and landscape buffer

Building related to sidewalk / street

Street-trees and sidewalk

9.5 *Suggested new design standards by Landers, Atkins for Mayport Road in Jacksonville and Atlantic Beach seek to overcome typical problems by incremental changes.*

the zoning map, although the community has the power to do so in accordance with a comprehensive plan.

4. Mapped, and developed, stable or deteriorating

In many places commercial corridors have been mapped in places that don't have anything like the market potential to fill all the land with successful businesses. The result is a familiar mix: some small office buildings, franchise restaurants, automobile repair, failing strip malls, old motels. Given the competition from other kinds of retailing, the future of these areas is in some kind of redevelopment. Along the Mayport Road corridor in Jacksonville and Atlantic Beach, redevelopment is anticipated as a new highway connection at the north end of the strip makes the area more accessible. The city is adopting standards, prepared by Landers, Atkins to improve individual properties as they redevelop. Standards include bringing buildings out to the street with parking behind, improved landscaping, connections between developments, coordinated parking and stormwater detention (9.4. 9.5)

These photo montages developed for the town of Hercules, California, in Contra Costa County northwest of San Francisco by Dover, Kohl and Partners illustrate how enacting such standards at selected points along a commercial strip can produce a town center. (9.6, 9.7, 9.8)

Mashpee Commons, situated near a traffic circle on Cape Cod, is a place where something like this transformation has already happened. A redevelopment of a conventional strip shopping center, Mashpee Commons is ultimately planned to be the town center for a residential development, although it will continue to draw customers from a much larger trading area. The shopping has been rebuilt as street-front retail, but much of the parking is still in perimeter lots. (9.9, 9.10, page 162) A related example is the town center for the Kentlands/Lakelands development in Gaithersburg, Maryland. Located on a main road where it can draw customers from a larger trading area, the retail streets are well integrated into the surrounding residential development. (9.11, page 163) Both plans are by Duany/Plater-Zyberk.

5. Mapped, developed, maybe too successful

In Brookfield, Wisconsin, Blue Mound Road is lined with development that is approaching downtown intensity, with a regional mall, smaller malls, substantial office parks, and hotels all within about a mile of highway frontage. Brookfield is closer to the center of the metropolitan region than Milwaukee, so that this road, originally a country lane, is a main street for a substantial section of the region. The combination of intense use and heavy traffic leads to serious congestion problems and is having a negative impact on development plans.

9.6, 9.7, 9.8 Incremental redevelopment of a typical commercially zoned highway in Hercules, California, as planned by Dover, Kohl and Partners.

9.9 Mashpee Commons on Cape Cod has a shopping center location at a traffic circle and a lot of perimeter parking.

9.10 Once inside the center, it is designed to feel like a town. When the development is completed, the shopping will be attached to new residential neighborhoods. The plan is by Duany/Plater-Zyberk.

9.11 *Downtown in the Lakelands/Kentlands development in Gaithersburg, Maryland. As at Mashpee Commons, the retail is located on a main road, and there is some perimeter parking, but here the streets connect directly into residential neighborhoods. Plan by Duany/Plater-Zyberk.*

The master plan for Brookfield by the Cunningham Group suggests alleviating traffic congestion on the most intensely developed segment of Blue Mound Road by creating two parallel local streets on each side. This is a different strategy from the more commonly used service road, as the secondary road is a block away from the highway. Instead of simply widening the corridor, these parallel streets create a street grid, as in a conventional downtown, so that left turns don't need to be made from mid-block locations along the highway. Instead, traffic crosses the highway at signalized intersections, and then makes the necessary turn.

This proposal to separate through-traffic on Blue Mound from local traffic that could use the new streets was met with strong opposition by homeowners whose back yards bordered the proposed parallel street south of Blue Mound Road. They were able to organize almost their entire neighborhood to protest. The future success of commercial development on Blue Mound Road is vital to the whole community, as the taxes from this development keep residential property taxes relatively low and commercial property tax revenues from businesses along Blue Mound Road also help support one of the most successful school districts in the region. Even the opponents of the new

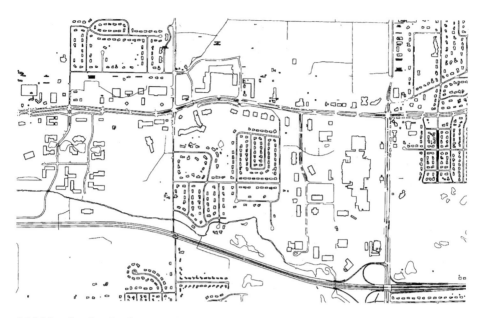

9.12 Map showing development along Blue Mound Road in Brookfield, Wisconsin.

9.13 Plan by the Cunningham Group to add two parallel streets to Blue Mound Road, creating a traffic grid as in a town, separating local and through traffic and making access easier. This proposal has provoked strong opposition from neighbors to the south, although everyone agrees the improvement is needed.

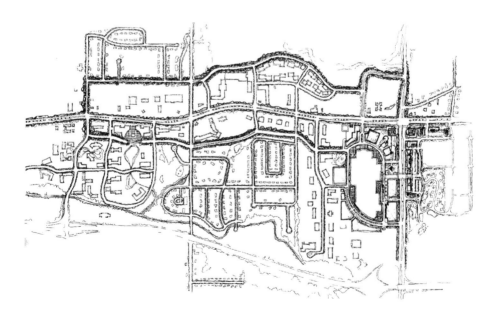

streets agree that they would make commercial development more viable and would help preserve the economic health of the commercial district in the future. The community has a tough political choice to make. (9.12, 9.13)

It is in corridors like Blue Mound Road, where some development has reached almost urban intensity, that rapid transit in the suburbs has the best chance of succeeding. Rapid transit stops also help give structure to a commercial corridor, encouraging more concentrated development near stations.

The Example of Arlington County

When the Washington Metropolitan Transit System was being planned in the 1960s, Arlington County recognized the potential for the transit system to support new development. As noted in Chapter 3, plans for one of the transit lines called for it to run through Arlington down the center of Route 66. The stations would be islands in the middle of the highway, which would mean little influence on development in the areas immediately surrounding the stations. The county was able to put together the additional financing to have the metro built in a tunnel that runs parallel to the highway about half a mile to the south, more or less along the route of Wilson Boulevard, a traditional commercial corridor. The tunnel rejoins the highway about halfway across Arlington County and the line continues in the center of Route 66 out into Fairfax County. There are five stops in Arlington County: Rosslyn, Court House, Clarendon, Virginia Square, and Ballston. This corridor was actually identified by Joel Garreau as an Edge City, but it is very different from the automobile-based development pattern in most such suburban locations. Wilson Boulevard, with the adjacent Clarendon Boulevard, forms a one-way pair and continues to be a major traffic corridor. This area has been given a completely new structure by the transit, particularly at Rosslyn and Ballston, at either end of the corridor, which have become very like traditional downtowns. (9.14)

Pentagon City and Crystal City, also in Arlington County but on a different branch of the transit system, have also developed as concentrated urban districts. The Arlington County examples show what could happen in the next generation if rapid transit systems are added to commercial corridors that already have a high intensity of development.

9.14 *Intensive urban development in a former commercial strip location, Ballston in Arlington County, Virginia. A stop on the Washington Metro makes the density possible.*

CHAPTER

10

Turning Edge Cities into Real Cities

In *Edge City, Life on the New Frontier*, published in 1991, Joel Garreau defined an edge city as a geographic area with jobs, shopping, and entertainment. To meet his definition there had to be at least five million square feet of leasable office space; 600,000 square feet of retail space or more; a significant increase in daytime population on weekdays; and—most important—a location somewhere that 30 or 40 years ago was farmland or a suburban residential neighborhood. Garreau's book helped people understand a phenomenon that had grown up while most professional planners and academic theorists were looking the other way, at the problems of older cities. Intent on urban decline, they had ignored the obverse, that rapid growth of metropolitan regions had created urban areas in many non-traditional places.

Garreau is not just an observer, however, he is a partisan. The book begins: "The controversial assumption undergirding this book is that Americans basically are pretty smart cookies who generally know what they're doing." Garreau fully deserves the recognition he has received for his original and effective research, his ability to give a vivid name and definition to urban development in the suburbs and exurbs, and his superb abilities as a story teller. But what about his "controversial assumption?" Yes, Americans are smart cookies. But Garreau fails to allow for the possibility that the collective effect of a lot of smart decisions could be a lot less than smart. Because Garreau has confidence in the efficient functioning of the marketplace, he is optimistic about overcoming the obvious defects of Edge Cities: That most can only be reached by car, which is also needed to drive within them and through them, that their buildings are isolated amid wide expanses of parking, that there are few public spaces and public amenities— in Garreau's view all these problems are just growing pains. Someday, he believes, something as wonderful as the great traditional cities will grow out of the parking lots and scattered buildings he describes.

Robert E. Lang of the Fannie Mae Foundation, writing approximately a decade after Garreau, has identified another phenomenon that he calls Edgeless Cities. Lang's research indicates that a majority of new suburban office space is not going into places that meet Garreau's definition of an edge city, but into a much more diffuse pattern of commercial corridors and isolated office parks that are spread out over hundreds of square miles and are not recognized by the public as being part of a single destination. Lang does not believe that this kind of development is likely to coalesce into any kind of city. He sees it as a defensive response to traffic congestion, and a symptom of the continuing rapid advance of sprawl.

The vitality and rapid growth of both edge cities and edgeless urbanization has impressed other observers, notably Rem Koolhaas, whose wonderstruck descriptions about highway-oriented development in his recent compendium, *S, M, L, XL* have gained the attention of many academic theorists of city planning and architectural design. Here is the future, they say, like it or not.

Garreau and Koolhaas fail to acknowledge the distortions introduced into the real-estate marketplace by governmental decisions about transportation and land development regulation.

Highways and Edge Cities

While Joel Garreau catalogues a few transit-oriented locations, like Arlington, Virginia, as edge cities, most are located at highway junctions. The U.S. Interstate Highway System is the great enabler of edge cities; highway administrators have had a blind spot about the land-use consequences of highway construction from the beginning of this program, as documented by Tom Lewis in his book, *Divided Highways*. The 1991 ISTEA legislation and accompanying amendments to the Clean Air Act sought to make the state transportation departments and the metropolitan planning organizations that approve new highways take induced real-estate development into account, at least for estimating air pollution. Knowledgeable observers, like Stephen Putman in his essay in *Planning for a New Century*, say that—except in Atlanta, where the regulators were constrained by a lawsuit over non-enforcement—the federal EPA is not implementing these provisions, because few new highways could be built if such legal requirements were taken seriously.

Federally funded highway construction has conferred huge land-development values on various pieces of private property as an unintended consequence of decisions about satisfying existing traffic demand. Smart cookies have taken advantage of these decisions, and sometimes manipulated the highway planning process, but the actual highway plans are anything but smart. Even today, the highway utilization forecast continues to be the de facto regional plan for most areas. The public, and even other governmental entities, never see this forecast, or evaluate the consequences. Usually the forecast is wrong, explaining why so many highways, designed to serve for a generation or more, reach their capacity only a few years after they open— their planners had not considered the effect of induced development.

Because edge cities were the unplanned consequences of highway policies designed to move people between previously existing destinations, edge cities grew up without the infrastructure of streets and public transportation that supports traditional urban centers.

How Conventional Zoning Shaped Edge Cities

When the interstates were first built, they ran through open country, and resembled in this respect the "townless highways" proposed by Lewis Mumford and Benton MacKaye in the1920s. MacKaye was a regionalist best known for proposing and promoting the Appalachian Trail; Lewis Mumford was famous as the Jeremiah of city planning. They advocated that regional highways should be outside the town and that people should drive to the town from the highway.

However, after intercity highways were built, there were proposals to re-zone the area around the interchanges, so it would be possible to have some gas stations and some motels and other things which would serve people on the highway. Local governments generally responded by zoning an area for commercial development around the highway interchange. As they did not want to show favoritism to any property owners, they often drew the zone roughly as a circle with the interchange in the middle.

Unfortunately, this even-handedness puts the interchange in the place that would be the center of civic consciousness and the most valuable development in a traditional downtown. Instead, the interchange is always a built-in void that splits development apart. As the quadrants around the interchange develop, they inevitably are planned as separate parcels: a hotel in one, maybe some light industry, office buildings and, in the most accessible location, a shopping mall. Shopping malls generate opposition from merchants on nearby Main Streets, but the potential increase in real-estate tax revenues usually persuades local authorities to approve them. Some of the local stores move to the shopping center and others are put out of business by the competition.

Eventually the highway interchanges became the access points for development that statistically adds up to a downtown. In big metropolitan areas these highway locations would meet Garreau's definition of an Edge City, in smaller communities, it might just be the new development "out on the bypass."

When development around interchanges is connected by local traffic or service roads, urbanization can coalesce into corridors, either forming an edge city, or the more diffuse edgeless city pattern that is becoming the norm in suburban development.

Mapping commercial zones for many miles along highways produced a surfeit of land zoned for commerce, but not enough at any one point to create a complete urban center, the same problem at a larger scale as is found with commercial strip zoning on arterial streets. For example, Hillsborough County in Florida mapped enough commercial land along Interstate 75 to produce more than 800 million square feet of commercial development, something like twice the commercial space on Manhattan Island. Developers had no incentive to use land efficiently, because so much commercially zoned land was available, and in any case there was usually no room on any given site in the commercial corridor to do a big, multi-use project.

The characteristic appearance of edge cities reflects the lack of smart governmental decision making, no matter how adept the individual developers may have been in working with these conditions. The dispersed nature of the development is a direct response to zoning. The separation of uses in most edge-city development is also a response to zoning. Often, high-density residential development is not permitted in commercial zones. The parking lots that separate individual buildings are a response to total dependence on automobile access from the highway. The highways supporting most edge cities have long ago reached their capacity at peak hours, making it difficult to expand development, or consolidate existing development into more normal urban patterns. Not only are destinations not close enough together to be served by public transit, but there is not even a complete local street system to support, say, a shuttle bus. The failure of planning that produced the lack of local streets means that the main highway has to be used for access even to close-by destinations, helping to produce the often-described edge-city gridlock, particularly at lunch hour.

Are Edge Cities and Edgeless Cities an Accidental New Discovery or Just an Accident?

Are all these problems merely growing pains? Is speaking of more normal urban patterns evidence of an outmoded outlook? Have edge cities, however accidental their origins, developed new urban patterns that can evolve into something more desirable than the traditional city center? It is exciting to contemplate such a possibility, but the research into behavior of people in urban places indicate that the traditional city centers evolved as they have for good reasons, summarized by Danish architect Jan Gehl's succinct aphorism: "Life takes place on foot." Gehl, William H. Whyte, and other like-minded researchers have demonstrated how important being able to walk from one destination to another is for the success of urban centers. The advantages of synergy among land uses, and the relative stability of investment in a 24-hour environment are also well-documented advantages of traditional urban patterns.

As highway plans, interchange locations, and zoning approvals all took place in accordance with deliberate government actions, often after extensive study and public hearings, the cure for failed policies also lies with government action. There are alternatives that could have happened if public policy took a different course. The highway could have been left to run through a corridor of natural landscape, in accordance with the theories of Mumford and MacKaye. Only one quadrant of the interchange could have been rezoned for high-intensity commercial activity. The others could have been mapped as residential zones. There is an objective criterion, which could have been used, which is that the quadrant nearest to an existing town is the one that ought to be rezoned for commerce. There would be no favoritism in doing that. The local authorities could have planned a street system within the quadrant of the interchange they selected and the same mix of uses that are normally scattered around the interchange could have easily been accommodated in that one quadrant, creating something much more like a traditional city where people could walk among the various destinations and development would be compact enough to be served by rapid transit as well as cars.

There have been some recent examples of the private market building just such a compact mixed-use development. In downtown Boca Raton, Florida, the city acquired a failed two-department-store mall and made the site available to developers. The development that replaced the mall, Mizner Park, designed by Richard Heapes, then at Cooper, Carry architects, is built around a new main street, a wide boulevard running parallel to U.S. Highway 1 (at right in the photo 10.1 on page 172). Arcaded shops line this street on both sides. There are offices over the retail on the side nearest to U.S. 1 and apartments over the stores on the quieter more residential side. All the parking is in garages, except for a few on-street spaces. The next street over, wide and landscaped, is the edge of single-family residential neighborhood. Mizner Park's garages on that side are lined with narrow townhouses, in scale with the houses across the street. The use of such "liner buildings" is an important technique for creating lively streets and for integrating new high-density development into lower density surroundings.

RTKL and Sasaki's design for The Reston Town Center, a somewhat larger

10.1 Mizner Park in downtown Boca Raton, Florida, was built on the site of a failed shopping mall to a design by architects Cooper, Carry. The wide central esplanade is lined with shops. There are offices over the shops on the right of the photo, towards U.S. 1 and I 95, with residential buildings on the quieter side adjacent to nearby single-family houses. Within its boundaries, this is a true urban development.

10.2 The Reston Town Center in the northern Virginia suburbs of Washington, D.C., is becoming a real urban place, and attracts people looking for a downtown with streets, shops and plazas. However, right now the urban experience is only one block deep on each side of the main street.

development, organizes a series of office buildings along a main street with shopping on the ground floor. There are movie theaters and a hotel, and an apartment tower at one end of the street. (10.2) Other apartments and town-houses are developing nearby, part of the trend towards living within walk-

10.3 *The Park Place townhouses designed by Pappageorge, Haymes are located within walking distance of the Reston Town Center. Someday not too far in the future these two islands of urbanity will be linked as the land in between is developed.*

ing distance of shops and entertainment described in the next chapter. (10.3)

Redesigning Highway Interchanges to Relate to Development
Highway interchanges have been designed to allow cars to make the transi-

tion from one highway to another at as high a speed as possible, while holding down construction and land costs, especially land costs. What if highway interchanges were designed to fit into future development, instead of being isolated objects that divide the development they help induce? One example of such an alternative design is the highway interchange for the town center at Daniel Island in Charleston, South Carolina. I was part of the planning team, along with Cooper, Robertson and Partners and Duany/Plater-Zyberk. The circumstances are unusual as the highway is rising from grade on to a bridge in order to cross the Wando River. The original plan was for a conventional four-way, cloverleaf interchange at the highway's low point, before it begins rising to go over the bridge. The interchange included an additional bridge to take the local road over the highway. As planners for the island we proposed an alternative. Why not let the local road go under the highway as the road was rising anyway to go over the river. In addition, why not bend the access roads so they went into the town center, and use the connection between them as the town center's main street? The state highway officials were uncomfortable with the design, because it mixed public and private property, and they were used to interchanges which were completely isolated, and thus totally under state highway department control. However this proposal was millions of dollars cheaper than a conventional interchange. Eventually, it has been built much as we proposed, so that people driving off the highway arrive immediately at the center of town. (10.4, 10.5)

   Unfortunately there are not a lot of comparable examples in other locations, and this one took advantage of special circumstances. However, every interchange situation has some special, local characteristics. Once the principle of designing interchanges and development together is accepted, there could be many possible solutions.

A Changing Market Means New Regional Growth Patterns

People used to say that the typical development constructed around highway interchanges works perfectly well and makes money for the owners, so how can it be criticized for not following a hypothetical better model? The answer is that this kind of highway-oriented development is rapidly becoming a problem because it no longer makes money for the owners. Many of the first-generation retail malls are failing: Their department stores have closed; some storefronts are empty and others aren't paying any rent. New super-regional malls have opened in these markets and the older malls can't compete with them. The first generation of highway-oriented hotels can't compete with newer and better hotels located in or near office parks that supply a steady stream of customers. Some highway hotels are being used as temporary housing for people on welfare. Highway-oriented office buildings are

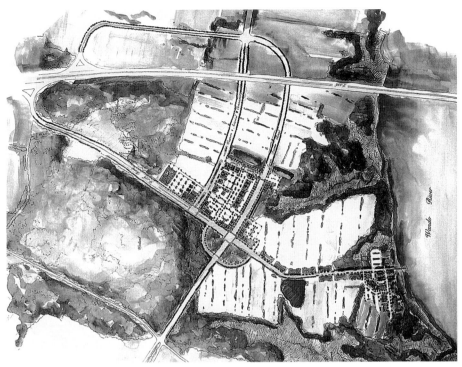

10.4 Plan by Design Works for the first phase of the Daniel Island Town Center.

10.5 Aerial photo shows the first development of the Town Center under construction; it fits into the highway interchange, instead of being separated from it.

nowhere near as attractive a working environment as offices in newer suburban office parks and so are partly vacant. Much development along the highway is not just a mess as urban design, it is a failure as real estate.

Retrofitting Edge Cities

Can failing shopping malls and isolated office parks evolve into something more like a traditional urban center?

The Legacy Town Center in the middle of a vast office park north of Dallas is one extremely interesting example. The office park had been having some trouble attracting and keeping employees because of long commuting times and a lack of any close-by housing or retail. The Town Center, designed by RTKL, provides somewhere to go at lunchtime and after work for tenants in the big corporate headquarters buildings, a place to live that could be selected by some employees, and a setting for buildings accommodating smaller office tenants. (10.6, 10.7, 10.8)

Addison Circle in Addison, Texas—a northern suburb of Dallas—has both a highway location and a future stop on the Dallas Area Rapid Transit Line. Much of the area had already developed in the typical edge-city pattern of buildings surrounded by at-grade parking, but local officials promoted making Addison a real urban center to give it a competitive advantage as the region spread farther out. The plan by RTKL provides for 3,000 apartments, street-front retail, and up to four million square feet of offices. The site is only about 80 acres, the same size as Seaside, and thus has to have real urban densities to meet the planned objectives: 55 units to the net acre. (10.9, 10.10, 10.11)

The Congress for the New Urbanism sponsored a study by PriceWaterhouseCoopers of regional shopping malls. The study concluded that 7 percent of these malls were older structures in poor competitive positions with low rents and empty stores. The study characterized these malls as Greyfields. Another 12 percent are vulnerable and could become Greyfields in the next few years. These shopping malls, as they lose their original economic rationale, can provide a key to retrofitting an edge city, because of their large parking fields and accessible locations, frequently in one quadrant of a highway interchange. They are excellent building sites that can support offices, apartments, and street-level retail.

10.6 The Legacy Town Center is being developed in the midst of a big office park north of Dallas.

10.7, 10.8 Photos of the initial development at Legacy, designed by RTKL. The architecture follows an urban pattern.

    In 1998 The Eastgate Mall in the Brainerd section of Chattanooga, Tennessee, (10.12, page 183) was only 25 percent leased. The city resolved to make the mall the centerpiece of an urban renewal area that would give Brainerd a real mixed-use urban center. Dover, Kohl and Partners prepared a plan (10.13, page 183) that showed the mall connected by a new street to a nearby office park, and the mall and its parking lot broken up into traditional city blocks. A town square location was identified, with the mall owner donating the land and the city putting up the money to landscape it. A failed department store was remodeled into a telemarketing center, with a new

10.9, 10.10 Development at Addison Circle in Addison, Texas, also designed by RTKL to look like a downtown in a substantial city.

10.11 The Plan of Addison Circle shows how this intense urban development, adjoining a future stop on the Dallas Area Rapid Transit line, fits into its edge-city context.

windowed exterior instead of the blank brick walls. The first phase of the redevelopment is now complete, and the mall properties in their new outward facing configurations are almost fully leased.

Dover, Kohl has made other studies of how malls can be transformed into compact, mixed-use centers, including an ambitious plan for Kendall, Florida, designed with Duany/Plater-Zyberk, which proposes a system of new streets, blocks, and public squares around the highly successful Dadeland Mall. Instead of the typical edge city townscape, the plan requires that developers provide colonnaded sidewalks and line the streets with "habitable spaces," liner buildings, as shown in these photomontages. (10.14, 10.15,10.16, 10.17, pages 184, 185) The design maps out a complete transformation of the area, from isolated buildings surrounded by parking to a dense urban environment. (10.18, pages 186, 187) The new zoning code that has strict requirements, but it also represents a substantial upzoning, justified by Kendall's two stations on Miami's rapid transit system. There has been significant interest from private investors. Several retail and apartment projects and a hotel have already been designed in accordance with the plan.

The Redmond Town Center in Redmond, Washington, designed by LMN Architects, occupies a site where a developer tried for 18 years to develop a conventional mall. Today there is a street and block system connected to the existing downtown, with a central retail plaza attached to a parking deck, and the rest of the site developed as offices, with streetfront retail, a hotel, and some additional retail buildings.

Parking Lots as Housing Sites

Most edge cities have a big reservoir of land devoted to at-grade parking. As land values increase, it becomes possible to decant some of this parking into garages, creating sites for new development. In many edge cities, existing zoning permits such additional development by right, as the initial structures are below zoning limits, because of the constraints of at-grade parking. However, the gridlock on surrounding highways limits the feasibility of additional commercial development. As a result, high-density residential development is beginning to be constructed in edge city locations, bringing with it a demand for streetfront retailing and other characteristics of a normal urban center. The recent development of extensive new housing in Tysons Corner in Fairfax County, Virginia, is an example of this trend, but the superblocks and high-speed arterial streets make a true urban pattern impossible.

The Galleria District in Houston, one of the nation's oldest edge cities, has recently become a tax increment reinvestment zone. A portion of the property tax is going to construct, retroactively, the streets and parking systems needed to support high-density development. The decision to take action was caused by competition from newer development on the rapidly expanding edge of the Houston metropolitan area. One feature of Uptown Houston's plans is a transitway along Post Oak Boulevard, which could connect into Houston's rapid transit system as it develops. A similar process is taking place in Buckhead, a comparable uptown location in Atlanta.

These early indications suggest that the future dynamic for edge cities is to evolve into more traditional downtowns, with a balanced mix of uses, the potential to add enough residential development to become a "24-hour city" and enough density to support rapid transit as an adjunct, at least, to automobile access. Local governments that support these incipient trends with appropriate zoning and transportation policies are likely to accelerate the process.

In areas that are still developing, the highway connections that make edge

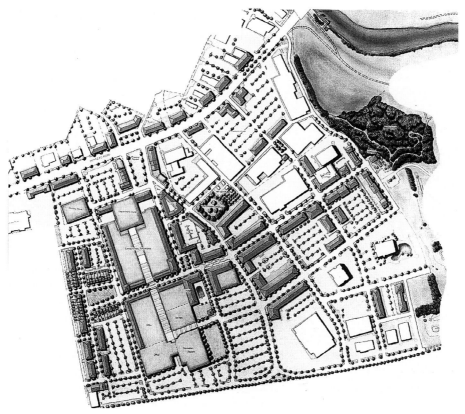

10.12 The Eastgate Mall in Chattanooga; at the time of the photo it was only about 25 percent rented.

10.13 Plan for redeveloping the Eastgate Mall site by Dover, Kohl and Partners

10.14, 10.15 *Kendall Drive in downtown Kendall, Florida, before and after implementation of the downtown plan.*

cities possible have to be recognized for what they are, and the desirability of creating new edge city locations has to be evaluated before a highway is built. There are still many new highway plans that could produce edge cities. Proposed outer beltways or ring roads to facilitate peripheral commuting multiply the potential for edge cities geometrically, as can be observed in the extraordinary dispersal of urban growth taking place in Houston. If a particular highway connection is seen as a desirable location for an edge city, specific plans for the area should be created in advance. These plans should include configurations for the interchange and other highway connections that are compatible with future development. Local zoning has to become a template for a desirable future, and not just a vague set of instructions that will be interpreted only after a development is proposed. If a highway location is not considered appropriate for an edge city, planning policies should

10.16, 10.17 *Dadeland Boulevard in downtown Kendall, again before and after the plan is implemented.*

be followed to keep it from developing in this way, by not extending the necessary water and sewer connection, as one example.

Putting more money into regional transit systems, and not just highways, would permit edge cities to become part of a transportation network, and would alleviate regional gridlock problems. At the same time, edge cities would have to become more dense and more walkable, so that they could be served effectively by transit.

Americans are basically pretty smart cookies and when they make a mistake, they can generally figure out how to fix it.

The north side of Dadeland Mall is renovated with restaurants, neighborhood serving retail, offices, and studios facing the Snapper Creek Canal.

A new canal segment adds waterfront to enhance the residential neighborhoods north of Snapper Creek.

The "island" created by the new canal is a prestigious place to l The buildings on the edge of the island surround a hidden parki garage. The roof of the garage landscaped garden.

One of several neighborhood squares.

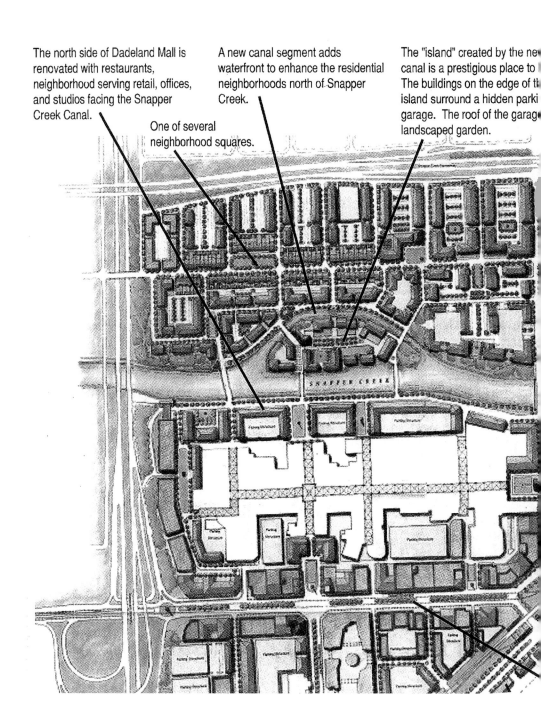

d values have increased to the
t where existing condominiums
purchased, demolished, and
veloped.

Land underneath the Snapper Creek
Expressway is utilized as
playground or other active
recreation such as basketball courts,
handball courts, etc. Certain
portions serve as overflow parking
lots.

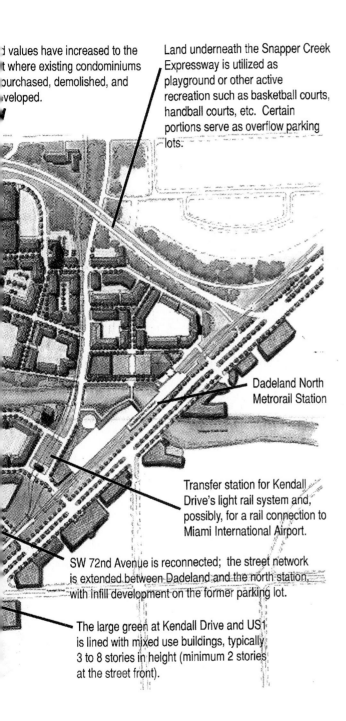

Dadeland North
Metrorail Station

Transfer station for Kendall
Drive's light rail system and,
possibly, for a rail connection to
Miami International Airport.

SW 72nd Avenue is reconnected; the street network
is extended between Dadeland and the north station,
with infill development on the former parking lot.

The large green at Kendall Drive and US1
is lined with mixed use buildings, typically
3 to 8 stories in height (minimum 2 stories
at the street front).

*10.18 The Downtown Kendall
plan is a radical restructuring of
local zoning enacted by the Dade
County Board of Commissioners.
Substantial developer interest
shows that the county's proactive
stance was the right policy.*

11

Keeping Downtowns Competitive

Christopher Leinberger, real-estate developer and market analyst, has concluded from his research that about a third of all U.S. households would like to live in a small town or a rural area, if they could have what they wished. Another third prefers conventional suburban living. The remaining third would like to live in an urban community where it would be possible to walk to shops, restaurants, and entertainment. It is this third preference that is driving the neighborhood revival in suburbia, the transformation of edge cities, and a remarkable new interest in living in traditional downtowns. The revival of downtown as a place to live is a favorable new chapter in a long saga: the perils of downtown.

City centers were once the only possible place for the most important offices and the best retailing, but today a traditional downtown is just one among many competing business locations, and even Midtown Manhattan and downtown San Francisco need to be well managed to maintain their position as important regional office and retailing centers. The threat of terrorism has now added another factor to the competitive position of big city downtowns.

A city's original location was determined by navigable waterways or railway junctions, and its continued importance in the region has much to do with the placement of local airports. Downtown Boston, a short transit ride from Logan International, retains primacy in its region, while downtown Detroit risks becoming just another edge city in a metropolitan area that centers on Southfield and Birmingham, no farther from the airport than downtown.

If the principal airport is close to the fashionable side of the metropolitan region, as in St. Louis or Los Angeles, downtown activities are more likely to be drawn into suburban or uptown centers, such as Clayton or Westwood. In

Pittsburgh, Cleveland, or Atlanta where the airport is on the other side of downtown from the traditionally wealthy neighborhoods, it has acted as a counterweight, helping to keep downtown relatively healthy.

Keeping Downtowns Competitive

Regardless of this diversity of geographic factors, every downtown has had to respond to competitive pressures from suburban office parks, and from retail and office development along highways. Beginning in the late 1950s federal urban renewal money was used to assemble and demolish groups of old buildings to make way for new downtown offices, hotels and apartment towers. Federally funded highways, double-edged, kept downtown connected to the region but accelerated suburban development, and often damaged urban neighborhoods.

Attempts to emulate suburban shopping centers by turning downtown streets into pedestrian malls have mostly failed, with expensive installations of trees and paving quietly taken out again in order to restore conventional streets. Transit ways, such as Denver's 16th Street and the Nicollet Mall in Minneapolis, where bus service is maintained on what is otherwise a pedestrian street, have proved more successful. The Third Street Mall in Santa Monica, a series of short pedestrian blocks in an otherwise active downtown street grid is also a successful model. The Grand Avenue in Milwaukee and other indoor downtown malls, often created by a combination of infill structures and connections to existing buildings with pedestrian passages, can be successful environments but draw life off the surrounding streets.

Despite active business retention efforts by cities, corporate headquarters for most manufacturing businesses moved out, leaving downtown to banks, utilities, insurance companies, law firms, and brokerages, which always relied on large back-office staffs. It was these financial businesses that occupied the new downtown office towers built during the 1980s and early 1990s. Today major structural changes in the banking industry and the new information technology are again raising questions about the future of downtown's role as an office center. The terrorist attack on the World Trade Center and the Pentagon in September 2001 also raises questions of security: A high-profile downtown office location suddenly seems dangerous, as in the 1940s and 1950s, when decentralization of offices and industry to the suburbs was seen as a response to the vulnerability of city centers to air raids.

Downtown as a Tourist Attraction

"Festival" retailing began in cities that were already attracting tourists, for example, Ghirardelli Square in San Francisco and the Faneuil Hall Market Place in Boston. Extending this strategy to other cities that did not have a strong history of attracting visitors has worked well in some places, like Baltimore, and much less well in other places, like Toledo. Success requires a coordinated effort to attract suburbanites and out-of-town visitors.

One support for festival retailing in downtown Baltimore is the presence of the National Aquarium a few blocks away. Baltimore has now developed a whole cluster of attractions around the Inner Harbor including the Power Plant, an entertainment retail destination, the Maryland Science Center, and the Port Discovery Children's Museum.

Many other cities have emulated Baltimore in placing a cluster of tourist attractions near the city center, such as the Rock and Roll Hall of Fame and Great Lakes Museum at Northcoast Harbor in Cleveland, or the Museum of Modern Art, the Children's Museum, and the Metreon—an entertainment destination—near the convention center in the Yerba Buena district of San Francisco.

Convention and exhibition centers remain a primary way to bring visitors downtown, and cities find themselves locked into an expensive competition to keep providing the biggest and best. Despite improvements in information technology, meeting planners continue to demand more and more space for ever larger groups. Another reason for enlarging a convention center is to hold multiple events on a staggered schedule, as set-up and takedown time for each event permits active use of meeting and exhibit spaces only 40 percent of the time. Continuous events at the convention center are needed to fulfill its purpose of supporting local hotels and restaurants.

Sports Franchises as Downtown Anchors

While suburbanites will come to an automobile or boat show at the convention center, a more dependable way to draw them is to locate arenas, baseball, and football stadiums in or close to downtown. In the 1960s and 1970s cities built multipurpose downtown stadiums designed to accommodate both baseball and football, although the necessary compromises meant that these stadiums were far from perfect for watching either. In 1992, when the Orioles' Camden Yards stadium opened in downtown Baltimore, it reminded people of the intimacy and individuality of traditional urban baseball parks, setting in motion another expensive competition among cities to create new, old-fashioned places to watch baseball, with the addition of the skyboxes that owners now require.

The parking spaces built for downtown office buildings are almost always available for baseball games, overcoming the usual advantage of a suburban location: inexpensive at-grade parking. Providing a parking garage only for skybox patrons permits a baseball stadium and arena to fit right into city, as at Jacobs Field and the Gund Arena in Cleveland, where

11.1 Jacobs Field and the Gund Arena in Cleveland were designed to follow the city's design guidelines. They are buildings on an urban street, not isolated structures surrounded by parking lots. They draw on downtown itself for most parking needs, with garages only for the skybox holders (Master plan by Sasaki Associates). Arena architects were the Ellerbe Partnership, the stadium was designed by HOK.

the ballpark and arena are urban buildings right on the street, not distant objects seen across a parking lot. (11.1) People walk to Jacobs Field and the Gund Arena on evenings and weekends from their downtown parking spaces, passing local restaurants and bars on the way, so that the sports destinations anchor downtown streets—that might otherwise be almost empty—in the same way that department stores draw patrons through

shopping malls. There is a big government investment in these two sports locations: the payback is urban vitality.

However, another consequence of replacing multipurpose stadiums is the need to build a new football stadium. There is less justification for government involvement in helping to pay for football, as there are so few home games each year. Having a major-league sport franchise is important to a city's sense of itself; cities and states usually end up paying most of the bills for the stadium. The revenue from the skyboxes generally goes to the owners, which helps them pay the players' salaries. Thus a side effect of using sports franchises to revitalize downtowns is that the taxpayers end up directly subsidizing the owners and indirectly subsidizing the players.

Downtown as a Center of Arts and Culture

One advantage that older city centers have over newer suburbs is a long history as a center of art and culture. The art museum, the symphony, opera and dance companies, resident theater companies, and theaters for touring productions all continue to draw patrons and subscribers who have moved to the suburbs. Not all these institutions are downtown. The art museum is likely to be in a park in an "uptown" district on the fashionable side of the city. The concert hall also may have moved to the same area as the art museum, for example, Severance Hall in Cleveland.

Heinz Hall in Pittsburgh is one of the first old downtown theaters restored as a concert hall, bringing the Pittsburgh Symphony downtown from the Oakland district near the art museum. In its early years Heinz Hall also served the Pittsburgh Opera, but later another old theater nearby was restored as an opera house. Under the leadership of the Heinz foundations, Pittsburgh now has a complete cultural district, with a repertory theater, galleries, and film theaters in addition to the concert hall and opera house.

Downtown cultural activities are not without competition. Universities in the suburbs often have extensive concert series and art and drama programs. But in most places the downtown cultural activities are still the most important in the region, and civic leaders work hard to keep them that way. Playhouse Square in Cleveland and The Avenue of the Arts development in Philadelphia are examples of districts that have been created from a mix of existing and new performing arts facilities, while the Performing Arts Center in Portland, Oregon, the Kravis Center in West Palm Beach, and the new Greater Miami Performing Arts Center are examples of performing arts centers created to make sure that downtown has the ability to draw visitors and suburbanites that performing arts centers provide. City Place, a new development in downtown West Palm Beach adjacent to the Kravis Center, is a demonstration of the way in which arts centers help anchor downtown retail and residential development. (11.2, 11.3)

Business Improvement Districts

There is a huge investment in infrastructure and property values tied up in downtowns. The financial interest in downtown properties includes many national banks and insurance companies, real-estate investment trusts, and publicly held companies, as well as anyone who holds municipal bonds. Many pension funds are partly invested in downtown real estate. Taxes from downtowns are also a principal support of most city budgets.

However, downtowns do not have a lot of votes in local elections and have been losing out on the provision of sanitation, street maintenance, public safety, and other services to the city's neighborhoods, which, of course,

11.2, 11.3 City Place in downtown West Palm Beach, Florida, mixes destination retailing with apartments and town houses. It is next door to the Kravis Center for the Performing Arts. Another anchor for the development is the Himmel Theater, formerly a church, behind the arches in the photo above. There is also a Macy's, as a more conventional retail anchor. At right, apartments over the kinds of stores that used to be found only in shopping malls—a new downtown mix. Urban designers are Elkus/Manfredi Architects.

also need them. Meanwhile, suburban shopping malls and office parks, downtown's principal competition, all allocate money for special management services: maintaining common open spaces and parking lots, providing private security guards, keeping the public environment clean, orderly, and attractive. Even in the days when downtowns were dominant, they were never maintained this way; at the time the public had no other choice.

The remedy in many communities is for downtown properties to tax themselves an additional amount, with the money from this increment devoted to improving services downtown. These special tax districts, usually called business improvement districts, began as a device for neighborhood commercial revitalization, but are now in force in many big-city downtowns. Midtown Manhattan has three business improvement districts, and there is another in the Wall Street area. The use of business improvement districts is starting to make a significant difference in downtown Washington, D.C., and has had impressive success in downtown Philadelphia. All districts use their special funds to supplement city services, providing additional street cleaning, private security guards, and special advertising—all the benefits that suburban office parks and malls receive from their management.

Philadelphia is among the cities that has extended the life of the business improvement district to 20 years, permitting the revenues from the district to be used to pay back bonds. By capitalizing the district revenues, the district has been able to make major street improvements as well improve daily operations.

The Main Street Program

The return of retail to the shopping streets in small towns, smaller cities, and commercial districts in urban neighborhoods owes much to the Main Street program originated by the National Trust for Historic Preservation. The Main Street Program is a process, there is no special secret ingredient. It applies the managerial techniques used in shopping centers and business improvement districts, but it also mobilizes community and nonprofit resources; the bottom-line is not only the success of local businesses, but also the preservation and restoration of historic districts. The program began as a demonstration study in three communities between 1977 and 1980: Galesburg, Illinois, Madison, Indiana, and Hot Springs, South Dakota. The National Trust provided the funds for a full-time manager to set up and manage the Main Street process in each community. The process has four stages: organization, promotion, design, and economic restructuring.

Each Main Street district is begun by creating a board and committee system that organizes the work of many volunteers. The program follows with such promotional efforts as holiday parades and celebrations, special retail offers and marketing, farmers markets and street fairs. Then there is a design plan that builds on the architectural strengths already present in the community, which often includes gaining approval for listing a historic district on the National Register maintained by the U.S. Department of the Interior. For income-generating properties, there is a 20 percent federal tax credit for renovating buildings that are listed on the National Register or are eligible to be listed. There is a 15 percent tax credit for properties built before 1936. The plan also deals with street landscaping and the design of street furniture, and usually includes some kind of handbook that shows individual property owners how to restore their buildings to meet the criteria in the plan and the Department of Interior standards for eligibility for the tax credit. Finally the plan deals with retail economics of the whole street: What should be its position in the regional market place?

As the program became known, thousands of communities applied to the National Trust for help. The trust turned to the states, asking them to set up Main Street prototypes. Originally six states participated, now almost all do. Between 1985 and 1988, the trust enlarged the program to apply to shopping streets in urban neighborhoods. Now there are also citywide Main Street programs in Boston, San Diego, and Baltimore.

Generally the community pays for the office and the salary of the Main Street manager, the state or city pays for the outside assistance. The National Trust administers the program with a staff of about 24, plus some 250 consultants who can be called upon in various parts of the country. The trust also runs training sessions and has developed handbooks based on a growing body of experience.

The trust has figures indicating that about 17 percent of the Main Street programs have failed: That is, the organization created to implement the program has gone out of business. This usually happens between the early catalyst phases and the growth phase, and may reflect difficulties in finding the right managers as well as intractable economic problems. The trust staff has observed that the local visionaries who get the Main Street program started are not always the best people to manage it once it gets going.

If 17 percent have failed, that would indicated that the great majority have succeeded, or are in the process of succeeding. A recent trust publication tells the success stories of some 45 communities. It is a formidable achievement.

The Return of Streetfront Retailing
Many people are getting tired of shopping malls, one of the factors that has helped energize historic main streets. Malls are not efficient if your objective is to buy one or two specific items, rather than to spend the day shopping. Malls are confusing, to some extent deliberately, as retailers hope to lure

shoppers into purchases they had not originally intended to make. However, there is a lot to be said for being able to see where you are going before you get there, and to understand where you are when you arrive. This kind of understanding is acquired with little effort by driving down a city street. The street also provides access to other activities like offices and residences, so that the people on the sidewalk are not a herd of shoppers but a diverse crowd bent on different destinations.

All over the United States downtown shopping streets are coming back, and stores that used to be seen only in malls are appearing in streetfronts. Some people are concerned that mall stores are crowding out local businesses, but these new kinds of destination streets like Third Street in Santa Monica, California, contain a mix of mall stores with local restaurants and specialty shops.

King Street in downtown Charleston, South Carolina, had suffered in the 1980s when the two department store anchors both closed. The city responded by helping to finance a new hotel and conference center which also included 30,000 square feet of high-quality specialty stores at street level, a higher grade of shopping than was then available in the Charleston area's suburban malls. This new retail destination proved popular, and has expanded into shop fronts on King Street. It also attracted a Saks Fifth Avenue, built on a site that had previously been cleared of historic buildings to make way for a small branch bank. Much of King Street shopping still consists of locally owned specialty stores, restaurants, and antique shops, creating a retail district that continues to appeal to tourists as well as local residents. (11.4, 11.5)

One of the problems with streetfront retailing has been that it lacks the ability to concentrate stores like a multi-level shopping mall. By designing downtown retail frontage as a "sandwich," densities can be created that rival those of a three-level mall. In the sandwich design, smaller stores open directly off the street, bigger stores are upstairs or in the basement, but have street-level entrance lobbies. Passersby see a sign for a big box bookstore, inside is a small part of the book store, with escalators leading up to a second floor that fills the whole building. A few doors down, an entrance to a big store for recorded music can have escalators leading down to a basement level that also is a large area. At present this kind of concentration of streetfront retail is usually found in big cities, as along New York's Fifth Avenue, but it can be used in smaller urban centers as well.

Downtown Bethesda

Downtown Betheseda, Maryland, which was once a modest suburban shopping district, has become an urban center with office buildings, hotels, and

11.4 *Looking south on King Street in downtown Charleston, South Carolina. At left are specialty stores in a downtown hotel and conference center actively promoted by the city. At right, the taller building houses a Saks Fifth Avenue, attracted by the revival of downtown shopping.*

11.5 *Looking north on King Street, Banana Republic, which started out in the retail arcade in the hotel/conference center, is now in larger space out on the street, which has a mix of local businesses and the stores more usually found in malls.*

apartment towers, partly because it is a stop on the Washington Metro system and partly because it is the geographic center of some of the region's most affluent residential districts. The initial effect of redevelopment was to replace local shops with the kind of restaurants and convenience shopping found in office districts, like eyeglass stores and travel agents. However, an amazingly large and diverse regional restaurant district, supported by public parking garages, has developed in storefronts along a network of small streets close to the center. Now, a new generation of diverse, streetfront retail is being created by a developer, Federal Realty, following a plan by Richard Heapes of Streetworks. In the first phase, a public parking garage occupies the center of a block, surrounded by streetfront retail. (11.6) The sidewalk is widened by setting the buildings back, an exception to the proposition that downtown buildings should be built up to the front property line. Pedestrians walk close to the buildings; but between the pedestrian and the street is a zone that can be used for outdoor cafes, landscaping, bicycle racks, and kiosks. (11.7, 11.8) The result is a streetscape that has many of the advantages of a pedestrian mall, but is closely connected to the local traffic system as well as the buildings. Retail is generally one level, but the Barnes and Noble on the corner has two. Other upper floors are occupied by offices.

Downtown Housing

Polls of downtown office workers show that substantial percentages of people who work downtown would like to live downtown—or near downtown—if suitable housing were available. Suburbanites whose children are grown or away at college, proverbially tire of maintaining large houses and long for the freedom of urban apartment or townhouse living. Young people just starting out want to live in a place where there is always something going on. All of these groups create a market for downtown housing, or housing in neighborhoods close to downtown. Until recently the real-estate industry has been busy satisfying the market for suburban houses and apartments, and has not paid much attention to opportunities in urban areas. Now, however, the size of the potential urban market is understood, and there is much more developer interest.

This market trend interacts with policy determinations by many cities that center-city housing should be a priority because it supports retail and restaurants, and helps attract office tenants. Cities are using land assemblage, tax abatement, and other incentive programs to overcome the cost advantages of building housing on vacant land in the suburbs. Many downtowns have a stock of older office buildings with floor plans suitable for conversion to apartments, notably some of the famous old buildings in lower Manhattan.

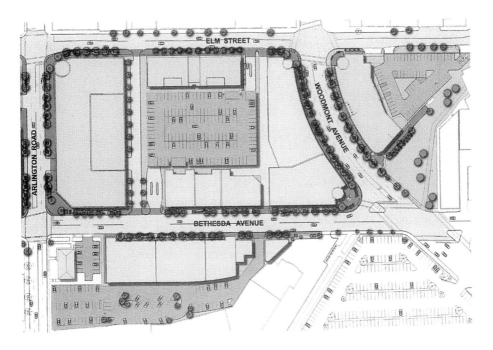

11.6 *Retail development in downtown Bethesda, Maryland: a ring of stores around a parking garage, not a ring of parking around a store. Urban design by Streetworks.*

11.7 *Buildings in this downtown Bethesda development set back to make room for a new sidewalk, while what would usually be the sidewalk is well landscaped and provides space for cafes, benches, bicycle racks.*

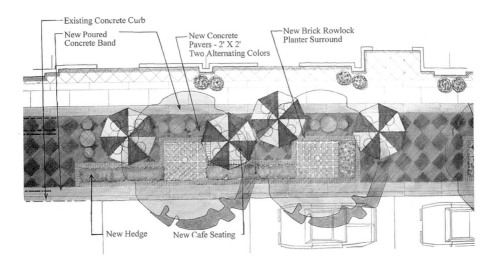

11.8 Landscaped sidewalk space in downtown Bethesda, Maryland. Pedestrians use the setback next to the buildings, while the sidewalk becomes a tree-lined, multi-use space.

Downtowns also have close-by zones of vacant or underused light-industrial and service buildings that are suitable for new residential development.

Uptown Dallas

Uptown Dallas was a pre-World War I upper-income residential district where many houses had been torn down to make way for small service-commercial establishments, while other houses had been broken up into apartments or converted to business uses. At the same time, some upscale stores, restaurants, and hotels remained, and the area continued to occupy an advantageous location between downtown Dallas and the affluent Turtle Creek area. Following plans coordinated by the city of Dallas, several thousand new apartment units have been built in the area since the mid-1980s. Typically they are four-story elevator buildings built up to the sidewalk in the traditional urban manner. They have interior courtyards and interior parking garages. There are ground-floor shops on the main streets. Enough of these buildings have now been constructed that they are defining a walkable neighborhood. (11.9, 11.10)

Downtown Albuquerque

Albuquerque today is a decentralized city that has grown by annexation; much of the new development has bypassed the downtown. A plan for strengthening the traditional business district is built around a new parking garage, lined on the street frontages with stores and offices, a multi-theater complex, and extensive investment in new residential buildings. A block of townhouses is part of the first phase, as a relatively small number of such buildings can quickly produce a new image for a large area. Higher density residential buildings are in the next phase. (11.11, 11.12, 11.13. 11.14)

Live-Work Units Downtown

Predictions about the ways in which information technology will change society have often suggested that people who have the option to work at home will choose to live on a mountain top or a beach. It turns out that many people who do have this option would rather live near the center of a small town, in an urban neighborhood, or in downtown itself. There are new live-work units in downtown Los Angeles, near downtown Portland, Oregon, as well as the live-work units that have been converted by enterprising owners from existing houses and industrial buildings. Despite the instant communications available by e-mail, fax, and telephone, people want to get away from their computer screen and see other people, and they miss the social network of a more traditional office. Being able to go out to a café for coffee, being close to other people in the same kind of work, being close to culture and

11.9 *Uptown Dallas, just north of the city center, has been redeveloped with mid-rise apartments built around courtyards and internal parking garages.*

entertainment all make downtown, or neighborhoods close to downtown, attractive locations for combined live-work housing. The National Association of Home Builders is very aware of this trend, and made three prototype live-work units a key exhibit of their 2001 national meeting in Atlanta.

Downtown's Competitive Advantage: It's a Real Place
From the 1960s through the early 1980s, big city downtowns tried to compete with the suburban office parks and retailing by being as much like the suburbs as possible. Urban streets were turned into pedestrian malls in imitation of early suburban shopping centers. As noted on page 190 , in most cases, these downtown malls have been failures. Later, cities built indoor shopping malls in imitation of the big suburban regional shopping centers. This strategy has been somewhat more successful, but often created dead spots along downtown streets, so that there was life inside the mall but not much urban activity around it. Old buildings were cleared to make parking lots, so that once you went off the main downtown streets, buildings became separate objects surrounded by parking. Smaller towns and cities gave up on their main streets, and the city hall and public library followed the strip malls and

11.10 Development in Uptown Dallas is built to the street front; ground floors on main streets have shops and restaurants.

franchised restaurants out to the commercial strip along the bypass.

Then in the 1980s, the process began to turn around. Partly the change was a victory for historic preservationists and urban designers through the Main Street Program and the efforts of planning and redevelopment agencies in big cities. Some of the change was created by cities merchandising their cultural and tourist destinations, and building convention and exhibition centers. Some of the success came from the great inventory of historic buildings in older urban areas, which were finally recognized to be an asset, and not an encumbrance preventing the "highest and best use" of the land. Cities began to improve their quality as places: restoring old buildings, landscaping streets, fostering the arts and culture.

This revival of the traditional attractions of big cities, originally motivated to bring in tourists and meeting participants, has lead to a change in the regional marketplace. The flats and warehouse districts in Cleveland prospered with some discreet help from the city, but most of their success came from local entrepreneurs working with cheap real estate to create a restaurant and entertainment location that was more interesting and more fun, than going to a place out on the highway. Some of their business comes from

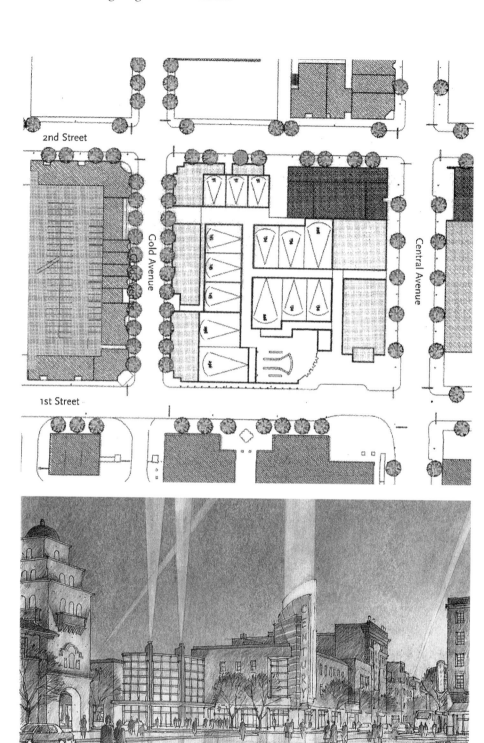

11.11 Residential development and entertainment retail are the basis for redevelopment plans in downtown Albuquerque. A new parking garage surrounded by stores is the first step, then multiplex movie theaters.

11.12 The theaters are at the center of this drawing, showing how residential buildings with stores on the ground floor will fill in vacant downtown sites. Urban designers are Moule and Polyzoides.

downtown workers, visitors and convention goers, but suburbanites actually come into town after work to go there. In many other cities, entertainment and restaurant destinations have created a nightlife scene that draws people from the region downtown after work and on weekends.

Some of the people who come downtown for entertainment become interested in living there. A few urban pioneers began living in converted warehouses, in imitation of the artists who were colonizing the Soho district in New York City. Soon loft-living downtown became a trend; now it is a recognized real-estate category. When the developers run out of old buildings to convert, they start building new ones. Developers had been building townhouses in the suburbs. When the Hovnanian company opened up a development of new townhouses in the devastated First Ward adjacent to downtown Newark, the development sold rapidly.

With more bright, highly educated younger workers interested in living downtown, some of the businesses that compete for them began to take another look at downtown office locations. The trend is well-established in a few cities, such as Denver and San Francisco, although recent cutbacks in "new-economy" employment have slowed things down.

It generally takes a turnover of four or more people per seat to create a successful destination restaurant, which is why it almost impossible to find really good restaurants in places where they have to subsist on lunch business alone. The occasional exceptions are very expensive, are restaurants where there is also a brisk catering business, places that open for breakfast, or hotels, which combine several of these factors.

When there is strong business in the evening from downtown residents and people who come downtown after work, the food can be better than at the restaurant near the mall or at the office park. Being able to walk from place to place is also an advantage usually found only downtown. If one restaurant has an hour-long wait, what about the one next door?

The phenomenon can be self-reinforcing: The more people come downtown for entertainment, culture, or food, the better these offerings can become. The more inviting the downtown scene, the more attractive it is for offices and housing.

11.13 *Townhouses are part of the first phase of downtown Albuquerque's redevelopment.*

11.14 *Apartment buildings will be the next phase.*

The salvation of downtowns, it turns out, is not in being the dominant office market or in imitating malls. Much of the change in the last four decades is permanent. Competing office and retail centers in formerly suburban locations will only become more important. Building on downtowns' unique advantages is their best chance for future prosperity: their central location, their compactness, their inventory of historic buildings, their variety and incident. Every cheap, older building can be an asset because it gives scope to entrepreneurs who can't afford to occupy a new structure.

Most of all, people are attracted to main streets and downtowns because they are real. They are the products of hundreds of decisions made over long periods of time, which create an ambiance almost impossible to duplicate even by the most imaginative themed developments. Downtowns are already real places, and most of their competitors still have a long way to go.

Implementation

12

Designing the
Public Environment

The public environment includes all areas of a city or town that are publicly owned and open to the public: streets, parks, government buildings, bridges, airports, and transit stations. Privately owned areas also can be part of the public environment: malls in shopping centers, and lobbies of hotels and office buildings, for example.

The Street as the Essential Public Space

Streets can represent something like a quarter of urban land area, and are almost always the most important part of the public environment. In traditional cities and towns, much of the life of the community took place in the streets. The advent of heavy wheeled traffic created conflicts; busy downtown streets no longer seemed big enough. In the 1920s theorists suggested separating pedestrians from traffic. Cars, trucks, and buses would be confined to sewerlike channels designed for efficiency of traffic flow, while pedestrians followed elevated walkways or paths through parks and gardens. It was a plausible theory, and after World War II, many cities put it into practice. Unfortunately, it didn't work. Walkways and open space separated from buildings and passersby are not safe, even in orderly societies like Sweden. The famous pedestrian bridges and upper level walkways of Stockholm's Hotorget district are closed, although the ground-floor pedestrian precinct is still in use. The open spaces in and around mid-twentieth century public housing projects are generally unsafe, in retrospect it would have far better to site the buildings on conventional streets and blocks, rather than on the superblocks that architects and planners confidently thought would be a better alternative.

12.1 *The mall on State Street in Chicago has been replaced by a restored street and enhanced sidewalk. A landscaped zone between the pedestrians and the street is the most important part of the design by Skidmore, Owings and Merrill.*

As noted in the previous chapter, making shopping streets in the heart of a city available only to pedestrians has worked in Europe where most of the people arrive at these central districts by transit. Lincoln Road in Miami Beach and Third Street in Santa Monica do work because the blocks are short, the cross streets are kept open to traffic, and the pedestrian precinct is only a few blocks long, But most pedestrianized streets in the United States have been opened up to traffic again.

Today, people who accept the theory that walking is a prime means of creating community in urban places also accept that pedestrian routes should be primarily on sidewalks along streets. The former mall on State Street in Chicago (12.1) has been reopened to traffic, but the sidewalks have been carefully designed to be attractive to pedestrians. How to make traffic streets that work and still accommodate pedestrians comfortably is a central issue of good city design.

Designing Urban Streets and Street Furniture

In old engravings of cities, buildings relate directly to streets and squares; often there are not even sidewalks, as in the engraving of the place in front of the Theatre Italien in Paris in 1818 (12.2, see page 216), although in other locations pedestrian areas are clearly defined, as shown in the London street scene at about the same time (12.3, see page 216). Visible in both pictures are a few lanterns that would be lit at dusk by a lamplighter, but there are no traffic signals, no utility wires and poles, no traffic information signs, fire hydrants, mail collection boxes, fire and police call boxes, newspaper vending machines, trash baskets, telephone booths, or other elements of street furniture, and, most important of all, no parked cars. There are also no street trees, as the tree-lined urban street is rare until much later in the nineteenth century, and becomes a standard practice only relatively recently.

Many of the ways of improving street design and organizing street furniture were invented for mid-nineteenth century Paris by Jean Alphand, the landscape architect working for Baron Haussmann who directed the reconstruction of the city during the reign of Emperor Napoleon III. The selection and planting of trees that can survive on a street, the design of tree grates, curbs, bollards and railings, of street lights, street signs, and kiosks, were all solved so well that they continue to be used up to the present time. American architects and landscape architects familiar with Paris brought these designs back for use in "City Beautiful" plans early in the twentieth century. The street lights on Chicago's State Street are a modern adaptation of this kind of street furniture, as is the streetscape in New York's Battery Park City. (12.4, see page 218)

Today, while buildings continue to define the space of streets, the street itself now has another intermediate layer of one-way signs, wires, parking

12.2 *The place in front of the Theatre Italien in Paris in 1818. There is no distinction between roadway and sidewalk and no street furniture except for lanterns. The buildings define the space of the street.*

12.3 *Broad Street in London's Bloomsbury district in 1829. There are sidewalks and street lamps, but no traffic signals and signs or other street furniture. Buildings still define the space of the street.*

meters, and traffic signals, plus parked cars and delivery trucks, that were not anticipated in designs for historic Paris. While people may not consciously notice the visual confusion this intermediate level creates, they react favorably to its absence. In the last decades most cities and towns have done something to improve the design of their most important streets, while a few places have been able to extend such design improvements to a whole downtown or historic district. The following are some of the measures needed to extend design to every urban street.

1. Leave Enough Room for Pedestrians
In most urban areas streets need to serve both pedestrians and automobiles. If, as is often the case, sidewalks were cut down to make room for extra lanes of traffic, pedestrian space can be too narrow. In places that urbanized after World War II, there may never have been appropriate sidewalks to begin with. In Uptown Houston, as noted earlier, a special taxing district has been created to retrofit the area with a public environment that will both move traffic better by adding to the street network and encourage walking by providing usable sidewalks on every street.

A sidewalk needs to have about eight feet clear, the amount of space needed so that two couples walking in opposite directions can pass each other comfortably without having to shift into single file. The four-foot sidewalk that has been typical of Uptown Houston is not really wide enough even for two individuals to pass comfortably, although there was sometimes a grass verge in addition to the sidewalk that gave enough room for pedestrians to slip by each other.

Sidewalks also must have room for street lights, and the centerline of the supporting pole needs to be about 18 inches back from the curb to protect it from cars. There also needs to be space for the hydrants, call boxes, postal boxes, newspaper vending machines, and telephones. If there are to be street trees, the trees need a planting area around five feet wide.

As a result, the minimum width for an urban sidewalk is about 13 feet, enough to leave a comfortable clear area for pedestrians and a five-foot band adjacent to the curb that can accept the trees, as well as the parking meters and other necessary street furniture elements. Eighteen feet is the minimum that leaves room for a sidewalk café, or display cases on a sidewalk, as in designs by the ROMA Design Group. (12.8, see page 220)

2. Turn arterial streets into boulevards
U.S. cities and suburbs are full of wide arterial streets designed to move traffic efficiently but making no allowance for street trees, no bicycle paths, and no consideration for pedestrians walking along the street, or trying to cross it. In

12.4 Revival of traditional street furniture designs in New York's Battery Park City, where low traffic volumes make signals and signs less necessary. Note simple tree planting details.

12.5 It is hard to know when and if you can park in Manhattan. The Grand Central Business Improvement District is trying to help, by putting all the relevant signs in one place, in an orderly format.

the next generation some of these arterials will become transit streets, which can provide the occasion for a comprehensive redesign. These street sections, also by the ROMA Design Group, show the conversion of an urban arterial first to a five-lane street plus a service road and parking that relates to a retail frontage and then ultimately to a transit street. (12.6, 12.7, 12.8, see page 220)

3. Organize the Signs and Street Furniture
Parking information signs, way-finding signs for ballparks and convention centers, information about bus services—the potential number of signs is extensive, and several different agencies are likely to be responsible for putting them up. Typically, when a new sign is needed, a crew arrives in a truck and attaches the sign to a light pole using stainless steel bands—even if the pole is painted some other color than silver. If there is no pole near enough to where the crew wants to put the sign, or if there are already too many signs on the pole, the crew drills a hole in the sidewalk, inserts a slotted metal pole, fills the hole with grout and attaches the sign to the pole. Nobody seems to worry if the whole pole is leaning at an angle and the sign is turned so it is hard to see. In a big-city downtown this process creates an amazing amount of clutter and confusion, to the point where the information that is supposed to be conveyed by the signs becomes hard to find. This sign pole in the Grand Central Business Improvement District in midtown Manhattan is an example of one attempt to deal with complex sign requirements. (12.5)

The Downtown Alliance, a business improvement district in Lower Manhattan, has started implementing a radically simplified design for street lights and other street furniture, the work of urban designers, Cooper, Robertson + Partners in association with landscape architects Quennell, Rothschild & Partners, who have worked on streetscape designs for other business improvement districts in Manhattan. Instead of the slotted sign metal poles there will be special round black sign poles, designed as part of the same family of shapes as the street lights. (12.9, see page 222)

4. Make Street Lighting Friendly to Motorists and Pedestrians
The standard 450-watt sodium-vapor light deployed on a davit 30 feet over the street is an efficient means of delivering foot candles to the roadway, but the fixture creates glare in the eyes of oncoming motorists and bathes the pedestrian in an unnatural orange glow. Shopping streets should have relatively closely spaced light fixtures 13 to 15 feet high, with illumination from sources that put people in a sympathetic light. Lower Manhattan's Downtown Alliance light poles for pedestrians are 14 feet high and use an "electrodeless induction" light source, that works like a fluorescent bulb but with a color close to incandescent light. The roadway should be lighted from 30 foot poles

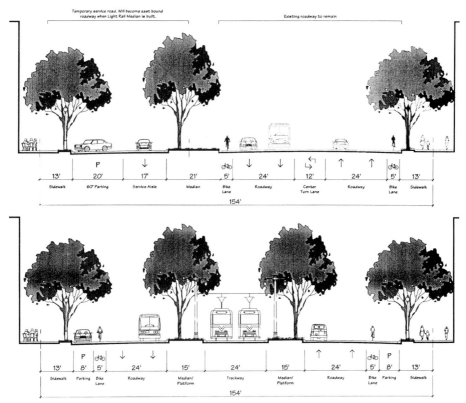

12.6, 12.7 Drawings by the ROMA Design Group show the conversion of a wide arterial street, first with added parking and a service aisle to support retailing and then, later, reconfigured to accommodate rapid transit.

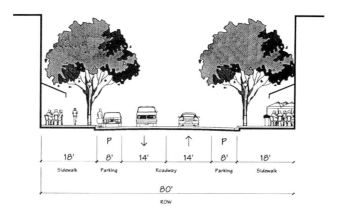

12.8 Where there is streetfront retailing, there needs to be plenty of room for both pedestrian and sidewalk activities, as in this design by the ROMA Design Group.

using cut-off light fixtures that reduce glare. Preferably, they should have a white light, like the metal halide bulbs used by the Downtown Alliance. Replicas of historic cast-iron fixtures based on Parisian, Washingtonian, or other models were not designed to provide modern levels of illumination. The Washington "Acorn" fixture designed for the 1904 McMillan Plan looks well on a pedestrian street in the daytime, but with a high-wattage sodium lamp it creates a terrible amount of glare at night. The best pedestrian illumination comes from a low-glare fixture, using a cut-off around the light source, reflectors, or a diffusing shade, as in the Downtown Alliance fixture.

The Manual On Uniform Traffic Control Devices for Streets and Highways, published by the U.S. Department of Transportation, requires that traffic signals be located where they can be seen from a distance, the distance increasing with the prevailing speed of cars approaching the signalized intersection. Meeting the requirements of the manual, as shown in diagram (12.10, see page 223) generally requires that at least one traffic signal is placed out over the roadway on a boom. The boom is often festooned with additional traffic information in the form of street identification signs and information about lanes and turns. Because these traffic signal booms intrude into the space of the street, they become a prominent part of the streetscape. Improving their design can make a big difference to the street.

Organizing street lights and signs into a panel system has been tried in a number of cities but the frames have to be strong enough to withstand wind loads, as well as the cantilever over the street, and can easily become so massive that the benefits of a more organized design are lost. Frames work best in cities, such as Jacksonville, Florida, where the street lights are deployed horizontally. A simple boom system, preferably with horizontal traffic signals, is probably the best answer in most cases.

5. Traffic Signals Don't Have to be Yellow

A provision of *The Manual on Uniform Traffic Control Devices* says: "To obtain the best possible contrast with the visual background, it is desirable that signal-head housings be highway yellow." The manual has three levels of language to describe its provisions. If the manual says *shall*, the instruction is mandatory. If the manual says *should*, the instruction is considered advisable. If the manual says *may*, it is not officially a design requirement. The phrase "it is desirable," used to describe using yellow paint on signal-head housings, corresponds to none of these three levels. To those familiar with bureaucratic language, the wording is significant; it is just an observation. If other desirable factors are considered more important, such as painting the signal heads to match the black or dark green light poles in a historic district, a locality is free to do so.

Unfortunately, however, this one sentence in the manual has had a big

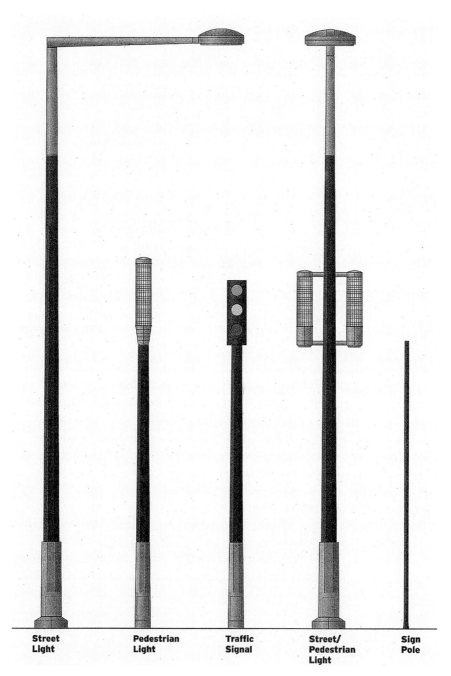

Street
Light

Pedestrian
Light

Traffic
Signal

Street/
Pedestrian
Light

Sign
Pole

12.9 New coordinated designs for street furniture prepared for the Downtown Alliance in Lower Manhattan by Cooper, Robertson + Partners and Quennell, Rothschild & Partners.

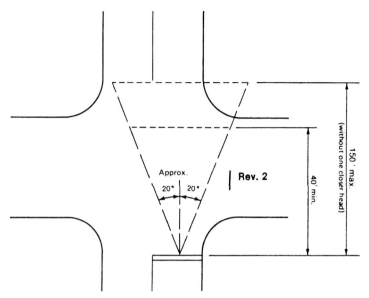

12.10 Required locations for placing traffic signals from The Manual On Uniform Traffic Control Devices for Streets and Highways.

effect on the streetscape in U.S. cities. Traffic signal heads come from the factory already painted highway yellow. For some reason, the casings for walk/don't walk signals also come in high-visibility yellow. Many cities and towns install them just as they come from the box. Yellow isn't necessarily a bad color, but often it is an inappropriate color. Washington, D.C., paints all its street furniture a uniform gun-metal gray, signal heads, walk/don't walk boxes, and all. Many other cities paint traffic signal heads black. Logic is on their side. It is difficult to understand what the advantage is to having the sides and backs of the traffic signal housing painted yellow, as they are the sides not visible to oncoming drivers. Where there is concern about the visibility of the traffic signals themselves, there is supposed to be a back-plate installed behind the signal so that the signals are seen against a dark gray or black background. Incidentally, the reverse of such a back-plate is not painted yellow, and the plate covers up the backs of the traffic signal housings. Unfortunately, many downtown main streets and local historic districts with carefully designed light fixtures in black, dark green, or other special colors, have inappropriate yellow signal housings presumably in the mistaken belief that the color is a safety requirement.

6. Keep Street Trees Alive
When trees grow beyond the capacity of their root systems, they begin to die.

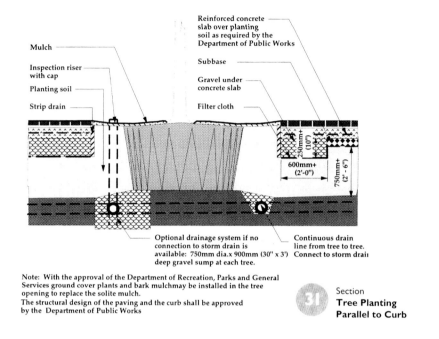

Mulch

Inspection riser
with cap

Planting soil

Strip drain

Reinforced concrete
slab over planting
soil as required by the
Department of Public Works

Subbase

Gravel under
concrete slab

Filter cloth

250mm+
(10")

600mm+
(2'-0")

750mm+
(2' - 6")

Optional drainage system if no
connection to storm drain is
available: 750mm dia.x 900mm (30" x 3')
deep gravel sump at each tree.

Continuous drain
line from tree to tree.
Connect to storm drain

Note: With the approval of the Department of Recreation, Parks and General
Services ground cover plants and bark mulchmay be installed in the tree
opening to replace the solite mulch.
The structural design of the paving and the curb shall be approved
by the Department of Public Works

31   Section
**Tree Planting
Parallel to Curb**

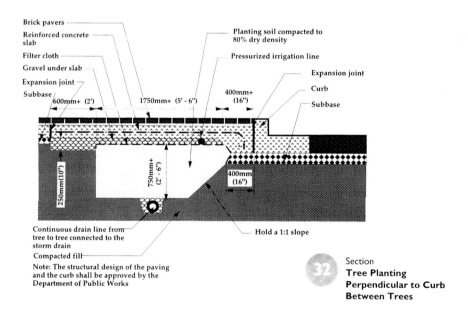

Brick pavers

Reinforced concrete
slab

Filter cloth

Gravel under slab

Expansion joint

Subbase

600mm+ (2')

Planting soil compacted to
80% dry density

Pressurized irrigation line

Expansion joint

Curb

Subbase

1750mm+ (5' - 6")

400mm+
(16")

250mm(10")

750mm+
(2' - 6")

400mm
(16")

Continuous drain line from
tree to tree connected to the
storm drain

Compacted fill

Hold a 1:1 slope

Note: The structural design of the paving
and the curb shall be approved by the
Department of Public Works

32   Section
**Tree Planting
Perpendicular to Curb
Between Trees**

*12.11 Planting details by landscape architect James Urban for keeping street trees alive by
giving their roots room to grow. Roots are not confined to a tree pit, but can work their way
under the sidewalk, which is reinforced to form a bridge over compacted fill.*

When trees are planted in a typical sidewalk tree pit, their roots have only a limited space to grow. One solution is to keep cutting the tree back. Pollarded street trees, as are often seen in European cities, stay healthy even if planted in confined spaces, but few U.S. cities have the staff of foresters needed to maintain trees in this way. The alternative is to design a tree pit that allows the tree roots to continue to expand. Putting trees in a continuous planting strip, rather than in pits, is one way to do this. Segments of sidewalk between the trees can be designed to bridge over the planting space, as in these details by landscape architect James Urban. (12.11) Another of James Urban's methods, still experimental, is to install a series of vertical polyvinyl sheets in the tree pit. The roots spread upwards along these sheets, creating multiple sets of tree roots within the tree pit, which seems to have the same benefit as root expansion over a wider area.

If a tree is too small when it is installed on a city street, it will have trouble surviving. The diameter of the tree at planting should not be less than 2 1/2 inches. Transplanting large trees is expensive, and, unless the immediate effect is important, it does not ordinarily make sense to transplant trees that have a caliper of more than 4 inches. An optimum size is often considered to be 3 1/2 inches.

There needs to be some kind of system for keeping a tree watered for its first two years of life. Ideally, watering is done by the abutting property owner, or the staff of a parks department or business improvement district, only on days when it is needed. The alternative is an automatic watering system, but the tree pit needs to be well-drained as the system will operate even if it is raining already, and too much water can kill a young tree as effectively as drought. Automatic systems eventually fail, but by that time the trees on the street should be well established

The area around the base of the tree should be pervious to water, but in urban areas people also need to walk near the base of the tree. A tree grate is a typical solution. (12.12) The grate has a hole in the center for the tree trunk and is designed to have knock-out elements so the hole can be enlarged as the tree grows. If this maintenance is not done, the grate can eventually kill the tree by cutting through the bark as the tree grows against it. There is also a problem with rubbish going through the grate and being hard to extract, and people wearing shoes or boots with high heels will have difficulty walking on it. Some landscape architects suggest omitting the grates and just using mulch, which is easy to clean and replace. Tree pits in New York City's Grand Central district are treated as flower beds, with some loose Belgian block right around the base of the tree, and two bollards to protect the tree from trucks backing into it. (12.13)

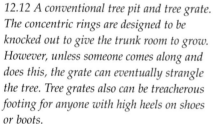

12.12 *A conventional tree pit and tree grate. The concentric rings are designed to be knocked out to give the trunk room to grow. However, unless someone comes along and does this, the grate can eventually strangle the tree. Tree grates also can be treacherous footing for anyone with high heels on shoes or boots.*

12.13 *The Grand Central Partnership dispenses with tree grates and plants trees in beds with flowers or ground cover. The bollards are to protect the tree from trucks backing into it, the wickets are meant to protect the tree from dogs.*

7. Choose a Paving Material That Can Be Maintained

Many sidewalks in Paris are asphalt, a material that is not permitted on downtown sidewalks in most U.S. cities except as a temporary measure. The authorities in Paris prefer to spend their money on trees, lights, and kiosks, although they do use special paving materials in high-visibility locations. The problem with specially designed sidewalks, unless the street is being completely reconstructed, is that the sidewalk finish or pattern is going to be interrupted by utility access points, fire hydrants, or storm drains that occur at unpredictable intervals. Another problem: If the sidewalk has to be broken through to gain access to an underground pipe or conduit, repairs are seldom as skillful as the original paving work. Often the surface is just patched with concrete or asphalt. Some downtown streets are designed with a special access strip of removable pavers close to the curb. In theory, underground utilities will all be under this strip, where access will be relatively easy. Unfortunately, even when utilities actually are under the strip, the work crews are unlikely to remove the pavers without breakage, or to put them back properly. Special sidewalks are best used in business improvement districts or other locations where extra funds for maintenance and repair are available.

Brick sidewalks laid in a simple repeating pattern adapt relatively well to incidents like circular utility covers in varying diameters, hydrants, and call boxes, which are randomly spaced and difficult to move. Brick sidewalks are also relatively easy to repair.

There is a lot to be said for using conventional concrete sidewalks, which are easy to repair and accept random incidents easily, putting the money that would have gone into more expensive paving into bigger trees and better quality streetlight poles.

Designing Suburban Streets
1. Make Streets Connect
As discussed in Chapter 6, suburbs need an interconnected street system. If there are too few through streets, they become over-loaded, producing the familiar suburban gridlock. Neighborhoods should have interconnected streets as well, as over reliance on dead-end streets makes houses hard to find and discourages pedestrians. However, a connected street system does not have to mean high-speed traffic cutting through neighborhoods or pedestrian-oriented districts: street patterns can be artfully designed so that motorists have to slow down, as in the Wildwood Town Center plan shown in the prologue (pages 4, 5).

2. Keep Street Widths Appropriate
There was a time when highway planners believed that every low-density residential street would one day be redeveloped as a higher density urban neighborhood, and every local shopping street would one day be a downtown. It seemed prudent to design streets, not for their current use, but for their eventual future use. This prudence persists in many local regulations, even when changing development patterns render it unnecessary.

In discussing street width, there are three measurements: the right of way, which is the whole area reserved for the street, the paved area for traffic— called the roadway or the cartway—and an area between the edge of the roadway and the right-of-way on both sides of the street that is reserved for the sidewalk and landscaping.

The 100-foot-wide arterial streets that border a neighborhood can be designed as boulevards, as in these designs by the ROMA Design Group. (12.14, 12.15) A 60-foot right of way, reserved for traditional prudential rea-

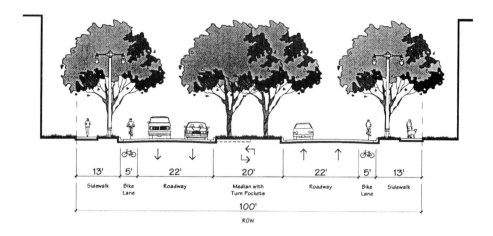

12.14, 12.15 *Arterial streets can be treated as boulevards, as in these drawings by the ROMA Design Group. The landscaped median makes it much easier for pedestrians to cross the street.*

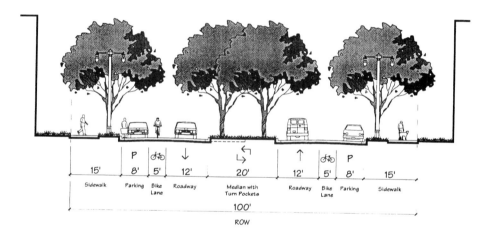

sons, does not automatically have to produce a 36-foot wide roadway, an absurd amount of paving for a local neighborhood street. The paved part of the street can be as narrow as 20 feet, which permits one slow-speed lane in each direction. That leaves 20 feet on each side for sidewalks and landscaping. What about parking cars on the street? Two 8-foot parking lanes, one on each side, brings the paved area up to 36 feet. But, in a low-density neighborhood, is continuous parking for cars needed on both sides of the street? What about a parking lane on one side, as each individual house has its own off-street parking? Or what about just permitting parking on one side of a 20-

foot paved roadway, and letting traffic work its way around the occasional parked car. Another alternative: the section in Chapter 6, page 111, which shows one wide traffic lane and two narrow parking lanes.

The right answer obviously depends on the density of development along the street and how the street fits into a larger traffic pattern. The point is that the minimum paving widths enshrined in many local subdivision ordinances are much too wide.

If traffic is meant to move through a neighborhood of narrow streets at speeds of 15 or 20 miles an hour, the radius of curvature of streets at the corners should be designed to go with these roadway widths and speeds, and can be as small as 20 or even 15 feet. A 35-foot radius at corners, plus 36-foot roadways, are invitations for cars to go around corners at 30 or 40 miles an hour, not desirable in low-density neighborhoods with lots of small children, and not desirable for adult pedestrians either.

The paved width of arterial streets in suburbs can often be kept to two lanes, or two lanes plus a passing lane, except at major intersections, where turn lanes can be added. By only widening arterials at intersections, formidable rivers of asphalt are held to a minimum. A street with two lanes in each direction plus a turn lane is an undesirable barrier in residential neighborhoods.

3. Provide for Pedestrian Circulation

If you believe that being able to walk is an important part of creating a community, having a sidewalk on at least one side of a local street is important. Sidewalks do not need to be as wide as they should be in urban areas. A four- or five-foot sidewalk is adequate. Walking in the street is only a safe alternative in very low density areas. If there is room, a bicycle path is also highly desirable.

A superblock discourages walking, unless there is an internal greenway system within the block. A maximum block size might be between 600 by 300 feet and 700 by 200 feet, that is a maximum perimeter block area of 1,800 feet. A bigger block can be constructed if there is a pedestrian way through it that brings the perimeter area of the sub-block down to 1,800 feet or below. (12.16, page 230) A maximum perimeter for blocks is a useful requirement in a subdivision ordinance to help ensure a walkable street plan. Alleys should not be counted as reducing a block perimeter because they are meant for service, not for walking.

4. Create a Sense of Destination

If people are going to walk, they need a destination, and research has shown that a visible destination needs to be no more than five minutes away. Thus what a person sees at the end of the street is important. A street vista that

12.16 *Mid-block pathways keep long neighborhood blocks walkable, as in this example at the Kentlands, designed by Duany/Plater-Zyberk.*

terminates on half a garage door is not as great an inducement to a stroll as a street that terminates in a park or a community building.

Having houses within shouting distance of the sidewalk is a way of keeping people interested while they are out walking, front porches are highly functional in this respect if people are willing to use them.

Designing Parks and Public Spaces
Research by William H. Whyte, Jan Gehl, and others have given us some simple principles for the design of public spaces, which can be summarized under the following nine headings.

1. Make Public Spaces Legible
Savvy pedestrians are not going to enter a public space if they can't see how they can get out of it again. Sunken and raised plazas are usually not attractive for this reason, neither is any kind of enclosed dead end. A successful public space needs several clearly visible entrances and exits. The same considerations apply to subcomponents of the public space. There shouldn't be any secluded pockets or inaccessible corners. (12.17, page 232)

Interior public spaces need openings to the outdoors so that people can figure out where they are. Bridges in skyway systems generally have windows that provide orientation, underground concourse systems should look out on occasional sunken courtyards. Works of art and distinctive storefronts can help people find their way, but they don't provide any reference to familiar landmarks outside of the building.

2. Plan for a Pleasant Microclimate
As the public open space is sometimes a residual element in the design of the building, it can end up having an unfavorable orientation. A north facing plaza that gets almost no sunlight is not likely to be attractive, even in a warm climate. New York City's plaza regulations require a southern exposure whenever possible. Wind tunnel tests are usually done for tall buildings to evaluate special conditions on the exterior walls that might cause windows to pop out or create other structural failures. At the same time, tests could be done to see if there are any unusual wind conditions created on the plaza. The shape of the tower can interact with winds from a certain direction to create augmented air currents across plazas. These locally created winds can be strong enough to knock people over.

People like to sit in the sun on a cold day and be protected from the wind. On hot days they look for shade and a cool breeze. Good public space design should be able to create both conditions. Well-placed trees and a fountain can create a pleasantly cool microclimate on hot days; chairs or benches in front

12.17 *A park at Battery Park City in New York. A public park should be easy to enter and leave, with no hiding places. The simple lawn is a versatile space.*

of a south facing wall that stores heat and blocks wind can produce a favorable environment when the weather is cooler. The fountain at the Reston Town Center creates its own sense of place. (12.18) The Esplanade at Battery Park City, designed by Hanna, Olin creates a variety of microclimates from deep shade to bright sun. (12.19, page 234)

12.18 This fountain at the Reston Town Center in Reston, Virginia, attracts people to sit a while where it is a little cooler and where they can watch and listen to the water. The landscape architects are Sasaki Associates.

3. Make Seating Available

The essence of an inviting space is the ability to sit down and linger as long as you wish. The seating does not have to be benches or chairs. Ledges on buildings or the edges of planting boxes—without spikes—will do very well if they are placed at three feet or less (but more than a foot) above the plaza, a height where sitting is easy and comfortable. Flights of wide shallow stairs

12.19 The esplanade at Battery Park City has several different microclimates, from deep shade protection to bright reflective spaces in full sunlight; the landscape architects were Hanna, Olin.

lend themselves to all kinds of impromptu seating arrangements.

Whyte recommends individual movable chairs, such as are rented out for a small sum in French parks, over fixed arrangements of benches. The chairs can be moved about to create all kinds of groups, pulled into the sun or shade, and just generally rearranged to give individuals a feeling of comfort. If fixed, backless benches are used, Whyte suggests making them wide enough that strangers can sit on either side without making each other uncomfortable.

Furnishing a public space with movable chairs means that there must be a guard or attendant present, which is desirable for other reasons: Even the best designed spaces need someone to keep order and deal with emergencies. Bryant Park, in New York City, redesigned by the Olin Partnership, uses movable chairs on the central lawn, on the terraces, and along the walkways under the trees. (12.20, page 237)

4. Create Opportunities for People-Watching
One of the principal attractions of being in a public space is the opportunity to watch other people. Seating areas should face out over circulation paths. Studies have shown that benches or other fixed seating oriented away from traffic flow will go unused, or will be used in what Jan Gehl calls "untraditional ways." He illustrates his point with a photograph of two Danish matrons seated back to front on a park bench, with their legs through the gap between the seat and the backrest, watching the crowds walk by.

5. Provide Food
A concession that sells sandwiches, salads, soft drinks, and desserts enhances a public space and is an economical way of making sure that there are responsible people around to keep an eye on what is going on. The only problem is if the concession is permitted to take over the space and make it uncomfortable for anyone who hasn't bought their food or drink.

6. Provide Good Lighting
Even cities that have given a zoning bonus for a public plaza should allow it to be closed from the late evening to the early morning. However, lighting is still an important factor in extending the use of the space and making sure it is not misused at night. Floodlights glaring down on the plaza from tall poles or surrounding buildings are efficient, but can create a penitentiary atmosphere. Although harder to maintain, some of the light should be reflected off trees, come from built-in fixtures near ground level, and from street lamps in scale for pedestrians, with light sources that give a pleasant illumination.

7. Encourage Surrounding Activities

The most important factor in the design of an urban plaza is what happens around it. New York City's regulations governing plazas that qualify for a zoning bonus require that 50 percent of the building frontage on the plaza be devoted to retail—defined as not including banks, brokerages, airline offices, and travel agencies. This is a shrewd requirement as the typical New York zoning plaza, before these regulations were written, belonged to an office building. If the office tower had any ground-floor uses at all, they were likely to be a bank, a brokerage, or a travel agency, dignified activities that were useful for office tenants but didn't do much to enliven a plaza, compared to a restaurant, a shop selling take-out food, or a bookstore.

Jan Gehl goes further, saying that tall buildings should not directly adjoin a public space or even, if at all possible, a sidewalk. His reasons have to do with keeping buildings and their activities in scale with pedestrians. Someone leaning out a third-floor window is still recognizably a human being to a person walking by at ground level. Of course, most modern office towers are sealed buildings, even on the lower floors, but that is exactly the point Gehl is making. A street or a public square is a three dimensional place, for it to be at its best it should relate to activities on the second floor and perhaps above. Shopping malls are now designed this way, so that, if you are walking along on level one, you can see that there is a food court on level three. On the same principle, retail streets and public places should be designed with a liner of low buildings with active uses, with the taller buildings set back within this matrix of traditional relationships.

In residential neighborhoods, the same principle suggests that houses be designed in relation to streets and public spaces. As noted above, this is the basis for the front porches and small front yards characteristic of "new urbanist" communities.

8. Design for Walkable Distances

According to Whyte's observations, the distance that people were likely to walk in New York City was five north-south blocks, which adds up to about 1,250 feet, or a little less than a quarter of a mile. This finding agrees with the experience of shopping center developers who have found that 1,200 feet is about the practical limit to the distance between major destinations, such as department stores, in a shopping mall.

It also agrees with the diagram in Chapter 6 from Clarence Perry's famous article, *The Neighborhood Unit*, showing a walkable area contained within a circle a half-mile in diameter—that is no more than a five minute walk from a central point.

These are modern figures applying to people who are used to driving a

12.20 *William H. Whyte's prescription for movable chairs is followed at Bryant Park in New York City. Landscape architects for the park redesign were the Olin Partnership, the architects, Hardy, Holzman, Pfeiffer.*

car or taking public transit. The five-minute threshold is not about physical stamina but about the onset of boredom, and the fact that people today feel that they need to use time efficiently. According to Whyte, New Yorkers, living in a transit-rich environment, will start thinking about taking a bus, the subway, or a taxi if a trip is going to take more than five minutes on foot. In a more typical city, someone leaving the office to go to lunch will start thinking about getting the car out of the garage if the distance is more than a short walk.

9. Create the Right Environment for Pedestrians
Whyte found that to get people to walk for even five minutes meant that you had to keep them interested. In environments where buildings flanking the sidewalk had long stretches of blank walls, Whyte found that pedestrian traffic was low. Again, this confirms the experience of shopping-center owners that even a few vacant storefronts near a prominent corner could be enough to discourage shoppers from entering a whole section of a mall. The interest factor turns out to be far more important than ease of pedestrian movement.

   As noted previously, planners and designers used to believe that the best way to promote pedestrian movement was to remove "conflict" between pedestrians and vehicles and to protect pedestrians from the weather. This is the theory behind the skyway systems in Calgary, Minneapolis, St. Paul, Charlotte, and other cities and also the underground pedestrian concourses in Montreal, at Rockefeller Center in New York, and in downtown Dallas and Houston. Whyte measured the pedestrian traffic in skyways and concourses and found that the numbers of people dropped off sharply as he went farther from the center of the system. Not only did a skyway or concourse system not overcome the five-minute limit, but, unless there were shops along the way, people did not even walk that far.

   The weather protection provided by a concourse or skyway system is clearly useful, but, on a winter day in Montreal that was so cold that his camera froze, William H. Whyte found as many pedestrians on Ste. Catherine Street as in the nearby underground concourse of Place Ville Marie.

   Separating people from cars is more helpful to drivers, by getting rid of delays at crosswalks, than it is for pedestrians, who generally prefer a direct route at street level to the bridges or underpasses placed for their safety at busy urban intersections.

   The effect of a skyway or underground concourse system is to divide the pedestrians into numbers that are too small to support retail at both street level and the skyway or concourse. Except perhaps in Asian cities with a tradition of very dense multi-level shopping, the protected level will become

12.21 *The Lechmere Canal restored and incorporated in a park by landscape architects Carol Johnson and Associates. It forms the centerpiece of a new urban development in Cambridge, Massachusetts.*

dominant, leaving the street level without much in the way of shopping, which means it is too boring to attract pedestrians, and doesn't look safe enough.

Whyte's studies left him much impressed by the efficiency of walking and the instinctive skill with which people avoid collisions on busy sidewalks. He was also bemused to note that the places where people stopped to talk were generally at street corners, right in the middle of the pedestrian traffic stream.

No! — due to st lights!

Correcting Problems in the Public Environment

The public spaces of many cities were invaded by railway rights of way, and paved over for highways. These expedient decisions gave little consideration to the comfort of the public, or the values of surrounding property. Today, when the public environment can be part of an area's competitive advantage, some of these errors are being corrected.

For example part of the Lechmere Canal, lost within derelict industrial property in Cambridge, Massachusetts, has been restored and incorporated into a park as the centerpiece of a new development. The design is by Carol Johnson & Associates. (12.21)

In Providence, Rhode Island, architect William Warner organized an effort to reopen a river that ran through the center of the downtown. The river had been completely decked to create a vast arterial road. Warner's design for the River Park gives the city a new centerpiece, while still leaving plenty of room for streets along the river and bridges across it. The park design is enlivened by Waterfire, by the artist Barnaby Evans, a series of metal grates for bonfires in the middle of the water. (12.22)

Another major improvement in downtown Providence has been the implementation of a plan by Skidmore Owings and Merrill to reroute the railway tracks that were a barrier to the expansion of downtown. (12.23, 12.24, see page 242) The new downtown blocks created have been landscaped by an extension of the River Park. Some new buildings have been constructed, other sites are still available.

In Cincinnati, the highways that swing past the downtown cut the city off from the riverfront. Now the right-of-way for the highway has been narrowed and the highway decked over, allowing for the seamless connection of downtown streets to a new riverfront development, which includes baseball and football stadiums, replacing the old multiuse stadium.

In San Francisco, the stub of the controversial Embarcadero Freeway, whose construction had been terminated by a public opposition, has now been torn down, permitting the creation of a grand new public space designed by the Roma Design Group in front of the Ferry Building at the foot of Market Street. (12.25, 12.26, see page 244) Of course, the most spectacular

12.22 *The Providence River, which had been decked over, has been opened up following the designs of architect William Warner. The metal baskets and lights are part of an art installation, Waterfire, by artist Barnaby Evans.*

12.23, 12.24 *The railway tracks in downtown Providence have been moved back toward the State Capitol, away from the business center, adding new blocks to downtown, and correcting the mistake that brought the tracks through the center of town. The new station and the urban design plan are by Skidmore Owings and Merrill.*

restoration of this kind is the demolition of the Fitzgerald elevated express-way in Boston and its replacement with an underground highway, the multi-billion dollar "Big Dig."

Highways everywhere create undesirable air and noise pollution for build-ings next to them. Modest, but moderately effective, mitigating measures are the sound walls, being built to protect many suburban neighborhoods. (12.27, see page 246)

The Design of Public Buildings

Up to World War II, bridges, post offices, and courthouses were all designed with a sense that a public structure or building required a certain amount of extra expenditure to convey the importance of their public role. After World War II, as a by-product of the modernist movement in architecture, this sense of obligation was replaced by a more utilitarian desire to save the public as much money as possible. This attitude was reinforced by the scarcity of money for such public uses, as the United States remained in what was effec-tively a war economy until the early 1990s. Recently, a renewed sense of the importance of public buildings and the return of peacetime priorities is changing public building back once again in the direction of better architec-ture and the legitimacy of expenditure on public art and fine materials. Pub-lic buildings should continue to be given this kind of attention even as the United States pursues a war on terrorism and strengthens homeland security.

In Europe, the architects of important public buildings are usually selected after a design competition. Competitions lessen the likelihood that the untal-ented, but politically connected, will get the work, and open the possibility that a gifted unknown will beat out the established names. The competition system has a major defect: It forces the architect to come up with a concept with little or no response from the eventual client and user because, to pre-serve fair play, contact between the competitors and the competition organiz-ers is discouraged. In theory, the competition is intended to select the archi-tect, not the design, but the architect has invested a lot of time and energy in the original idea. The design has now been selected and published; it is hard to make major changes, even if the original design concept turns out not to be the best solution once the designer has a better understanding of the prob-lem. Nevertheless the competition is a recognition that public buildings are an important element of the city, and, precisely because they are paid for by the public, should be the product of more than usual care and forethought.

An alternative is a competitive selection process for a building: It should be in two stages, a request for qualifications and a request for proposals. Anyone can respond to the request for qualifications, and then a short list is selected to make proposals and come to an interview. This system gives pref-

12.25, 12.26 *The removal of the stub of the Embarcadero Freeway in front of the Ferry Building in downtown San Francisco has created the opportunity for a grand civic space, designed by the ROMA Design Group.*

erence to established firms that have done similar buildings before. A new firm may make the short-list, but only if they have a substantial portfolio of built work. The Public Buildings Service of the U.S. General Service Administration has recently compiled an impressive record of giving important commissions to talented architects who produce excellent buildings. They are reminder that states, cities, and towns should do no less.

Public Spaces in Private Buildings
A shopping mall is a space that has no meaning unless it is open to the public, but it is privately owned. As more and more communities find that their most important public spaces are privately owned, questions come up about public life. Do people have the right to ask for signatures to a petition in a shopping mall, the way they can in a public street or square? A complicated question: Apparently under the federal constitution, no, but if the state constitution permits it, yes. A demonstration? This has not been decided definitively, but the owner could well have the right to prevent anything that obstructs business in a private space.

New York City has encouraged building privately owned public plazas and indoor public spaces through its zoning code. In Manhattan there are 503 of these spaces. The owners received a bonus in floor area for building them, in return for legal obligations to the public. In *Privately Owned Public Spaces*, lawyer and Harvard planning professor Jerold Kayden evaluates these spaces. Some fulfill their public obligations well; others have been effectively privatized, or are so uninviting that no one wants to use them. Keeping an appropriate public interest in spaces that are open to the public but located on private property is a matter for development regulation, the subject of the next chapter, but Kayden's book is a reminder that enforcing these legal obligations is also an issue.

12.27 A landscaped sound barrier along a highway. So far, these are usually built to protect suburban neighborhoods. They are needed in the inner cities also.

CHAPTER

13

Shaping Cities Through Development Regulations

Development regulations are among the most powerful forces shaping the built environment. Almost every city, county, and town in the United States has a code that separates manufacturing, commercial, and residential zones. These zoning codes also contain height and setback requirements that have a decisive effect on the placement and appearance of individual buildings. Subdivision codes govern the layout of streets and lots on greenfield sites. Many other laws affect development in specific locations. Landmark buildings and historic districts are protected. The environmental impact of large federally funded projects must be assessed before they go forward, and some states have comparable requirements. Other federal laws specify what can be built in floodplains and how to build there, and what develops in a coastal zone is subject to review. More indirect, but still decisive requirements come from federal laws regulating air and water pollution, and from state growth management legislation.

What is being built today is very much the product of the limits and instructions written into codes. If we don't like what is happening, we need to adjust the regulations.

Zoning: Separating Uses, Protecting Light and Air
Zoning originated in Germany and the Netherlands at the end of the nineteenth century as a way of keeping heavy industries that were intruding into cities away from historic or residential districts. Separating factories from upper-income neighborhoods was one purpose of the 1916 New York City zoning, an early and influential ordinance in the United States; but its

247

framers also were interested in stopping tall buildings from blocking too much light and air from streets and neighboring properties. They turned for precedents to the laws governing the height and roof setbacks of buildings in Paris, which had been regulated since the eighteenth century. The Parisian system related the height of a building to the width of the street, with the roof sloping back above the height limit at a predetermined angle. (13.1)

In New York City, the same system was applied, but at the larger scale of elevator buildings, with the first setback occurring on wide streets at about the 11th floor, and then, instead of an attic, a series of additional setbacks under an imaginary "sky-exposure plane" set, like the Parisian roof line, at a predetermined angle from the street. To keep every building from turning into a pyramid, towers could go straight up once setbacks had reduced their area to no more that a quarter of the building lot. The design of the Empire State Building, a relatively slim tower on a big base, is closely determined by this ordinance.

Similar height and bulk controls were enacted in many other U.S. cities. Architects became interested in the designs that derived from applying these regulations. It was almost as if a building were sculpted out of an imaginary block, as shown in this illustration by Hugh Ferris. (13.2) Much of what we now think of as the Art Deco style of skyscraper design was influenced by the streetwall height limits and set backs of zoning codes.

Zoning Codes and Modern Design

The modern movement in architecture rejected these Art Deco shapes in favor of straight towers surrounded by open plazas. While it was possible to build sheer towers under the old zoning codes, the setback requirements limited the tower size. The Chase Manhattan Bank tower by Skidmore Owings and Merrill and Ludwig Mies van der Rohe's famous Seagram building in New York City were both built in the 1950s under the 1916 zoning code. The owners gave up potential space on the lower floors in order to achieve the desired shape and still meet the code. A revision to the 1916 zoning ordinance was already under study in New York City when these buildings were going up, and their influence helped bring about a fundamental change in the way the code was written.

Instead of relying on height and setback regulations to control building size, the newer code uses a floor-area ratio. The ratio is perhaps better described as a multiplier. If the area of the building lot is 10,000 square feet, and the floor-area ratio is 10, the permissible floor area is 10 times the lot area, or 100,000 square feet.

Floor-area ratios are intended to limit the number of people accommodated on a site, not the building's external shape. Unoccupied areas like mechan-

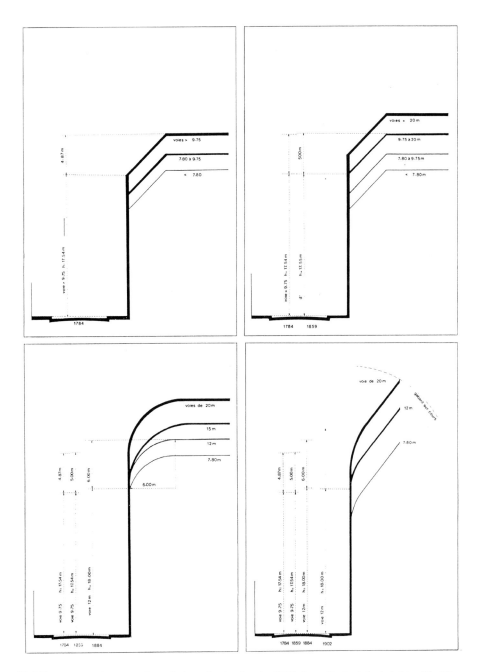

13.1 Four successive sets of regulations, beginning in 1784, have limited the heights of buildings in Paris in relation to the width of streets.

13.2 One of a famous series of drawings by Hugh Ferriss showing how architectural forms are sculpted out of New York City's 1916 zoning regulations.

ical equipment floors, basements, stair towers, and elevator shafts are generally exempted from floor-area calculations. Parking garages often are exempted also, even if they greatly increase a building's size.

The floor-area ratio chosen for the highest density business districts in New York City was 15, although there are various bonus devices that can raise the ratio. The Empire State Building, which has a floor area ratio of about 30, could not be built under the current New York City zoning.

New York City's 1965 ordinance removed the 25 percent restriction on tower sizes as related to the lot, going first to 40 percent and then, by amendments for various circumstances, to almost full coverage. To encourage the appropriate modernist setting for the new sheer towers, the New York City code gave as much as a 20 percent bonus in floor area to owners who provided a ground-level plaza, thus writing into the code the opportunity to develop more, and bigger, Chase Banks and Seagram buildings. The twin towers of the World Trade Center, destroyed by a terrorist attack in September 2001, did not have to comply with the 1961 ordinance's floor-area limits, as the developer was the State of New York, which can overrule local zoning. As the site was a superblock that included several closed streets, the towers were considered to be in compliance with the code.

The Effect of Modernist Zoning Codes on Cities

Most other cities have, like New York, switched from relying only on height and setback controls to setting absolute limits on building size with floor-area ratios. Some emulated New York City in encouraging plazas. The tower and plaza combination was fashionable and was used in many situations that were not influenced by zoning requirements.

Enabling architects to go from decorating a basic shape, predetermined by zoning, to controlling the form and design of the whole office tower, hotel, or apartment house permitted individual creative decisions. Some of the resulting buildings were very good, others were not. In most cases the image of the individual building took precedence over the image of the city. The predictable, if often dull, relationships of urban buildings were lost. The skylines became more spectacular, but the street frontages could become fragmented, confusing and discouraging to pedestrians. In residential neighborhoods, modernist apartment towers, enabled by the new codes, intruded into established relationships of houses and older, lower-scale apartments.

Old-style bulk-control zoning was relatively permissive about uses. Industrial districts were often unrestricted zones that permitted walk-to-the-factory housing. Commercial areas allowed a wide gradient of activities. Modern zoning codes have been much more explicit about separating different types of industry, and segregating industry from other uses. They also designate different zones for different kinds of commercial activities, and create a large number of residential districts based on lot size and the number of housing units permitted.

While these changes have helped get rid of some of the congestion and pollution prevailing in slum areas and around factories, the desirable juxtapositions traditional in cities, where you could walk past offices with stores on the ground floor, then a theater entrance, then a hotel, then around the corner into a street of houses, often can not be recreated under these modernist zoning codes.

Making Corrections to Modernist Zoning

Only a few years after New York City's modernist zoning came into effect in 1965, weaknesses in the code had appeared: Its expectations about land-use were simplistic, and the new separate towers encouraged by the ordinance did not fit well into the existing city. By the late 1960s, New York was already enacting amendments to preserve theaters in the theater district and shopping on Fifth Avenue. Over time, the plaza regulations were modified to require not just square feet of open space, but open space with a favorable orientation equipped with seating, lighting, and landscaping.

The importance of continuity in street frontages, especially where there are ground-floor shops, became evident as soon as a few plazas had interrupted them, and New York City eventually came up with requirements to maintain the "street wall," that is, build up to the front property line for at least a large percentage of the building, on streets with a strong retail presence. Other zoning measures have limited the heights of new buildings in relation to the surrounding context.

San Francisco, which also changed its zoning in the 1960s to a code much like New York's 1965 law, also has amended it to control height and placement of buildings. In many other cities, the zoning codes are nowhere near as restrictive, in relation to the real-estate market, as they are in San Francisco and New York. Many cities welcome a major new building, and zoning has only a marginal effect on what is constructed. The New York- or Chicago-style building has nevertheless become the norm: A tall tower, set off by a plaza.

Washington, D.C., as a Counter-example

Washington, D.C., enacted a height limit in 1894, soon after elevator buildings came into use, initially because of neighborhood protests over a tall apartment house. The law limited apartment buildings to a height of 90 feet and office buildings to 110 feet. This local law was confirmed by acts of Congress in 1898 and 1910. There have subsequently been minor increases in height for some downtown office districts, but the height limit has remained in effect.

The height limit, combined with L'Enfant's monumental street plan, a precursor of designs that were later executed in Paris, plus an excellent rapid transit system has made the center of Washington into a very urbane place, different from any other in the United States. Because of the limit of potential construction on any one property, downtown Washington has a much more even spread of development than can be found in cities where one 40-story building can mop up all the potential growth for years to come. Because developers wish to cram as much building as possible under the Washington height limit, construction generally goes right to the front building line, without setbacks. The combination of uniform height and frontages that line up along the edge of the street is producing boulevards of an almost Parisian coherence and grandeur. The architects for individual buildings have limits placed on their creativity—in most cases they are giving expression to a building shape predetermined by the interaction of real-estate economics and the regulations, but some very successful buildings have emerged from this process. The worst buildings, and some of them are pretty bad, are rendered almost innocuous by the design of the larger street ensemble. (13.3)

Washington also has developed powerful regulations for historic preservation, which has allowed some of the older commercial buildings, which are rebuilt and added on to instead of being demolished. Sometimes preservation in Washington has meant just the facade, or the facade and front structural bay of a historic building. Preservationists complain about these "facadectomies," which are not real historic preservation, but they do maintain variety and incident along the street

Washington's excellent Metro system helps maintain a coherent environment by reducing the demand for parking spaces. The regulatory system does not make it easy for individual entrepreneurs, but everyone is playing by the same rules and the demand is there, so it works.

The Manhattan-style skyline for U.S. cities makes for great photographs, but often the actual development among the towers is sparse and unconnected. Most cities would be better off using development regulations like Washington's for most of their central districts, limiting the size of new increments of development by using height controls and permitting tall buildings at special locations as exceptions.

Suburban Zoning and Subdivision as a Cause of Sprawl

Development regulation in the suburbs is just as influential as it is in cities. Much of the recipe for urban sprawl can be found in local zoning and subdivision regulations. As noted in earlier chapters, the endless ribbons of com-

13.3 Washington's height regulations coordinate these buildings along K Street NW. The architecture of the individual buildings, sometimes not very good, is subordinated to the overall ensemble.

mercial development along highways all follow zoning and so do the big tracts of suburban houses, each the same size on the same-sized lots. The subdivision ordinance, by setting a maximum grade for streets, is usually the reason for the drastic stripping and bulldozing of the landscape that so often happens when a suburban area is developed.

These problems come from two basic flaws in current suburban zoning and subdivision laws: They treat land as a commodity and not an ecosystem, and they protect the neighbors from negative influences rather than creating a positive template for the whole community.

How Development Regulation Has Failed to Recognize Environmental Factors

The experience of Wildwood, described in the prologue, shows that routine zoning and subdivision decisions can have an adverse effect on the environment.

The zoning and subdivision laws that do so much to shape cities, towns, and suburbs allocate land among different users and divide it up into lots, without considering it as a living natural system. As more and more land is urbanized, these regulations are causing great harm to the natural landscape and colliding with another set of legal requirements designed to protect air and water quality, wetlands, and coastal zones.

The landscape might as well be a Monopoly board or a billiard table, as far as the zoning laws that determine land use and intensity of development are concerned. In fact the billiard table is sometimes referred to as the theoretical ideal landscape when calculating how many lots and houses zoning permits on a given site.

The subdivision ordinances that set the rules for laying out streets and dividing tracts of land into individual lots do recognize that land has contours, by setting a maximum gradient for streets. If all streets in a subdivision may not slope at a grade of more than 5 percent, and the site is divided up by a conventional street system, the developer is likely to bulldoze the high points of the landscape down into the low-lying areas so that the lots have the same general gradient as the streets, which requires removing all the trees and other vegetation. It also means stripping the topsoil and putting any streams that cross the site into culverts.

Planned Unit Development

The problems created by applying conventional zoning and subdivision to any kind of terrain more complicated than a flat open field were recognized back in the 1960s. The cure was supposed to be an alternative procedure called Planned Unit Development, which most local communities have since incorporated into their zoning codes. As the name suggests, streets, lots, and buildings may be planned as a unit in ways that are otherwise not permitted; the site plan of streets and lots becomes the zoning and subdivision for the property. The procedure is sometimes called cluster zoning, as it is often used to cluster the permitted number of houses (determined by the billiard table analogy) into smaller lots on the most buildable portions of a site, leaving the most environmentally sensitive parts of the property undisturbed.

The alternatives in local zoning ordinances that permit cluster development are useful, but they have not, by themselves, been the expected cure for suburban development problems. The units of planning follow property lines, which seldom relate to natural boundaries like watersheds, so a site plan that appears to have some advantages in preserving the environment may not make sense in a larger context.

A true cluster of houses means an architectural grouping on small lots, where some houses might even share party walls. Many developers are unwilling to build such houses, because they see them as serving a different market from single-family homes, and many local governments are unwilling to approve them.

Yet another problem has been that a street plan that serves an individual development may be more responsive to the local landscape but less a part of any overall traffic system. A lack of connection among local streets puts more traffic on the streets that do connect, making suburban traffic more congested and circuitous. This particular problem with planned unit development has received a lot of attention from Andres Duany and other new urbanists, who have denounced planned unit development as the cause of bad suburban design. However, Seaside, Duany/Plater-Zyberk's most famous project, is itself a planned unit development. It could not otherwise have been built under the Walton County, Florida, zoning code. Planned unit development is a procedure that can be put to many uses, both good and bad.

In any case, local governments have found it much easier to reduce minimum lot sizes than to change street-grade requirements in the subdivision ordinance. As a result, grading in a planned unit development is often little different from a conventional subdivision.

The biggest problem with typical regrading practice is the cumulative effect on the regional ecosystem. Trees and shrubs retain rainwater, when they are removed the flow of water across the landscape is accelerated. Land contours have reached an equilibrium over time, when they are disturbed and then subjected to powerful flows of water, erosion can take place with great rapidity.

An individual subdivision or planned unit development may have an internally consistent grading system, but what about its relationship with surrounding properties? Have they also been regraded? If not, there is likely to be an escarpment or a ditch at the property line, both unstable, erosion-prone conditions. If the neighboring property also has been regraded, the problems of accelerated runoff are likely to be multiplied.

Many localities are discovering that floods of a magnitude that was once expected to occur every 100 or even 500 years are now a frequent occurrence.

Environmental Zoning and Subdivision

Why shouldn't there be a reduction in the permitted development, if the carrying capacity of the land doesn't support it? As mentioned on page 83, this is the issue raised by Lane Kendig in a book entitled *Performance Zoning* published in 1980. Kendig questioned the billiard-table theory of zoning entitlement. If a 100-acre parcel has only 70 acres of buildable land, why shouldn't the calculation of permitted development be based on the 70 acres? Why create development rights on unbuildable land, and then transfer them to the land that can be developed, causing it to be built on at a higher density than is specified in the zoning?

These are good questions. In most zoning ordinances, the area of land under development is the basis for calculating how much building is permitted. Kendig proposes a simple amendment to local zoning that discounts the land area for calculation purposes, based on the land's sensitivity to environmental damage. Land under water would be discounted 100 percent, hillsides above a certain steepness 85 percent, lesser slopes a lesser percentage and so on. There is no need for the local authority to map these areas itself. A map at two-foot contours identifying any special-category land listed in the ordinance is provided by the developer as part of the application process.

This environmental zoning procedure clearly protects public safety, health, and welfare by reducing erosion and flooding. It is elegantly simple. It is based on objective considerations. It applies uniformly to everyone. In other words it should meet the constitutional tests for zoning. A local community can adopt it without any other changes in its zoning ordinance. Local communities can go a long way towards protecting the natural environment from the bad effects of future development by using environmental zoning in concert with planned unit development, plus specific environmental protection provisions added to the subdivision ordinance.

As the subdivision ordinance is the part of local development regulation that controls the specifics of land planning, adding environmental provisions can make it more effective in protecting the local ecology. The subdivision ordinance can specify that there should be no major changes to natural drainageways and steep hillsides, and require the developer to show how buildings will be kept away from sinkholes, sites of previous landslides, or any floodplains and wetlands. There also can be restrictions for places with easily erodible soils, or land formations susceptible to erosion.

In addition, there can be water retention requirements that say that water should leave the property no faster after development than it did before. If this goal cannot be attained by conserving the natural landscape, it is possible to channel runoff water into detention ponds.

Putting such specific requirements into the subdivision ordinance makes it harder to waive them in a planned unit development, conversely meeting these requirements without a reduction in the permitted density probably requires planned unit development.

Grading and Tree-Cutting Ordinances

What prevents a developer from stripping and bulldozing a property before applying for zoning and subdivision approval? Nothing, unless a community also has laws that require permits for grading and for cutting down trees larger than a specified size, usually a 6- or 8-inch caliper. The key phrase in such regulations is to require that grading or tree cutting be done in accordance with an approved development plan. Good draftsmanship can provide exceptions for working farms and for individual homeowners who want to do a small amount of tree-cutting and clearing.

While it makes sense for every community to adopt environmental protection provisions, such codes, by themselves, may only make sprawl worse by spreading development more thinly. They need to be accompanied by other code provisions that encourage neighborhoods and compact business centers.

Traditional Neighborhood Development and Neighborhood Zones

It is possible to make residential zoning into a positive template for a neighborhood rather than solely a way of protecting homeowners from negative influences. A new concept called a Neighborhood Zone can create this template and achieve the flexibility otherwise unavailable except under planned unit development.

As noted in Chapter 6, designating residential districts by lot size often makes neighborhood planning difficult or impossible. Once the separation of lot sizes by zoning is understood as a mindless practice rather than a theory about how to improve living conditions, it is easy to suggest some alternatives. Andres Duany and Elizabeth Plater-Zyberk came up with the idea of associating different types of houses with different lot sizes, and then making each house-type compatible with the others by subjecting them to similar rules, such as having them all built to the same front setback line. Then they came up with the even more interesting idea of making all the lot sizes in a neighborhood multiples of each other. If you want to build an attached rowhouse you buy one 25-foot lot. If you wish to build a sideyard, "Charleston-style" house, you buy two 25-foot lots. You need three lots for a small detached house and four for a larger one.

Duany/Plater-Zyberk have elaborated the principle of relating lot sizes to building types into codes that apply to the many communities they have designed. These codes are not literally zoning, although like the Seaside Code they can be approved as part of a planned unit development. As the planned community is originally under one ownership, the code is enforced through the purchase agreements that go with each building lot.

However, Duany/Plater-Zyberk also have drafted a more generic version of their code, which combines elements of both zoning and subdivision, calling it a Traditional Neighborhood Development ordinance, or TND. The contrast between their traditional neighborhood concept and conventional separate subdivisions is shown in the cartoon on the next page, developed in the office of Duany/Plater-Zyberk and naturally intended to show their ideas to advantage. (13.4, page 260) Like a subdivision ordinance, the TND has instructions about street layout and width, block sizes, requirements for open space. Like zoning it specifies the location for different building sizes and different mixes of activities. TNDs have now been adopted by a number of jurisdictions. They are generally available as an alternative to conventional zoning, and are thus an option like a planned unit development, but with a lot of the rules for approval spelled out in advance.

A Proposal: N Zones

A Neighborhood Zone would be a mixed lot-size residential district that applies as of right to all properties within the given area. The community can still limit the overall density of a N district. For example, a district designated N-4 can have an average density of four housing units to the acre. However, within the district, properties could have a variety of sizes, not just the quarter-acre lots of conventional R-4 zoning. For the variety to be meaningful, the overall size of a district would have to cover a whole neighborhood. As noted on page 99, if a neighborhood's size is determined by walking distances it would be about 160 acres. The neighborhood could include rowhouses, apartments, small houses, big houses, even big estates. In order to be fair to all property owners, the zoning district would have to be accompanied by a plan that covered the whole area and assured all property owners the right to build at a lower baseline level. Once the combination of built units plus permitted baseline units had reached a total of 640, the maximum permitted in N-4, the neighborhood plan would be completed.

This N zoning could be applied to existing neighborhoods, to replace the typical patchwork of different R districts. The degree of future development

TRADITIONAL NEIGHBORHOOD

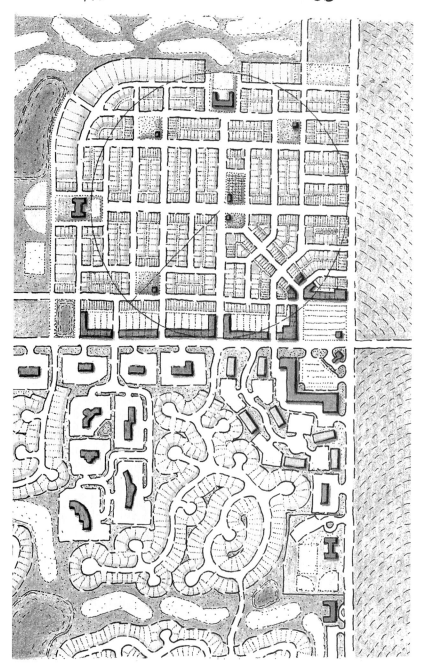

SUBURBAN SPRAWL

permitted, such as the subdivision of larger lots, would be determined by the overall density designation. Once the neighborhood reached that density, it would be built out.

This effect, as of the music stopping in a game of musical chairs, is typical of all zoning. The necessary record keeping by the building department might have been difficult before the computer, but now it is feasible. The difference between this hypothetical N zoning and conventional R zoning is that large and small lots could continue to co-exist. The larger properties could not all be subdivided down to the smallest permissible lot size, which is what tends to happen under conventional zoning.

Street Plans

The ability to map streets is one of the oldest and most unquestioned powers available to local government. However, since World War II, it has become customary to wait to map local streets until the owners of the properties apply for subdivision approval. The subdivision ordinance regulates the way larger pieces of land are subdivided into individual streets and lots to meet the zoning code. It contains performance standards and dimensions for streets that will be acceptable to the local government, but the actual layout is left to the planners and engineers employed by the applicant, subject to review and approval.

This custom makes some sense if an owner is applying for approvals under planned unit development or a TND, as streets and buildings can then be planned together. However, leaving the streets to individual owners inevitably disconnects each development from the one next door. As only the major streets are mapped by the local authorities, and all the subdivisions are connected to these main streets, most travel from one subdivision to another takes place on these major streets. In older cities and towns there is a more complete street network so that traffic is more distributed, and the stress on any one street can be reduced—although people may complain about through traffic taking shortcuts through their neighborhood.

When Wildwood, Missouri—the community described in the opening pages of this book—retained Duany/Plater-Zyberk to develop a detailed plan for their town center, their first step was to map out a street plan for the whole district, despite the land being divided among many different owners. Most of the remaining decisions in the plan follow from this initial step.

If development regulation is to be a positive template for development, communities need to resume responsibility for the design of more of the

13.4 (left) Cartoon by Duany/Plater-Zyberk comparing traditional neighborhood design with their rendition of conventional suburban development.

street network. To do this effectively requires an understanding of the terrain and it also means making assumptions about future land use and densities.

Specific Plans or Special Districts

The strategy, described in Chapter 9, for redesigning commercial corridors as a series of mixed-use zones located at key intersections, will usually require that special provisions be added to local development regulations. In California there is a well-established procedure called the Specific Plan, which is intended for just such a purpose. The specific plan is comparable to a planned unit development, but it applies when an area is divided among different owners. Unlike Urban Renewal, which also could impose a plan on multiple ownerships, there is no need to make a finding of blighted conditions. A local government can initiate a specific plan, including streets, site plan, location and size of buildings; if it is adopted, it becomes the zoning for the area and is binding on all the property owners. Oregon and Arizona have enabling legislation that also permits specific plans.

In other states it is possible to get to the same result, but it requires more steps. A community can adopt a master plan for a specific area. The master plan can include a street plan and a zoning plan. As zoning is always supposed to be the implementation mechanism for a master plan, the existing zoning districts within the area covered by the plan can be changed to reflect the plan's objectives. If the right kinds of zoning districts do not exist in the current code, new zoning districts can be created.

In addition, a local government can enact a special zoning district, which is an overlay that applies only to the area in the plan. The special zoning district can include provisions like build-to and setback lines to govern building placement, height limits, required pedestrian connections and other similar provisions. Because they are part of zoning, these overlay districts are necessarily more abstract than the drawings in a planned unit development or a specific plan, but, if appropriately crafted, they can achieve similar objectives.

The major obstacle to the approval of such a plan is, of course, the assent of the property owners. The owners can be overruled by the specific plan or by a master plan and zoning overlay, but the decisions become more difficult politically, the more objections are voiced by property owners. It helps if the specific plan or new zoning increases development over what was permissible before the plan was drawn. It also may be necessary to add incentives to make it worthwhile for property owners to agree to the plan. The local government can provide assistance in building streets and utilities, and in dealing with parking and stormwater management. As the plan is likely to increase future tax revenues, these revenues can be set aside to pay back the

13.5 Signs on buildings in New York City's Times Square are mandated by the zoning. Here is one sign that is more famous than the building itself.

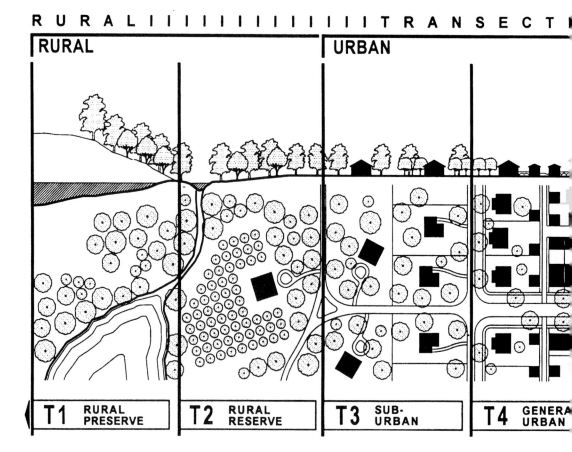

R U R A L I I I I I I I I I I I I I T R A N S E C T

RURAL		URBAN	
T1 RURAL PRESERVE	**T2** RURAL RESERVE	**T3** SUB-URBAN	**T4** GENERA URBAN

13.6 *The Transect by Duany/Plater-Zyberk, a way of organizing development regulations by scale and context.*

costs for elements—like streets and utilities—needed to make the project happen. This technique is known as tax-increment financing. The tools for such proactive local planning are generally available, if the community has the political will to use them.

A special zoning district is more general and abstract than a specific plan, but can be used to promote a special design character for a particular area. A good example is the special district enacted for Times Square in New York City. Historically, Times Square had been the center of a district of big electric advertising signs: "The Great White Way." As new corporate office buildings were constructed in the area, the Municipal Art Society and other citizen groups became concerned that Times Square's distinctive character would be

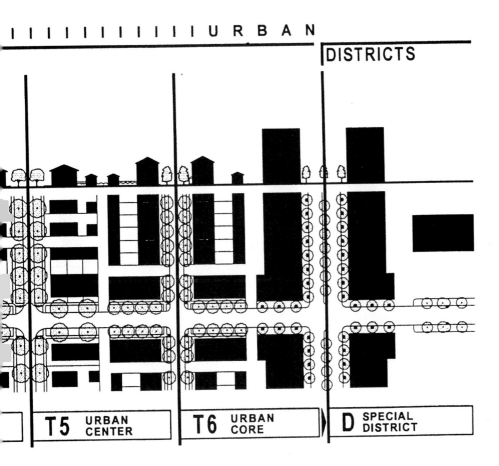

I I I I I I I I I I I I U R B A N

DISTRICTS

T5 URBAN CENTER   T6 URBAN CORE   D SPECIAL DISTRICT

sanitized out of existence. In response an ordinance was enacted that speci-fied minimum areas for electric signs on the lower floors of building facades. Initial resistance from developers vanished when they discovered how much money could be made from leasing the signs. Ingenious methods were devised to permit occupants on lower floors to look out their windows through the signs. The character of the area has been reestablished by the zoning. There are more bright lights on Broadway and Times Square than there ever were before. (13.5)

The Transect and The Smart Code
Andres Duany is attempting to rethink all of development regulation from first principles, rather than trying to modify the zoning and subdivision laws and practices that have accumulated over the years. He sees his code being adopted as an alternative to whatever regulations a community may have in

place, and has named it the Smart Code, implying that it promotes Smart Growth, and that communities and developers who are smart will use it.

The organizing principle is a gradient of building densities, which Duany calls a *transect*, another name for a cross-section. It is an analogy to the cross-sections drawn by landscape architects, for example through an off-shore sand bar where there is a succession from ocean to beach, to the primary dune, through a trough behind this dune, to a secondary dune, then to the backdune, the bayshore, and the bay.

Duany's succession goes from rural preserve, to rural reserve, then: suburban, general urban, urban center, urban core. He also reserves another category, special districts. (13.6)

The transect appears to relate to the Valley Section, drawn by pioneer city planner, ecologist, and geographer Patrick Geddes through a hypothetical region in his native Scotland in the early twentieth century. This drawing, a landmark in the history of city planning and urban geography, describes a gradient of activities from resource extraction, through farming, to the fishing village and on to the town, which Geddes pointed out was made up of activities that drew on what was happening in rural areas.

The relationships Geddes observed among centuries-old settlements in Scotland have long since become far more complicated. Modern transportation and communication have allowed urban activities to locate almost anywhere, and no one would use Geddes's Valley Section to describe regional geography today. Duany agrees that a gradient from rural to central place no longer describes metropolitan areas, and explains that categories from his transect can occur in different relationships across a region. Apparently, the transect is a device for illustrating the context and relationships of streets, parks, and buildings within a specific type of development such as a suburb or an urban center, not, as it may first appear, a proposal for mapping all land uses according to a gradient that runs from city center to rural areas.

The Smart Code pulls together earlier Duany initiatives, including codes relating building types to lot sizes and the principles of the Traditional Neighborhood District. Most development regulation says what you can't do, and describes what ought to happen only by indirection. The Smart Code is one of the few attempts to rethink all development regulation as city design. It could become a major theoretical advance, although today it is still a work in progress.

Historic Districts and Design Review

Historic districts are among the earliest forms of development regulation to have a specific design component. The Old and Historic District in Charleston, South Carolina, was first enacted in 1931, the Vieux Carre in New

Orleans became a historic district in 1937, the historic district in Alexandria, Virginia, dates from 1946, the preservation of Beacon Hill in Boston from 1955. In all these places the existing building fabric was to be maintained and new construction reviewed to ensure that the design would be in harmony with its historic surroundings.

The Federal Historic Preservation Act of 1966 included guidelines for the establishment of local historic districts and the preservation of individual buildings. This act also established the National Register of Historic Places. A listing on the National Register affects eligibility for tax subsidies and can protect a building or district from federally funded actions, but the real task of preservation and review is left to landmark and district designations established by local governments.

In a historic district there are two basic design questions. The first has to do with the appropriate way to treat an existing building: What paint colors are correct, how to make replacements of structurally deteriorated elements, what to do about the accretions from different periods? The second question concerns filling in gaps within the district. Should a new building counterfeit the appearance of an old building? If not, what constitutes an appropriate architectural expression?

The Board of Architectural Review in Charleston prefers to deal with most development within the Old and Historic District boundaries on a case by case basis, and has built up a long series of precedents over the years. Its counterpart in Nantucket operates with a complex set of published design guidelines. While it is not possible for guidelines to anticipate every problem, they have the advantage of articulating the important issues in advance, informing financial and design decisions even before the formal review process begins.

Design Review and Design Guidelines
The courts have upheld historic districts and historic district review procedures over the years because the criteria are based on well-understood general principles that apply to all properties within a district. Design review outside of a historic district has a somewhat different basis.

1. Design Review as a Condition of Ownership
In an urban renewal district, when a public entity assembles property and sells it to a private investor, design conditions can be made part of the property transaction. The deed can require the developer to fulfill conditions; the public agency can review plans for a proposed development to make sure it meets the conditions in the purchase agreement. The design guidelines for Battery Park City in New York are based on transaction requirements. When

13.7 South End Avenue in Battery Park City. Design guidelines were used to relate tall build-ings to lower structures. Note setback/expression line shared by apartment buildings and office towers. A tower of the now-destroyed World Trade Center is just visible in the upper right-hand corner of the picture.

you but the property, you buy the guidelines. You can see in this photograph of South End Avenue in Battery Park City that the design guidelines include a setback and expression line that is observed in the design of both the office and residential buildings. The gradient from primarily masonry to all glass as your eye goes up the face of the office building is also set down in the guidelines. (13.7)

The design codes that are part of many planned communities have a similar basis as part of a purely private transaction. When you buy a lot at Celebration, or at Seaside, you buy into their requirements. The owner retains the right to review plans and make sure they conform to the code.

These kinds of guidelines and reviews can be as detailed as in a historic

Residential floor to be no more than 5 feet above sidewalk.

Primary unit and building entries oriented to street at approximate intervals of 50 feet.

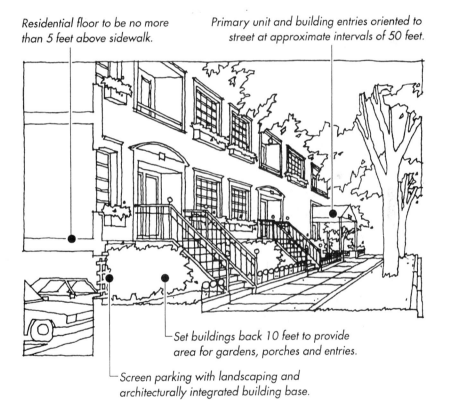

Set buildings back 10 feet to provide area for gardens, porches and entries.

Screen parking with landscaping and architecturally integrated building base.

13.8 On these and the succeeding three pages, four examples of the design guidelines by the ROMA Design Group from the redevelopment and reuse plan for the former Robert Mueller Municipal Airport in Austin, Texas. On this page, guidelines for buildings along a residential street.

Awnings to provide shade.

Maximize storefront transparency to create visual interest. Building entries oriented to street at approximate intervals of 50 feet.

Building generally built to property line with setbacks up to 5 feet for cafes, entries, etc.

High quality base materials (e.g. stone, tile, etc.)

13.9   *Guidelines for a street with commercial frontage.*

district, down to the building materials or the slope of the roof, and up to the overall size and shape of any building. There is no constitutional question, but there may be a conflict between brokers and salesmen, who want to make deals, and those who are trying to preserve the integrity of the original design.

2. Design Review as a Condition of Public Action
Cincinnati's Urban Design Review Board advises the city manager on any important downtown project that requires a discretionary approval or any kind of city action or subsidy to support the project. It becomes more immersed in the actual design process than most review boards. Recent design review legislation in Seattle gives the Review Board some of the powers of a zoning board of appeal. The design review process can lead to exceptions from the zoning, granted for appropriate design, rather than for hardship, which is the basis for exceptions from a board of appeal.

The Reuse Plan for the former Austin airport by the ROMA Design Group contains design guidelines that told prospective purchasers of the airport land what will be expected of them when they develop it. In addition to the streets and land uses, these guidelines give instructions about essential ele-

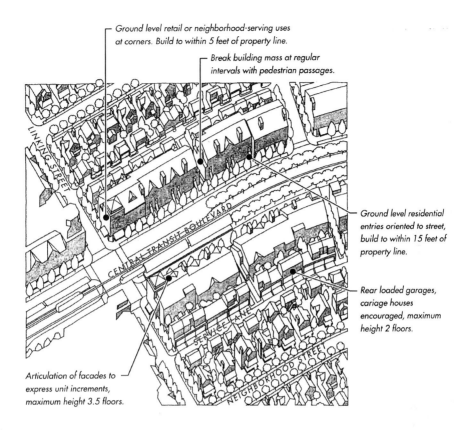

Ground level retail or neighborhood-serving uses at corners. Build to within 5 feet of property line.

Break building mass at regular intervals with pedestrian passages.

Ground level residential entries oriented to street, build to within 15 feet of property line.

Rear loaded garages, cariage houses encouraged, maximum height 2 floors.

Articulation of facades to express unit increments, maximum height 3.5 floors.

13.10 Guidelines along the central transit boulevard.

ments of the overall design, while leaving many details to the discretion of the architects of individual buildings. (13.8, 13.9, 13.10, 13.11)

3. Design Review as a General Requirement

The public interest in a more general kind of design review comes from the "police powers" of the state: The state delegates its "police power" to the local government, enabling it to insure public safety, public health, and general welfare. The more objective and generally applicable the review criteria can be, the more likely the review process can be sustained if there is a challenge to it in court.

Norfolk, Virginia's, zoning code makes all development downtown subject to a discretionary Downtown Development Certificate. The code lists the criteria by which a proposal will be judged, and the design review committee

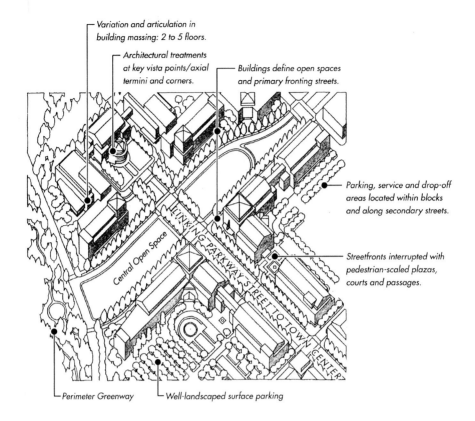

Variation and articulation in
building massing: 2 to 5 floors.

Architectural treatments
at key vista points/axial
termini and corners.

Buildings define open spaces
and primary fronting streets.

Parking, service and drop-off
areas located within blocks
and along secondary streets.

Streetfronts interrupted with
pedestrian-scaled plazas,
courts and passages.

Perimeter Greenway

Well-landscaped surface parking

Central Open Space

LINKING PARKWAY STREET TO TOWN CENTER

13.11 Guidelines for buildings at a central focal point of the plan.

and the planning commission adopt specific guidelines that apply to each
project at the beginning of the review process. The intent is to make sure that
applicants understand the criteria on which they will be reviewed before
design and budget commitments have been fully established.

Cleveland has adopted a series of mapped design guidelines for its downtown, which are the basis for review by the design review committee and the
planning commission. These guidelines are not part of zoning, but spell out
details of what the city is looking for before developers become completely
committed to a particular design. The Cleveland guidelines are mapped in an
abstract vocabulary that could be part of a zoning code, using such devices as
setback or build-to lines, and height limits. Special locations where exceptional buildings are encouraged are shown on the map by a star symbol.

Many other communities have a design review commission or design
review board that reviews proposals for compliance with special area plans,

compliance with requirements of a particular ordinance, or even for consonance with the established character of the community. Ordinarily the statute setting up the board sets qualifications so that some percentage of the members are design professionals. Almost all such boards have both preliminary and final reviews, so that the applicant has a chance to take the board's guidance into account before becoming too committed to a particular design. Often the board is advisory to the planning commission: Projects are referred to the board for comment before the planning commission takes action.

The advantage of a design review process is that it permits development regulations to be administered in a flexible way that relates to the specifics of a particular site and building program. There are inevitable difficulties as many of the issues that boards have to decide are at least arguable, and their judgments have to be in part subjective. The clearer the criteria for review, the better the process is likely to be.

14

Making The Designed City a Reality

Successful urban design needs support from individual citizens as well as advocacy by organized groups; it requires government regulations that promote a positive image of what a place should be, plus a strong design-review system to make sure that long-term urban design concepts are carried out. There has to be participation by real-estate investors who take a long view and intend to create permanent value; strong political leadership is also most important.

When I was director of urban design for the New York City Planning Department, Mayor John Lindsay came back from a ceremony marking the completion of a remodeled transit station and asked me to find out who had been responsible for the design. The walls of the station were covered with a strange mixture of blue, orange, and white tiles, and Mayor Lindsay was disturbed that a lot of money had been spent to make a station look worse than it had before. It turned out that the design had been done in-house by the Transit Authority's engineering department. The selection of wall materials had been left to a specialist in construction specification. In the absence of other guidance, he had picked blue and orange, the official colors of the City of New York, and, again as he had no other guidance, he had specified that the colored tiles be laid in a random pattern on a white ground.

This story illustrates a fundamental truth about urban design: Almost every decision that contributes to the design of a city is made by people who believe they are acting rationally, for perfectly good motives. The problem is the aggregate effect of all these seemingly rational decisions, not the people who make them.

A mayor often has the power to remedy this kind of problem. All construction on public property in New York City is supposed to be reviewed by the Art Commission. The transit authority had viewed the station remodeling as maintenance, not new construction; and had not brought the plans to the commission. The management of the authority was reminded that such highly visible changes did in fact require commission approval. One of the mayor's assistants remembered that the City Charter made the mayor ex officio a member of the Art Commission, although no one actually expected the mayor to attend its meetings. He suggested that the City Planning Department's director of urban design be the mayor's representative.

As a result, I attended Art Commission meetings on behalf of the mayor. My position was not as powerful as it sounds, as it is difficult for a mayor to cast a vote against the actions of city departments. The Art Commission, overburdened and understaffed, had also not been accustomed to acting as a strong guardian for urban design issues. However, I was able to get additional staff assigned to the commission, which before had functioned with only a secretary, so that a docket describing agenda items could be prepared and sent to commission members a week before the meeting. Not only could commission members make better-informed decisions, but I had time to get bad proposals off the agenda and sent back to the responsible department for additional work.

As agencies began to take Art Commission approvals more seriously, they began to get better professional advice before taking a proposal there. I was able to persuade most agencies to have a preliminary session before the Art Commission before making a final submission. This takes some of the pressure off a review body, which can otherwise be told that, by asking for changes, it is either making impossible demands on the budget or is holding up improvements that are already on a tight schedule. Without the implicit authority of Mayor Lindsay, none of these new procedures would have been possible.

The Mayor as Urban Designer in Chief
Mayor Joseph Riley of Charleston, South Carolina, has long recognized that a mayor is in a special position to influence the design of a city. Early in his tenure, which began in 1975, he made some important urban design decisions. As mentioned on page 132, he reached the conclusion that public housing projects just didn't work, and the money should be spent instead on scattered-site housing integrated into the community, often by restoring existing buildings. This has now become a consensus view, but Riley was a generation ahead of the consensus. Riley also refused to let a large parcel of public waterfront land be sold to private investors, but instead insisted it be turned

into a waterfront park. The city retained development parcels fronting on the new park, and the mayor held out until he could get precisely the kind of downtown residential development he wanted to have facing the park. It has taken a long time, but he has managed to have his public access to the waterfront and the waterfront development as well.

In 1985, Riley, who had been active in the U.S. Conference of Mayors and was later to serve as its president, wrote to Jaquelin Robertson, who was then the dean of the School of Architecture at the University of Virginia, proposing a program to help mayors understand their potential power to shape their communities:

> I have often said that I am the chief urban designer of my city. By that I mean that because of my position as mayor, I have many opportunities to affect development. Most large development plans come through my office. Either the general support of the mayor is needed, or specific city approvals, variances, etc., are required. I am often called on to be proactive, seeking and encouraging certain development. With many of these projects, there are opportunities to make them better for the city or to allow them to be ordinary—or worse. This is true for most mayors. A city's mayor has great opportunities to affect the quality of development there. The more sensitive the mayor is to good urban design, to issues of livability, scale, diversity, etc., the more willing and able he or she will be to help develop higher quality. If we could institute a program aimed at increasing mayors' sophistication and interest in urban design, we could have a substantial impact on the quality of development in American cities.

Riley and Robertson brought a proposal to Adele Chatfield-Taylor, then the head of the Design Program at the National Endowment for the Arts, and the endowment agreed to fund a series of institutes for mayors to be held at the University of Virginia. This program has continued, expanding to other universities nationally, and The Mayors' Institute on City Design is now a partnership of the National Endowment for the Arts, the American Architectural Foundation, and the U.S. Conference of Mayors.

Mayors are invited to participate in the institute, bringing with them an urban design problem from their community on which they would like some advice. There are generally only about eight mayors at any given institute and four or five design professionals as "resource people." All the costs of attending the institute are paid for, so that the mayors are not spending city money to attend. Mayors are meant to come alone, without their planning directors or other staff, and most honor this request. Mayors are often surprisingly nervous about being returned to something like a classroom situation, but they generally find what they hear to be useful. The design professionals are good at identifying problems and suggesting what could be done instead, but some of the best advice about how to handle a given situation usually comes from the other mayors.

Creating an Urban Design Constituency

A local government administration that takes urban design initiatives will go farther and faster if there is strong public support. Many communities have advocacy groups for historic preservation and for environmental issues, but advocacy for a more inclusive city-design program is still unusual. The Municipal Art Society in New York City, founded, as it name suggests, to promote the placement of statuary in public parks, has evolved into an advocacy organization with good city design as one of its prime objectives. A small group in a big city, the M.A.S. is influential because its expertise is respected and it knows how to get public attention. In addition to testifying at public hearings, the M.A.S. sponsors design competitions, commissions exhibitions and books, and creates photo-ops, such as organizing a crowd of people to form the outline of the shadow they said would be cast on Central Park by a proposed new development. The special district zoning for Times Square, described on pages 36 and 264, was the result of a Municipal Arts Society initiative.

Community design centers, usually attached to architecture and planning schools, began by advocating better planning and design for inner-city neighborhoods, such as the pioneering center at Pratt Institute in Brooklyn. Some of these centers now have a broader agenda. Examples include the Urban Design Center for Northeast Ohio in Cleveland, the Community Design Center in Pittsburgh, or the exceptionally successful center run by the University of Tennessee in Chattanooga. These centers draw on architecture and planning students and a small core-staff of professionals to carry out studies for neighborhoods and small communities. They are filling a gap, serving groups that could not otherwise obtain professional urban design services, or supplementing the work of government departments.

The Cityscape Institute was founded by Elizabeth Barlow Rogers in 1995, on the pattern of The Central Park Conservancy, also founded by Rogers, which mobilized private funding to restore and maintain Central Park in New York City. The Cityscape Institute is trying to adapt similar fund-raising and design advocacy to more dispersed streetscapes and public places, and also engages in urban design advocacy by sponsoring public lectures.

Urban Design Centers, partly sponsored by city governments, can be a continuing support system for long-term urban design objectives. In Minnesota, the St. Paul Design Center has been created as part of nonprofit Riverfront Development Corporation to help implement the city's 1997 Framework Plan. City employees from the departments of planning, engineering and public works form part of the staff, working half-time at the center. This hybrid organization is intended to overcome the resistance to outside interference that can be a problem in government agencies, while providing a long-term commitment to urban design policies, which might waver and change with different city administrations. Somewhat similar organizations are being set up in Charleston, South Carolina, and Nashville, Tennessee.

The 1000 Friends of Oregon, the prototype for many comparable organizations, was founded in 1975 to build support for Oregon's growth management laws and conserve Oregon's productive farm, forest, and range lands, To accomplish these objectives, it also had to promote such city design concepts as compact, livable cities, urban greenspaces and transportation choices. The 1000 Friends of Oregon and a newly founded group called Sensible Transportation Options for People—STOP (now called Citizens for Sensible Transportation) combined in 1991 to oppose the Western Bypass, long planned to run through rapidly developing Washington County west of Portland, Oregon. Billed as a way to relieve congestion, the plan had won the concurrence of Portland Metro, although part of the planned road would have run through farmland outside the growth boundary, opening up rural land to urbanization, and leading inevitably to expansion of the boundary, more sprawl and more congestion.

Knowing that effective opposition required an alternative design to the bypass, the 1000 Friends and other opponents of the bypass funded and produced a design alternative. This alternative would be incorporated into the environmental analysis of transportation options that is part of the required process for planning any federally funded highway—but is rarely more than a paper exercise. This alternative substituted a radial rapid transit line through Washington County for the bypass, and a system of compact development around transit stations for conventional urban sprawl. The alternative scored so much better than other options in the environmental analysis that it was adopted and funded, becoming part of Portland's 2040 Plan. (See page 57.)

Advocacy by Urban Design Professional Organizations
The American Institute of Architects and the American Planning Association both have interest-group committees devoted to urban design, although they have relatively little importance within the larger structures of these organi-

zations. The American Institute of Architects provides Regional Urban
Design Assistance Teams (R/UDATs), staffed by volunteers. These teams
conduct on-the-spot urban design workshops at the request of local sponsors.
The Urban Land Institute, a research organization created by the real-estate
industry, also takes an active interest in urban design issues. Like the A.I.A.,
it provides volunteer teams, through its Panel Advisory Services program,
that conduct workshops for local sponsors. While some of the issues they
study are financial, urban design proposals are usually a big part of each
advisory panel.

The American Society of Landscape Architects approaches urban design
through members' interests in parks and public spaces, and in regional conservation. The Institute for Urban Design, under the indefatigable direction of
Anne Ferebee, has provided a newsletter and forums for people interested in
urban design since 1979.

The most remarkable organization related to urban design is The Congress
for the New Urbanism, founded in 1993, (see page 39). More than a professional association, the congress aims to be an international coalition of
designers, developers, public officials, and interested citizens. Helped by the
growing concern for city design issues described at the beginning of this
book, the C.N.U. has been surprisingly effective in getting its agenda before
the public, exercising an influence far larger than would be expected from an
organization which currently has about 2,500 members. It is, however, far
from representative of any of its larger constituent groups: designers, public
officials, or developers.

Official Design Review

City planning commissions make urban design judgments when they review
design proposals in special districts, or when they approve a new project
where the zoning has essentially been negotiated. In many cities the planning
commission refers projects to official design review boards for advice, as in
Norfolk, Cincinnati, or Cleveland. Boston's Civic Design Commission
reviews any project larger than 100,000 square feet, serving as a quality control system for city-initiated projects as well as private development. More
and more cities and towns are creating design review boards, as complex
urban development proposals move outward into formerly suburban and
rural areas. They can either advise the planning or zoning commission and
become part of the approvals process, or they can advise the city's mayor or
city manager and be part of the administrative process.

Urban Designers as Staff or Consultants

Successful urban design requires designers to be present when important city development decisions are being made; this does not mean that designers should make all the decisions, only that they have a chance to influence them. When I first went to work for the New York City Planning Department in 1967, the only person on the staff with training in urban design was a special assistant to the chairman. My colleagues and I were being asked to set up an urban design capability within the staff. There were no appropriate civil service titles in New York and few precedents elsewhere, as I found out when I called other cities. Finally, the personnel director at the Boston Redevelopment Authority, one of the only cities at the time that had an in-house urban design capability, was able to give me the advice I needed to set up comparable civil service categories in New York.

Today, it has become routine for cities, counties, and even small towns to have people on their staff who are by title and responsibility urban designers. Staff at planning departments manage design review processes, and help set public policies through development regulations. Redevelopment authorities and local development corporations use urban designers to prepare plans, review development proposals and manage the development process. Urban design staff help landmarks and historic district commissions administer preservation laws, and work with community organizations to promote neighborhood conservation and renewal.

It is less usual for urban designers to have a voice in the site selection for schools and public buildings, which are often made as purely real-estate decisions. If urban designers are involved in major transportation decisions it is usually as consultants.

When I was first starting out in urban design there were perhaps only a dozen consulting firms in the whole United States that offered urban design services, now there are several hundred, well distributed across the country. Larger urban design studies for cities, such as downtown plans, neighborhood plans, plans for the reuse of railyards or military bases, or revisions to development regulations are generally done by consulting firms. Private investors use urban design consultants in preparing large-scale development proposals, particularly for their understanding of the public approvals process. Corridor studies for new highways and transit lines can also involve urban designers, although not as often as they should, and urban designers are also beginning to be hired to make regional planning studies.

Education for Urban Design
The University of Pennsylvania's Civic Design master's program was begun in 1957; Harvard's master's of Urban Design program followed in 1960. Today some 25 U.S. schools of architecture, out of more than 100, offer some kind of urban design concentration or certificate, while perhaps a dozen edu-

cational institutions offer a professional degree in urban design, almost always to people who already have a professional degree in architecture, landscape architecture, or city planning.

These programs typically center around a studio, an academic course where a real or hypothetical urban design problem is solved by the students. Usually students in a studio course are asked to simulate the experience of working as professional consultants, but occasionally they are encouraged to go off on a search for individual expression. The other courses in an urban design program can include introductions to law and real estate, the public and private-sector contexts for urban design decisions, plus the history and theory of urban design, and elective courses in such subjects as urban sociology.

Some educators in the design professions have an ambivalent attitude toward professional instruction in urban design. They are concerned that urban design considerations can dictate the design of individual buildings or spaces, and are distrustful of generic design concepts, like adhering to a build-to line, or the reliance on building typologies—office building, town house—that are staple elements of urban design. They also tend to teach that buildings should be designed from the inside out for the best accommodation of their internal functions, not from the outside in, by considering a building's place within an urban or environmental context.

Of course this tension between generic and specific design considerations is inevitable, and ought to be the stuff of a productive academic dialogue; if this were the only problem, probably it would be. However, these same design educators are frequently distrustful of government agencies and real-estate investment companies, the means by which most urban design ideas are implemented. They think there must be an alternative to government incentives and controls, and to for-profit real-estate development, although they can't as yet specify what it would be.

Concerns like these have unfortunately prevented professional education in urban design from being offered more widely in schools of architecture and landscape architecture.

Making the Designed City a Reality

Advocacy is the first step in improving the design of any place, whether it is a large city or a small town. Advocacy requires a positive vision of what should happen, not just an ability to organize opposition to bad projects. The leaders in Wildwood, Missouri, knew what they wanted to stop: an ill-considered highway and development practices that were causing soil erosion. But they were also aware of examples around the U.S. of the kind of environment and community they wanted to see in Wildwood. They circulated books, articles, and videotapes and sponsored lectures and meetings so that citizens were aware that what had been happening to their community was not inevitable: They had alternatives. As Wildwood has matured, urban design issues continue to be part of the campaigns for mayor and council. An important forum for urban design advocacy in Wildwood today is the website wildwoodtimes.com.

An essential step for Wildwood, and any other community, is to make sure that the official plans and development regulations mandate the kind of neighborhoods and commercial centers they actually want. It was critically important that Wildwood moved right after incorporation to prepare and adopt a master plan for the community. The plan provided the basis for changing the zoning and subdivision codes, and was the context for a more detailed plan for their town center.

Implementing the plans and administering the ordinances takes the constant attention of a dedicated planning staff. There is political controversy in any community, developers confronted by unfamiliar regulations threaten lawsuits—sometimes they actually bring them. Wildwood's plans and ordinances have stood up well to controversy and legal challenges.

The Wildwood Design Review Board has been an important factor in bringing potentially controversial changes to a good resolution. The board makes suggestions in an atmosphere of constructive criticism rather than confrontation and controversy. Wildwood's board, like most design review boards, derives it power from the planning commission, which refers proposals to it.

The story of Wildwood and the many other examples included in this book demonstrate that good urban design is not only possible but has actually been implemented in many places and in varying circumstances. Well-designed cities could be a reality everywhere, if there is informed advocacy for urban design in each community, if there is the political will to implement plans and development regulations that have positive objectives such as preserving the natural environment, creating walkable neighborhoods, and encouraging compact mixed-use centers; and if each community provides attentive administration and constructive design review.

Glossary

Brownfield: A vacant urban property that has been contaminated by industry, or is suspected of having been contaminated by industry, and must be cleaned up before it can be reused. The term is a play on greenfield, undeveloped land usually on the metropolitan fringe. See separate entry for Greenfield.

Business Improvement District: Where authorized by local law, a commercial district where an additional property tax is levied. The proceeds of the tax go to improvements within the district, such as better security and trash collection and are managed by a special organization created for this purpose.

Cartway: The actual paved street within a right of way that also includes sidewalks and possibly landscaped verges and medians. See Right of Way.

Cluster Development: An exception to usual zoning rules in order to permit development to cluster on one part of a property, without regard to the usual minimum lot sizes and setbacks. The advantages are that part of the land can be left in its natural state, a historic area can be left undisturbed, or the land can be shared for recreation. See Planned Unit Development.

Commercial: As a land-use category, commercial includes offices, hotels, shops, and restaurants, as well such activity centers as movie houses and bowling alleys. Zoning codes usually distinguish categories of commercial land uses, based on their potential impact on surrounding properties. See Zoning.

Deed Restriction: A clause incorporated in the deed of a property that limits use of the property in some way.

Design Review: A part of a locality's development approvals process that permits discretionary decision making about the appropriateness of a specific building proposal. Generally design review boards are advisory to planning commissions.

Edge City: Joel Garreau coined this term and used it as a book title in 1991. His definition of an edge city is a place that as recently as 30 years before was a bedroom suburb or a rural area. Today it has at least five million square feet of office space and 600,000 square feet of retail space, and is perceived as a regional business center. See page 167.

Environmental Zoning: The area of a property is usually the basis for computing permissible development in zoning codes. In an environmental zoning code, areas that should not be developed because of their vulnerability to erosion or other kinds of destabilization can be subtracted from the development computation. See page 83 and 257.

Equity: In urban planning and design, equity means balancing the needs of the majority against negative consequences for smaller groups, particularly those with less political power. Policies that result in concentrating poor people in places with the fewest resources, or in places full of undesirable land uses, are equity issues. The term Environmental Justice also is used to denote equity issues in planning and public policy. See Chapter 4.

Every-Day Urbanism: This term describes an area of study that elevates appreciation of city design decisions made by non-professionals and acknowledges concepts of Marxist social commentator Henri Lefebvre.

Exurban: This word was originally coined to describe rural areas beyond the suburbs where some of the residents commuted to jobs—usually executive jobs—in the city. Today, exurban means lower density suburban development on the edge of a metropolitan area. See Suburban.

Floor Area Ratio (F.A.R.): Floor area *multiplier* would be a better definition of this zoning control. If a plot is 10,000 square feet, and the F.A.R. is 5, then the maximum floor area for the building would be 50,000 square feet. Floor area for zoning calculations can exclude spaces such as fire stairs and mechanical equipment rooms, even above-grade parking garages.

Gentrification: This term, originally British, is a wry description of a process that improves neighborhoods but displaces poorer tenants. See page 140.

Grade: Grade is the official determination of ground level for the purpose of regulation. A height limit, for example, might specify that no house can have any element except a chimney more than 35 feet above grade. On a sloping site, determination of where the grade is located follows formulas set down in the regulations

Greenfield: A piece of rural land which is a potential development site. The implication is that the land is unspoiled, but agricultural land can be full of toxic chemicals. See also Grayfield.

Greenway: A greenway is a park that connects one place with another.

Grayfield: This term is a play on greenfield and brownfield and describes a vacant urban or suburban development with a lot of land paved for parking, a failed shopping center, for example.

Growth Management: Government regulation, usually at the state level, intended to shape new real-estate investment and development.

Infill: Development on vacant land or lots within an established urban area, as opposed to building on a greenfield site.

Inner-city: This term is used to describe older areas close to the metropolitan center, but only if poor people live there. In Boston, Roxbury is an inner city neighborhood, but affluent Beacon Hill—older and much closer to the center—is not.

ISTEA: The Intermodal Surface Transportation Efficiency Act of 1991. This act recognized rapid transit as an integral part of the national transportation system and opened up the use of some Highway Trust Fund money for transit.

Livability, as in Livable Communities: The combination of basic services and amenities that make life in a particular location as comfortable and pleasant as possible. Livability can be improved by design, but it is always a compromise. For example, it is difficult to maximize living space in locations that are also convenient and affordable. See Chapter 2.

Master Plan: A large-scale plan that directs other, smaller plans. Zoning codes are supposed to be the implementation tool for a city's master plan. Long-range master plans for a whole city have turned out to be very difficult to write and even more difficult to enact. Many planners prefer Comprehensive Plans to Master Plans, defined as both less directive and more inclusive.

Mixed-Use Development: Zoning codes traditionally separate activities into single-use zones, such as single-family residential zones, or industrial zones. Today, planning is moving toward the position that the only activities that require strict separation are industries that create pollution or hazardous conditions, and that most other districts can have a mix of different land-uses. However, there is still strong sentiment for separating uses that draw crowds or heavy truck traffic.

Mobility: Transportation has always shaped urban development. Originally the boundaries of urban settlements were determined by walking distances, then by wheeled vehicles drawn by horses, later by railways, automobiles, and now by air travel. Today some people speculate that electronic communication will at least partly replace transportation as a shaper of cities. See Chapter 3.

Neighborhood: In ordinary conversation your neighborhood is the area around the place where you live. In planning discourse, neighborhood has become a defined term, reflecting formulations like Clarence Perry's Neighborhood Unit. See page 97.

Neotraditionalism: According to Andres Duany, who has done much to popularize this term as it relates to city design, the Stanford Research Institute coined it as a way of characterizing the "baby-boom" generation tendency to follow traditional patterns in a modern guise. In planning, it means a revived interest in such city design strategies as symmetrical town squares and avenues centered on a public building, concepts rejected by the modern movement in architecture and planning. See page 40.

New Urbanism: Stephanos Polyzoides and Peter Katz coined this slogan, which combines *urbanism*, the term used in Europe to include city planning, city design and urban research, and *new*, the quintessence of American advertising. The Congress for the New Urbanism defines it in a charter covering 27 principles. See page 40.

NIMBY: An acronym, Not In My Back Yard, meaning opposition to new development because it is against one's personal interests.

Planned Unit Development (P.U.D.): As its name suggests, development where an approved plan replaces the regular zoning and subdivision requirements. Where permitted by a zoning code, a P.U.D. usually follows the same procedure as a change in zoning, including public hearings and approval by the local legislature as well as the planning or zoning board. It is a way of implementing cluster development or a planned community, as long as the original land is in one ownership. See Cluster Development.

Public Space: A place in a developed area that is open to the public and where many people are likely to congregate, at least sometimes. Public spaces can be publicly or privately owned. Streets and sidewalks are public spaces, although not usually described as such; a national park or a publicly owned golf course are also not normally described as public space.

Redlining: The practice of denying mortgage loans for properties in some areas of a city, now illegal. The term derives from actual color-coded maps once produced by U.S. government agencies. See page 65.

Right of Way: The land dedicated or mapped for a street or highway.

Section 8: A federal housing assistance program. Tenants whose incomes are below the specified limit can obtain vouchers from the local housing authority and use them to rent private houses or apartments. The tenant pays 30 percent of household income for rent, the authority pays the rest to the landlord.

Smart Code: A proprietary system, intended to replace zoning, devised by Andres Duany and named to take advantage of the promotion of *Smart Growth*.

Smart Growth: A clever slogan, as no one wants the opposite, to describe efforts to manage new development that avoids *sprawl*. The term is also a way to distinguish managing growth from trying to stop growth.

Snout House: A house with a front-facing garage close to the street in front of the main part of the house.

Sprawl: Low-density urban development rapidly spreading across rural areas. It may seem unplanned but is actually the result of complex interactions among government regulations and private initiatives.

Strip Development: Development strung out in narrow strips along an arterial highway, a pattern often mandated by a zoning code.

Suburban: Suburbs were originally the undesirable, unprotected areas outside a city's walls. The term was then applied to villages where some of the residents commuted to work in nearby cities. More recently *suburb* was used to describe primarily residential communities surrounding a central city. In today's decentralized metropolis, the term *suburban* refers to urbanized areas outside of traditional city boundaries.

Superblock: A large urban block created by closing intermediate streets, or planned from the beginning between widely separated streets.

Sustainability: Policies that preserve natural resources for future generations are said to make life on earth sustainable. The question is whether modern society is sustainable, given its reliance on coal, oil, and their chemical derivatives and the consequent destabilization of the world's ecosystem. See Chapter 5.

Tax-Increment Financing: A new park or other public improvement often raises property values in the surrounding area, so why not use the increased property values to pay for the improvement? This is the principle behind tax-increment financing, where an increment of increased property taxes in a special district is dedicated to paying back the money borrowed to build a public improvement within the district.

TEA-21: The Transportation Equity Act for the 21st Century enacted by Congress in 1998. It is the reauthorization and extension of ISTEA. See separate entry for ISTEA.

Traditional Neighborhood Development: A new development, usually on a green-field site, designed to emulate the kinds of neighborhoods that grew up in cities and suburbs before World War II. Traditional Neighborhood Development Ordinances legislate rules for such new developments, often as an alternative to a Planned Unit Development. See page 259.

Traffic Calming: Design techniques for slowing traffic, particularly in residential neighborhoods or along shopping streets.

Town Center: In ordinary conversation, the center of town, but in developer-speak a planned shopping center in a new location, often a long way from both the center and even the town. The term implies use of a street and block pattern for the stores, instead of an enclosed mall. Sometimes these shopping centers are part of a planned community and may actually become the town center.

Townhouse: A dwelling, usually of two stories or more, that shares side walls—called party walls—with neighboring houses is a townhouse, also called a rowhouse, and in Great Britain, a terrace house. Fire codes in many jurisdictions limit the number of attached houses in a row; end units can have windows on the side walls. Detached houses, or pairs of houses, are not usually called townhouses, even when close together in a town. Real estate advertisements sometimes call townhouses townhomes.

Transect: Short for a transverse section or cut-away view. In landscape studies it is a device for showing a succession of ecologies, such as from the shore, through the beach, to the dunes and beyond. Andres Duany is applying this term to zoning, not necessarily appropriately. See pages 264-265.

Urban Growth Boundary: A line on a map that separates urban development from open, rural land. This concept derives from the writings of Ebenezer Howard, who advocated surrounding cities with belts of parkland and agriculture. As pioneered in the United States by growth management legislation in Oregon, the UGB marks the limit beyond which a locality will not extend urban infrastructure, such as sewer lines.

Urban Renewal: This phrase obviously has a general meaning, but is also understood to be a technical term describing the practice where governments condemn private properties that are found to be blighted, take ownership, and sell to a new owner who will create more desirable development.

User Fees: The cost of a government service is assessed against those who benefit from it as a user fee, rather than paying for the service by taxes on the whole population.

Vest Pocket: Small. Vest-pocket housing is a government-aided housing project on a small, infill site; a vest-pocket park is an infill park, often on an individual vacant lot between houses. The term usually applies to government-aided projects because small projects are not considered efficient use of time in a bureaucracy. "Small enough to fit in your vest pocket" (for British readers, waistcoat pocket) is outmoded, semi-facetious writing, but the term is useful in defining a category of development.

Zoning: Zoning laws regulate land use and intensity of development. As the name suggests, the map of a locality is divided into zones, and the uses permitted in each zone are spelled out in the code. Intensity of development can be regulated by floor-area ratios (the amount of space permitted is a function of the area of the property) and bulk controls which include setbacks and height limits. In the United States, the power to write zoning codes belongs to the states, which almost always delegate these powers to local governments. See Floor Area Ratio, Planned Unit Development.

Illustration Credits

PR.1 Map courtesy of the City of Wildwood

PR.2 Photo by Jack Dann, courtesy of the City of Wildwood

PR.3 Photo courtesy Duany/Plater-Zyberk

PR.4 Plan courtesy of the City of Wildwood

PR.5 Envision Utah

1.1 NM photo

1.2 Diagram by Jan Gehl from *Life Between Buildings*, used with permission

1.3 From *Civic Art* by Werner Hegemann and Elbert Peets

1.4 From *The Social Life of Small Urban Spaces*, By William H. Whyte, 1980. Used with permission

1.5 Drawing by Jan Gehl from *Life Between Buildings*, used with permission.

1.6 NM photo

2.1 Drawings by Le Corbusier © 2002 Artists Rights Society (ARS), New York, ADAGP, Paris/FLC

2.2 Photograph from the 1940 Report of the Boston Housing Authority, *Rehousing the Low Income Families of Boston*, collection of the author.

2.3 Drawing from *Toward New Towns for America* by Clarence S. Stein, used with permission.

2.4 NM photo

2.5 Copyright 1998 by Congress for the New Urbanism, used by permission

2.6 Photo by Jim Adams

3.1, 3.2 Drawings by Stephen Kieran and James Timberlake, used by permission.

3.3 Sketch by the author

3.4 NM photo

3.5 NM photo

3.6 Map courtesy Portland Metro

3.7 Drawing courtesy Calthorpe Associates

3.8 Drawing courtesy Calthorpe Associates

4.1, 4.2 Photos courtesy Montgomery County

4.3, 4.4 Drawings used by permission of the New York Regional Plan Association

5.1 Drawing courtesy of the Cunningham Group

5.2, 5.3, 5.4 Photos courtesy Carol Johnson Associates

5.5, 5.6, 5.7, 5.8 Drawings by Stacy Moriarty copyright 1997 by TreePeople, used with permission

6.1 Photo by Alex S. MacLean used with permission of Seaside

6.2, 6.3 From the *Regional Survey of New York and Its Environs*, Regional Plan Association, 1929

6.4 Drawing from *Toward New Towns for America* by Clarence S. Stein, used with permission

6.5 Drawing by Le Corbusier © 2002 Artists Rights Society (ARS), New York, ADAGP, Paris/FLC

6.6 Drawing courtesy Duany/Plater-Zyberk

6.7 NM Photo

6.8 NM Photo

6.9 NM Photo

6.10 NM Photo

6.11, 6.12 Drawings courtesy ROMA Design Group

7.1 From the *Regional Survey of New York and Its Environs*, Regional Plan Association, 1929

7.2 Photographs from the 1940 Report of the Boston Housing Authority, *Rehousing the Low Income Families of Boston*, collection of the author

7.3 Photo courtesy UDA Architects

7.4 Photo courtesy UDA Architects

7.5 Photo courtesy Archive DS

7.6 Photo courtesy Archive DS

7.7, 7.8 Drawings courtesy Peterson and Littenberg

7.9, 7.10 Photos courtesy Weinstein Associates

7.11, 7.12 Drawings courtesy UDA Architects

7.13 Photo courtesy UDA Architects

7.14 Drawing courtesy Goody, Clancy and Associates

7.15 Drawing courtesy Torti Gallas and Partners

7.16, 7.17 Photos courtesy the Housing Authority of the City of Charleston

7.18 Photo courtesy Duany/Plater-Zyberk

8.1 Photo by Gary Hack

8.2, 8.3 Drawings courtesy Goody, Clancy and Associates

8.4, 8.5 Drawings by William Morrish, used with permission

8.6, 8.7, 8.8, 8.9 Drawing and photos courtesy the ROMA Design Group

8.10, 8.11 Drawings courtesy of Duany/Plater-Zyberk

9.1 Rendering courtesy of Johnson, Fain and Partners

9.2 Drawing courtesy Landers, Atkins

9.3 Drawing courtesy the Cunningham Group

9.4, 9.5 Drawings courtesy Landers, Atkins

9.6, 9.7, 9.8 Photomontages courtesy Dover, Kohl & Partners

9.9 NM photo

9.10 NM photo

9.11 NM photo

9.12, 9.13 Drawings courtesy the Cunningham Group

9.14 NM photo

10.1 Aerial photo courtesy StreetWorks

10.2 NM photo

10.3 NM photo

10.4 Drawing courtesy Design Works

10.5 Aerial photo courtesy Daniel Island Development Corporation

10.6 Photomontage courtesy RTKL

10.7, 10.8 Photos by Author

10.9, 10.10 Photos by Author

10.11 Drawing courtesy RTKL

10.12 Photo courtesy Dover, Kohl and Partners

10.13 Drawing courtesy Dover, Kohl and Partners

10.14, 10.15, 10.16, 10.17 Photos and photomontages courtesy Dover, Kohl and Partners

10.18 Drawing courtesy Dover, Kohl and Partners

11.1 Photo courtesy Sasaki Associates

11.2, 11.3 James Palma photos

11.4, 11.5 Photos courtesy City of Charleston

11.6, 11.7 Drawings courtesy StreetWorks

11.8 NM photo

11.9, 11.10 Photos courtesy Post Properties

11.11, 11.12, 11.13, 11.14 Drawings courtesy Moule and Polyzoides

12.1 James Steinkamp photo, courtesy Skidmore, Owings & Merrill

12.2 Author's collection

12.3 From *London in the 19th Century*

12.4 NM photo

12.5, 12.6, 12.7 Drawings courtesy of ROMA Design Group

12.8 NM photo

12.9 Drawing courtesy Cooper, Robertson + Partners

12.10 Drawing from *The Manual On Uniform Traffic Control Devices for Streets and Highways* 1988 edition.

12.11 From the *Downtown Norfolk Streetscape Handbook* prepared by Jonathan Barnett and James Urban

12.12 NM photo

12.13 NM photo

12.14, 12.15 Drawings courtesy ROMA Design Group

12.16, 12.17, 12.18, 12.19, 12.20 NM photos

12.21 Photo courtesy of Carol Johnson and Associates

12.22 NM photo

12.23 Douglas Dalton Photography, courtesy Skidmore, Owings & Merrill

12.24 Drawing courtesy Skidmore Owings and Merrill

12.25 Photo by Boris Dramov, courtesy ROMA Design Group

12.26 Photo by Ira Kahn, courtesy ROMA Design Group

12.27 NM photo

13.1 Drawing from *Paris projet no. 13-14*

13.2 From *The Metropolis of Tomorrow* by Hugh Ferriss, 1929

13.3 NM photo

13.4 Drawing courtesy Duany/Plater-Zyberk

13.5 NM photo

13.6 Drawing courtesy Duany/Plater-Zyberk

13.7 NM photo

13.8, 13.9, 13.10, 13.11 Drawings courtesy the ROMA Design Group

Suggestions for Additional Reading

PROLOGUE: The New Politics of Urban Design

Challenging Sprawl, Constance Lambert, National Trust for Historic Preservation, 2000.

Metropolitics: A Regional Agenda for Community Stability, Myron Orfield, Brookings Press, 1997.

"The Town That Took Hold of Its Future," Jonathan Barnett, *Planning*, November, 1999.

PART ONE: PRINCIPLES
CHAPTER 1: Community: Life Takes Place on Foot

A Theory of Good City Form, Kevin Lynch, MIT Press, 1981.

City: Rediscovering the Center, William H. Whyte, Doubleday, 1988.

Life Between Buildings, Jan Gehl, Van Nostrand, 1987.

"Fortress Los Angeles, the Militarization of Urban Space," Mike Davis, and "New City, New Frontier: The Lower East Side as Wild, Wild West," Neil Smith, in *Variations on a Theme Park*, edited by Michael Sorkin, Noonday, 1992.

The Conscience of The Eye: The Design and Social Life of Cities, Richard Sennett, Knopf, 1990.

CHAPTER 2: Livability: Urbanism Old & New

"Blurring the Boundaries: Public Space and Private Life," Margaret Crawford in *Everyday Urbanism* edited by John Chase, Margaret Crawford, and John Kaliski, Monacelli, 1999.

Charter of the New Urbanism, Randall Arendt et al., McGraw Hill, 2000.

Suburban Nation: The Rise of Sprawl and the Decline of the American Dream, Andres Duany, Elizabeth Plater-Zyberk, and Jeff Speck, North Point Press, 2000.

"The Elements of Architecture," Chapter 3 in *Architectural Composition*, Rob Krier, Rizzoli, 1988.

The Timeless Way of Building, Christopher Alexander, Oxford, 1979.

"Tom's Garden," Margie Ruddick in *Architecture of the Everyday* edited by Steven Harris and Deborah Berke, Princeton Architectural Press, 1997.

Urban Design as Public Policy: Practical Methods for Improving Cities, Jonathan Barnett, McGraw Hill, 1974.

CHAPTER 3: Mobility: Parking, Transit, & Urban Form

Divided Highways, Building the Interstates, Transforming American Life, Tom Lewis, Viking, 1997.

e-topia: "Urban Life Jim—But Not as We Know It," William J. Mitchell, MIT Press, 2000.

"Highway Planning and Land Use: Theory and Practice" Stephen H. Putman, in *Planning for a New Century, The Regional Agenda*, edited by Jonathan Barnett, pp 89-101, Island Press, 2000.

The Regional City, Peter Calthorpe and William Fulton, Island Press, 2001.

"Whatever Happened to Urbanism," and "The Generic City" in *S,M,L,XL, Office of Metropolitan Architecture*, Rem Koolhaas and Bruce Mau, edited by Jennifer Sigler, Monacelli Press, 1995.

CHAPTER 4: Equity: Deconcentrating Poverty, Affordable Housing, Environmental Justice

American Metropolitics: The New Suburban Reality, Myron Orfield, Brookings Press, 2001.

Crabgrass Frontier: The Suburbanization of the United States, Kenneth T. Jackson, Chapters 11 and 12, Oxford, 1985.

Foreword by David Rusk in *Planning for a New Century, The Regional Agenda*, edited by Jonathan Barnett, Island Press, 2000.

Inside Game/Outside Game: Winning Strategies for Saving Urban America, David Rusk, Brookings Press, 1999.

"Social Equity and Metropolitan Growth," John C. Keene in *Planning for a New Century, The Regional Agenda*, edited by Jonathan Barnett, Island Press, 2000.

CHAPTER 5: Sustainability: Smart Growth versus Sprawl

Design with Nature, Ian McHarg, Doubleday, 1969.

Green Urbanism, Timothy Beatley, Island Press, 2000.

Once There Were Greenfields: How Urban Sprawl is Undermining America's Environment, Economy, and Social Fabric, F. Kaid Benfield, Matthew D. Raimi, and Donald D.T. Chen, NRDC, 1999.

The Granite Garden, Urban Nature and Human Design, Anne W. Spirn, Basic Books, 1984.

PART TWO: PRACTICE
CHAPTER 6: Designing New Neighborhoods

Beyond the Neighborhood Unit Tridib Banerjee and William Baer, Plenum Press, 1984.

"The Neighborhood Unit" by Clarence Perry in *Neighborhood and Community Planning*, Volume VII of the *Regional Survey of New York and its Environs*, Regional Plan Association, 1929.

The Pedestrian Pocket Book: A New Suburban Design Strategy, edited by Doug Kelbaugh, Princeton Architectural Press, 1989.

"Safe and Productive Neighborhoods," chapter 18 in *Bowling Alone: The Collapse and Revival of American Community*, Robert D. Putnam, Simon & Schuster, 2000.

Site Planning, Kevin Lynch and Gary Hack, 3rd edition, MIT Press, 1984.

Towards New Towns for America, Clarence S. Stein, MIT Press, 1956.

CHAPTER 7: Reinventing Inner-City Neighborhoods

Defensible Space: Crime Prevention Through Urban Design, Oscar Newman, Macmillan, 1973.

Principles for Inner City Neighborhood Design, Hope VI and the New Urbanism, Congress for the New Urbanism and The U.S. Department of Housing and Urban Development, 2000.

Neighborhood Recovery, Reinvestment Policy for the New Hometown, John Kromer, Rutgers University Press, 2000.

The Urban Villagers: Group and Class in the Life of Italian-Americans, Herbert J. Gans, The Free Press, 1962.

CHAPTER 8: Restoring and Enhancing Neighborhoods

Crossroads, Hamlet, Village, Town: Design Characteristics of Traditional Neighborhoods, Old and New, Randall Arendt, American Planning Association Planning Advisory Service Report 487/488, 1999.

Making a Middle Landscape, Peter G. Rowe, MIT Press, 1991.

Rebuilding Daniel Solomon, Princeton Architectural Press, 1992.

CHAPTER 9: Redesigning Commercial Corridors

Ten Principles for Reinventing America's Suburban Strips, Michael D. Beyard and Michael Pawlukiewicz, The Urban Land Institute, 2001.

The Next American Metropolis, Ecology, Community and the American Dream, Peter Calthorpe, Princeton Architectural Press, 1993.

The Harvard Design School Guide to Shopping edited by Chuihua Judy Chung, Jeffrey Inaba., Rem Koolhaas, Sze Tsung Leong, Harvard Design School Project on the City, 2002.

CHAPTER 10: Turning Edge Cities into Real Cities

"Accidental Cities or New Urban Centers," chapter 2 in *The Fractured Metropolis: Improving the New City, Restoring the Old City, Reshaping the Region,* Jonathan Barnett, HarperCollins, 1995.

Edge City: Life on the New Frontier, Joel Garreau, Doubleday, 1991.

Edgeless Cities: Exploring the Elusive Metropolis, Robert E. Lang, Brookings Press, 2002.

CHAPTER 11: Keeping Downtowns Competitive

Cities Back From The Edge: New Life For Downtown, Roberta Gratz and Norman Mintz, John Wiley, 2000.

Main Street Success Stories, Suzanne G. Dane, National Trust for Historic Preservation, 1997.

Times Square Roulette, Remaking the City Icon, Lynne B. Sagalyn, MIT Press, 2001.

Transforming Suburban Business Districts, Geoffrey Booth et al., The Urban Land Institute, 2001.

PART THREE: IMPLEMENTATION
CHAPTER 12: Designing the Public Environment

Great Streets, Alan B. Jacobs, MIT Press, 1993.

How to Turn a Place Around, edited by The Project for Public Spaces, Project for Public Spaces, 2000.

Public Spaces, Public Life, Jan Gehl and Lars Gemzoe, translated into English by Karen Steenhard, Danish Architectural Press, 1996.

The Boulevard Book Alan B. Jacobs, Elizabeth MacDonald, Yodan Rofe, MIT Press, 2001.

CHAPTER 13: Shaping Cities Through Development Regulations

"The Elements of City Design," chapter 10 in *The Fractured Metropolis: Improving the New City, Restoring the Old City, Reshaping the Region,* Jonathan Barnett, Harper-Collins, 1995.

Performance Zoning, Lane Kendig, APA Planners Press, 1980.

Rural by Design: Maintaining Small Town Character, Randall Arendt et al., APA Planners Press, 1994.

Smart Growth, New Urbanism in American Cities, Andres Duany, Elizabeth Plater-Zyberk, and Jeff Speck, McGraw Hill, 2002.

CHAPTER 14: Organization Structures for Urban Design

"Urban Design" by Jonathan Barnett and Gary Hack in *The Practice of Local Government Planning,* 3rd Edition, edited by Charles J. Hoch, Linda C. Dalton, Frank S. So, ICMA, 2000.

Index